Plant Thinkers of
Twentieth-Century Bengal

Plant Thinkers of Twentieth-Century Bengal

SUMANA ROY

OXFORD
UNIVERSITY PRESS

Great Clarendon Street, Oxford, OX2 6DP,
United Kingdom

Oxford University Press is a department of the University of Oxford.
It furthers the University's objective of excellence in research, scholarship,
and education by publishing worldwide. Oxford is a registered trade mark of
Oxford University Press in the UK and in certain other countries

Published in the United States of America by Oxford University Press
198 Madison Avenue, New York, NY 10016, United States of America

British Library Cataloguing in Publication Data

Data available

Library of Congress Control Number:2024940100

ISBN 9780198929284

DOI: 10.1093/9780198929314.001.0001

The manufacturer's authorised representative in the EU for product safety is
Oxford University Press España S.A. of El Parque Empresarial San Fernando
de Henares, Avenida de Castilla, 2 – 28830 Madrid (www.oup.es/en or
product.safety@oup.com). OUP España S.A. also acts as importer into Spain
of products made by the manufacturer.

Contents

Phloem

Surely something unexpected—and unnoticed—had been happening in the last hundred years in Bengal.

A man trained as a physicist, with interests in wireless communication and the behaviour of metals, goes on to provide evidence of plants being 'living' things in the first years of the twentieth century.[1] At around the same time, Rabindranath Tagore, the scientist's close friend, whose poems and songs record a new poetic nomenclature of plant life, sets up, first, a school, and, soon after, a university[2] where trees and the seasons are at the heart of the cosmogony. In that university are artists—and art teachers[3]—whose manner of teaching art, drawing the human anatomy, for instance, references the analogous behaviour of plant life. In the decade when the university comes into being, a young man who has studied in Calcutta, unable to find employment in the city, leaves for the forests in the neighbouring state of Bihar.[4] There, as he supervises the cutting down of forests for agriculture, he records forest living in his diaries and in his autobiographical novel.[5] Another young man moves from Barisal to Calcutta, first for an education, then to seek employment—he finds and loses jobs as an English professor in the city.[6] His poems and stories and novels, most of which are discovered after his early death, create a space of ancient trees and grass where time and history can perhaps only be calibrated through plant life. This writer loses a life and a familiar land to Partition. Another artist, a filmmaker, whose films were a record of the trauma of Partition, would put trees almost obsessively—and perhaps even unconsciously—in his frames, whether it was Shillong or Kurseong, Calcutta or a riverside hamlet.[7] His contemporary, a Calcuttan who would go to Tagore's university to study at the department of art,[8] would go on to make a film based on an autobiographical novel by a young poet—the poet and his friends had gone to a forest on a weekend break from the city.[9] He would also, in a second career as an author of

Plant Thinkers of Twentieth-Century Bengal. Sumana Roy, Oxford University Press. © Sumana Roy 2024.
DOI: 10.1093/9780198929314.003.0001

detective stories, primarily for children, write stories about imaginary non-botanical plants with magical characteristics. A poet and writer, one among the four from the autobiographical novel about an outing in the forest, would write hundreds of poems that allowed him to imagine an ethics of plant life, one far more accommodative than human social structures.[10] He would die while teaching at the university established by Tagore. There were several others of course: a young man writing about life by the river Titash,[11] the changing behaviour of plants; and someone quite the opposite, a professional chartered accountant who would write about adventures in the jungles of eastern India, a forest life different from the travelogue about Palamou and Bhagalpur.[12] Another, a poet, responding to strained Hindu-Muslim relations, writes a song like 'Mora aeki brintey duti kushum, Hindu Mussalman', we are two buds on the same stalk—Hindu and Mussalman.[13] I name only the well known here, the men.

There were others—the anonymous, such as Maya-mashi, a refugee from Bangladesh, an illiterate woman who worked as house help in Siliguri, one of the many who used, lubricated, and, by adding their life histories to it, kept alive a unique oral culture of plant proverbs, perhaps without parallel in any other linguistic culture.

Who were these people? None of them were environmentalists, none of them had consciously set out to write about plant life, but they were all connected in some way or the other, related to each other, in life or through their habitat and art. It wasn't hard to see that a revolution had been going on. Why hadn't anyone noticed? It seemed like a continuation and manifestation of plant blindness. This book is about these plant thinkers, these revolutionaries who created a plant poetics that secretly changed the way a people would imagine and live with plants.

I came to write this book from as much a sense of wonder as of frustration. The more I read and spoke to people, particularly those who read primarily in the English language, I was struck by the absence of any consciousness about a tradition of plant thinking in the Indian subcontinent. It was clearly an effect of the Western colonization of academia—for almost everything I said, whether from 2,000 years ago or a hundred, the response, while always well-intentioned and eager to make connections, was about something similar in Europe or North America. In all—I say 'all', not 'most'—the books I read, no Indian thinker or scientist was mentioned, until it began to seem that there had never been a tradition of thinking about plant life in India at all. When I began writing this book, I knew that my approach, therefore, would not be comparative—not the well-mannered, see-the-convergences-in-thought discourse. As I read and wrote, I heard the word around me often: 'decolonization'. I also noticed, with sadness, the consequent good intentions and tokenism. And my resolve hardened—I wanted these plant thinkers to be read independently, on their own terms, through the cosmology that they had created, instead of their thoughts being compared incessantly, and often reductively, to those whose work had found circulation in Euro-American academia and publishing. That would also allow for the kind of immersive experience that their works demanded—not mere commendation through comparison. If anyone was genuinely curious, they would make a journey to these thinkers, not expect the Indians to make the journey to them, to meet them halfway. This book, then, is propelled by hope—that the unidirectional journey of globalization, where ideas from power centres travelled to those in the umbra and penumbra, without a journey from the opposite direction ever really taking place, might be reversed, that it might have other pathways. If they did at all, it had to be packaged appropriately for consumption in these places, sometimes through paraphrase, often through the smuggling of the comparative. In this book, there is neither—you meet these people and their thoughts in their habitat, not in an archive or museum or even a botanical garden.

None of these thinkers were 'environmentalists'. Perhaps it was this freedom from being anchored to any form of institutional thinking that allowed and compelled them to create a language, not of bureaucracy but of life. The language of bureaucracy has, quite clearly, failed to affect our minds and habits, drugged as we are by the saccharine of capitalism, it hasn't been able to rehabilitate us to a 'sustainable'—a bureaucratic word which implies co-sharing—manner of living. I read these thinkers closely, as I imagine I look at leaves and the bends of branches, imagining their need—and greed—for light in their shape. I read with hesitation and hope, as perhaps the structure of the book itself will reveal. It is to reintroduce my contemporaries, particularly my little nephew and niece, to the vocabulary of intimacy and cohabitation with plant life that I write this book—to record a history of living and thinking that I fear is on the verge of extinction.

Literary history is directly related to ecological history. Let me rephrase that. Literary history *is* ecological history. Why hadn't this, what I now intuitively recognized as obvious, been noticed? It was a surprise to me, often, therefore, when writing this book, that these people, most of them decidedly modernist in temper, had not been read for their thoughts on plant and animal life, or on the elements, on what is summarily—and almost insultingly—called the 'non-human' today. It wasn't the subject, nor the description, but consciousness, and its struggle to find 'roop' (meaning both 'form' and beauty'). My understanding of modernism was very basic: I saw it as the struggle of artists to record and report the world as they saw it; in trying to do so, the obstruction caused by the language or medium in reporting their truth made them respond in various ways, some of which were often playful. Avantgarde and the experimental were, quite obviously, a result of this search. These had been noticed, studied, analysed. Plant blindness—that humans have become conditioned to not noticing plant life in their surroundings, unless curated, as in the botanical gardens, for instance—was not just a condition of human life, it afflicted academic scholarship as well. As I waded through books and essays on these writers and artists, I noticed the brilliance and inventiveness of their commentators, but I also could not *not* notice their lack of critical thought on how the presence of plant life, the impress and pressure of philosophical traditions on their work, were what constituted their so-called modernity. European modernism had been studied as the effect of the wars—and later the introduction of technology—on a culture. Why hadn't Indian—Bengali, to be more specific—modernism been studied differently, as a response to the depletion of plant life, when so many writers were responding by writing about it?

What I seek to propose is, also, to modify our understanding of what constitutes 'theory'—how fiction and poetry are excluded from this corpus (perhaps because academics, who are arbiters and often producers of what counts as theory, do not usually write fiction and poetry), for instance. Not being a believer in the institutionalized binary between theory and literary texts, where the latter is used to illustrate the former in reductive, utilitarian, and sometimes even opportunist readings, I read writing and art and common adages as 'theory' itself. 'Theory', privileged over 'literature' today, has created its place in the hierarchy by virtue of it being espoused as argumentative. After all, the first arguments, whether about the creation of the world, or its critique, were made in kavya, poetry. 'After all, it was an ancient poet's description of a peacock-peppered wilderness in the rains that had inspired Kalidasa to imagine his messenger-cloud. For centuries, we have marvelled at the beauty of his epic poem, but had we realised that we were simultaneously also paying our respects to that fortuitous moonlit light, when the great poet read another's work by the golden light of his bedside lamp, and made it part of his own? To light a fire, after all, we need to already have some fire. A heap of ashes couldn't do the job. Neither could a flaming torch light a pile of ash on fire, even if it tried', writes Bibhutibhushan in *Pather Panchali*.[14] 'To light a fire, after all, we need to already have some fire'—the literary tradition where one advances and argues against one's ancestors. It is to continue the fire that I write this book.

Notes

1. Jagadish Chandra Bose.
2. Visvabharati University.
3. Nandalal Bose and Benode Bihari Mukherjee, among others.
4. Bibhutibhushan Bandyopadhyay.
5. Bandyopadhyay (2017).
6. Jibanananda Das.
7. Ritwik Ghatak.
8. Satyajit Ray.
9. Ray (dir.), Aranyer Din Ratri (1970).
10. Shakti Chattopadhyay.
11. Adwaita Mallabarman.
12. Buddhadev Guha.
13. Kazi Nazrul Islam.
14. Bandyopadhyay (2019), p. 299.

I spent several years in perfecting various instruments by which the plant attached to the recording apparatus is automatically excited by successive stimuli which are absolutely constant. In answer to this it makes its own responsive records, goes through its period of recovery, and I'm on the same cycle over again, without assistance at any point from the observer. In this way the effect of changed external condition is seen recorded in the script made by the plant itself.

—Bose

1

Jagadish Chandra Bose

'You are aware that in the West, the prevailing tendency at the moment is, after a period of synthesis, to return upon the excessive subdivision of learning. The result of this specialization is rather to accentuate the distinctiveness of the various sciences, so that for a while the great unity of all tends perhaps to be obscured. Such a caste-system in scholarship, undoubtedly helps at first, in the gathering and classification of new material.'[1] This is Jagadish Chandra Bose giving his presidential address on 11 April 1911 at Mymensing. The phrase 'caste system' stands out for obvious reasons—one doesn't expect it in a lecture by a scientist, and one doesn't associate it with the 'West'. There is a history to that ascription. A decade before this lecture, Jagadish Chandra had declared—and proved—to the scientific community that plants were 'living beings', and he had had to face criticism, harassment, and even mocking vilification for doing so.

Born in Munshiganj, in what is now Bangladesh, to a Brahmo Samaj family, Jagadish Chandra studied in Calcutta's Hare School and St Xavier's College, though he also spent time in Faridpur and Bardhaman, where his father was posted as Deputy Magistrate. Bhagawan Chandra Bose was insistent that his son study in a Bangla language school before he was forced to acquire the English language for professional reasons: 'At that time, sending children to English schools was an aristocratic status symbol. In the vernacular school, to which I was sent, the son of the Muslim attendant of my father sat on my right side, and the son of a fisherman sat on my left. They were my playmates. I listened spellbound to their stories of birds, animals, and aquatic creatures. Perhaps these stories created in my mind a keen interest in investigating the workings of Nature'. This affection and patriotism for his language would stay with him throughout his life. In the preface to *Abyakta*, a collection of

Plant Thinkers of Twentieth-Century Bengal. Sumana Roy, Oxford University Press. © Sumana Roy 2024.
DOI: 10.1093/9780198929314.003.0002

his essays published in 1922, he declares his desire and his ambition for Bangla to acquire a scientific vocabulary:

> The language that a man learns in his mother's arms is the language in which he expresses his happiness and sorrow. About thirty years ago, a few of my scientific writings and other essays had been written in English. I had started researching on electric waves and life, and that led to my involvement in several legal cases. The court for this is abroad, where arguments can only be made in the European languages. In this country too, a case is not declared closed until the judgment of the Privy Council.
>
> Isn't this insulting to our national life, to the life of our jaati? To redeem this, I have tried to establish a scientific court in this country. I might not live to see the fruit of this; the fate of scientific institutions is in the hands of god.[2]

Jagadish Chandra went on to study the natural sciences at the University of Cambridge and get his DSc degree from University College London, following which he returned to teach at Presidency College. He would eventually establish the Bose Institute in 1917, where most of his research instruments are still preserved. These details, though, tell us very little about his revolutionary imagination and courage.

Before I come to his work in the plant sciences, it would be useful to trace his research in the physical sciences and in wireless communication, for they lead to it, for what he's most remembered. In the early 1890s, Jagadish Chandra worked primarily on radio communication, and, in the middle of that decade, ignited gunpowder and rang a bell using millimetre range wavelength microwaves. Writing about it later, he declared the potential of radio waves for wireless communication. It was well received in England, reports of which we find in *The Electrician* and in *The Englishman* which, in its January 1986 issue, observed, 'Should Professor Bose succeed in perfecting and patenting his "Coherer", we may in time see the whole system of coast lighting throughout the navigable world revolutionized by a Bengali scientist working single-handedly in our Presidency College laboratory.'[3] A year before that he had met Marconi where they discussed radio wave wireless telegraphy—the two of them had been working on it independently, but while Marconi was interested in getting a patent and marketing his research, particularly to the British post office, Jagadish Chandra was uninterested in commercial telegraphy and the revenue his research might bring. At that time his focus was on analysing the phenomenon of radio waves, not tapping its potential in radio communication. He, in fact, shared details of his research, such as that on the galena crystal detector, while others like Marconi and Alexander Popov worked secretly and independently, working towards getting patents and individual recognition for their work. The first to use a semiconductor junction to detect radio waves, Nevill Mott, the 1977 Nobel Prize winner for his work on solid-state electronics, said that 'J C Bose was at least 60 years ahead of his time. In fact, he had anticipated the existence of P-type and N-type semiconductors.'[4] Simultaneous with this was his work on metal behaviour—subjecting metals to mechanical, thermal, electrical, and chemical stimuli, noting fatigue and recovery over varying time periods. At around the same time, in 1896 in fact, he wrote what is now considered to be one of the first pieces of science fiction by an Indian— 'Niruddeser Kahini' (The Story of the Missing One), whose title he later changed to 'Palatak Toofan'.[5] All of this now seems to be leading to the inevitable; if analysed in terms of trajectory, his work on radio waves and metal behaviour and in the short story were about communication and response. It was both, response and communication, that he would seek in plant life, and it was his experience in designing instruments and experiments in both the fields of radio research and metal behaviour that he would import into the plant sciences. One of the first hurdles in this would be what he, in his lecture at Mymensing, would call the 'caste system' in the sciences—a physicist trying to work in the botanical sciences.[6]

δ

But what exactly had brought him to the plant sciences? There is folklore about Jagadish Chandra stepping accidentally on *mimosa pudica*, called lajjabati in Bangla, meaning the 'shy one', and, surprised by the folding of its leaves, deciding to find out more about plant behaviour, their response and ways of communication. While we think of his botanical research, its ambition, design, and results, we must also allow ourselves to think of the ecosophical culture that indulged such thinking. Critiquing what he called the caste system in the sciences, watertight disciplinary boundaries, he turned to his own culture: 'The Eastern aim has been the opposite, namely, that in the multiplicity of phenomena, we should never miss their underlying unity. After generations of this quest, the idea of unity comes to us almost spontaneously, and we apprehend no insuperable obstacle in grasping it'.[7]

This 'Eastern aim' about the 'underlying unity' in 'the multiplicity of phenomena', a shorthand for an Upanishadic understanding of life, something that marks the plant philosophy of all the plant thinkers in this book, comes to Jagadish Chandra from the Brahmo Samaj, of which his father was an important member. He imports this understanding to the sciences and to everything in this neighbourhood of life. First his call to dismantle these artificial divisions between the sciences—notice how he stretches this to the 'artificial' division between life forms:

> This vast abode of nature is built in many wings, each with its own portal. The physicist, the chemist, and the biologist entering by different doors, each one his own department of knowledge, comes to think that this is his special domain, unconnected with that of any other. Hence has arisen our present rigid division of phenomena, into the worlds of the inorganic, vegetal, and sentient. But that this attitude of mind is philosophical may be denied. We must remember that all enquiries have as their goal the attainment of knowledge in its entirety. The partition walls between the cells in the great laboratory are only erected for a time to aid this search. Only at that point where all lines of investigation meet, can the whole truth be found.[8]

'Is there any possible relation between our own life and that of the plant world?' This question, which we find in many of Jagadish Chandra's essays, is a paraphrase of what propelled his research, which was only a manifestation of his belief in the life of all things. Light is invisible, he says, and yet we are aware of its working, the responses it generates in us. From light he takes us to its eater—for, as he famously said, we all eat light: humans and animals eat plants who eat light. But this eating of light is invisible, just as there is life in plants even if we cannot hear their voice. 'Unvoiced life'—that is the phrase he uses, one that is the vocabulary of response and communication. He names Western scientists who have refused to accept that plants are living beings; what he doesn't do is name European philosophers who have done the same. 'So distinguished a leader as the late Burdon-Sanderson declared that the majority of plants were not capable of giving any answer';[9] 'Pfeiffer, again, and his distinguished followers, have insisted that the plants have neither a nervous system, nor anything analogous to the nervous impulse of the animal'.[10] In this lecture at Mymensingh—and others—we find Jagadish Chandra refusing to distinguish between a 'poet and a scientific worker': 'Both poet and scientific worker have set out with the same goal, to find a unity in the bewildering diversity'.[11] He is aware of the pull of both in him—one rarely comes across scientific research written in such a moving manner—as he braces himself for the opposition to his research. Writing this letter to his friend Rabindranath Tagore from London, he says:

What I am doing is against accepted opinion. Just as cutting a tree from near its root leads to its fall, its rest on the earth, similarly with many old theories. Many things will need to be rewritten, and written afresh, and, for this, battles will have to be fought with old conventional thought. What I have discovered gives me a lot of courage, but patience—patience patience. This virtue we lack.[12]

A couple of months later, in January 1901, he writes:

Dr. Muirhead has asked me to keep my new discoveries a 'secret'; but my time here is limited, I have a lot to do, and if I become attracted to money-earning knowledge, then I will be able to do nothing. I cannot explain to you what a new kingdom I have entered, the new theories that I can see from here. I am unable to express this in words; that I will gradually be able to see them clearly I have no doubt; but I will have to strive for it with austerity day after day. If I am disturbed from this state, I will lose focus. What I have done until now is too little, there is much more to do. But, for that, time and money are necessary . . . I feel hurt that I have to publish my findings in this incomplete form.[13]

All through his stay in England, we find Bose reporting this hostility to his friend in India. Rabindranath's replies are warm, comforting, consolatory, curious, patient, affectionate, and always full of hope and details of his life and mental weather in Bengal. When Bose returns to India and moves for some time to Darjeeling, Tagore asks him for Himalayan plant cuttings for his gardens in Santiniketan. But that would happen later— before this was Bose's churning not for recognition, but for the acceptance of his work by the scientific community in England.

Thirteen years later, two months before the start of World War I, Jagadish Bose was giving a talk about 'Plant-Autographs and their Revelations' to the Royal Institution of Great Britain. This would be published by Macmillan in 1927.[14] For the Friday 'Weekly Evening Meeting', Bose is listed as 'Professor Jagadis Chunder Bose, MA, DSc, CSI CIE, Professor, Presidency College, Calcutta'. Bose's interest, in my understanding of his work, has always been with the nature of life: what constituted the living? 'Response' is an important category in the Bose universe—it is a mark of the living: to be alive is to respond. There are others too, and, in this talk, his argument for plants to be considered 'living' beings is moving, affectionate, completely idiosyncratic, even eccentric, slightly mad, but never unscientific. The talk often feels like a lawyer's argument, his desperation to prove the legitimacy of plants as citizens in the country of the living. The 'script' or 'handwriting' is important to Bose. It is a manifestation of response—he understands it as the claim of the living: to argue in language, to argue in 'writing'. And so he begins his talk with the 'science' of handwriting. It is pertinent that he characterizes this approach through a word that could be said to be at the other end of the 'scientific': 'mysticism', with its character of unquantifiability.

> There are professors of sciences bordering on the mystical, who declare that they can discriminate the character and disposition of anyone, simply by a careful observation of his handwriting. As to the authenticity of such claims, scepticism is permissible: but there is no doubt that one's handwriting may be modified profoundly by conditions, physical and mental. There still exist at Hatfield House, documents which contain the signatures of no less in person than the historical Guy Fawkes of the Gunpowder Plot celebrity. And those who have seen them declare that there is a sinister variation in these signatures.[15]

Bose recognizes the unreliability of such a science, but still chooses it to explain plant behaviour.

> Such, then, is the history that may be unfolded to the critical eye by the lines and curves of a human autograph. Under a placid exterior, there is also a hidden history in the life of the plant. Storm and sunshine, warmth of summer and frost of winter, drought and rain, all these and many more come and go about the plant. What coercion do they exercise upon it? What subtle impress do they leave behind? Is it possible to make the plants write down their own autographs, and thus reveal their hidden history?[16]

What Bose seeks, therefore, is not 'autograph' alone—through it he is seeking autobiography, the 'hidden history', the 'unsaid' ('abyakto') of the plants. Writing this during the high tide of modernism, when the autobiography was becoming the most interesting site for experiments in writing and art, and also an entry point for those who had been kept out of 'literature' and 'culture' by gatekeepers, this urge for both the autograph and autobiography of the plant seems natural—natural in the literary and cultural world, but not in the sciences. The sciences tell us someone's 'story'—of animals, objects, metals, the elements, the stars, and, of course, of plants. Bose is signalling for a move from literature about 'them', a world available to us only in reports and paraphrase, to a directness that has been denied to everyone besides those who have had no agency to speak to humans in a shared language. What he is trying to create, therefore, is language. This is as much the language of science, with its emphasis on quantifiability of the response, a manner of thinking that he inherits as much from the bureaucracy of Western science as he perhaps does from a conditioning in the temperament of Samkhya philosophy from the Indian subcontinent. What he is also challenging in the process is the hierarchy of 'living beings' since Aristotle, a conditioning in thinking of plants at the bottom of such a list. This championing of plant life to be recognized as on a par with the animal world, too, might have come to him from being surrounded by a Buddhist and Upanishadic understanding of what and who constitutes the category of the living, where, after acknowledging difference, there is an acceptance of the right of each plant, human, animal, stone, and the elements to life and this earth.

δ

'The Silent Life', an essay that I have translated from his book *Abyakta*, reveals this impulse repeatedly. We encounter his restlessness and his passion, his affection for the neglected. In the world of science and its performance of objectivity, of the suppression of emotions so that scientists are expected to behave with the neutrality of the instruments they use, this is, of course, an exception. Reading the prehistory of emotions that attended his experiments, something not granted to us by scientists, we become aware of the scientist's nerves as he sets out to discover and prove the nervous system in plants. It is these questions and these anxieties that become manifest in the first section of this essay:

The sapling, growing inch by inch, its growth invisible to the naked eye—how will I record its growth from moment to moment with a machine? Will an external injury affect the character and rate of its growth? Does giving it food—or depriving it of food—change it, and how long does it take for the change to begin? Will giving it medicine or poison cause it to change? Will it be possible for one poison to counteract the effect of another kind of poison in the plant? Can the amount of one poison undo the effect of another?

If a tree responds to an external injury, how long will it take for this response to materialize? Does the duration of that feeling change in a different situation? Will it be possible to get the tree to write about this time? How does the injury reach the tree's inside? Does it have a nervous system? If it does, how is the speed of the nerve's excitement communicated? Do favourable circumstances cause an increment in its speed? Do adverse circumstances prevent that? Are there similarities between our nervous system and the plant's? Can the changes in speed be recorded by the plant itself? Do plants have muscles like there are in the human heart? In the end, when death comes to a tree, is it possible to record that moment of nirvana? And does the tree respond fiercely to that moment before falling into an everlasting sleep?

Only a history of these different moments, captured by different instruments, will give us the true and uninterrupted history of plant life.[17]

There is also the attendant emotion of reading them in Bangla, a language colonial science did not consider suitable for scientific thought. This is the language of affection, of imploration, and, indeed, of activism:

To know the real history of plants, we must go to the plants themselves. That history is mysterious and complicated. To retrieve that history, machines will have to record every moment of a plant's life, from birth to death. The script will have to be written by the plant itself, and it must have the plant's autograph. This is because men are often deceived by their motive.[18]

And then we are allowed entry into the imagination that designed a variety of instruments, none of which seemed to have satisfied him completely, for he was always trying to design another one, one more sophisticated and acknowledging of the invisible life of plants—the electro-optic analogue, the shielded lens antenna, resonant recorder, phytograph, plant photograph, automatic potograph, Bubler instrument, plant sphygmograph, and, of course, the most well known among them, the crescograph. The design of these instruments came from his living in both the physical and botanical sciences. In this his sole collaborator was a tinsmith by the name of Putiram Das.

δ

Convinced that to know about plant life we must go to the plants themselves, to get their autobiography as it were, he designed his scientific instruments to be as 'sensitive' as possible. That is a word appropriate as much for the efficiency of these instruments as it is for empathy. What he wanted to record was response to various kinds of stimuli, of course, but, if one notices carefully, this is actually a record of injury, of hurt, a first information report of the effect of burn and cold, electric voltage or darkness. He wanted plants to write their own autobiography in their own script, 'torulipi', the plant script. His plant philosophy is one of the most non-anthropocentric practical philosophies that a human has possibly imagined.

> Injury startles every living creature. That contraction is life's response, the response of the living. When one is in the fullness of life, the response is the highest in degree; in a moment of exhaustion, the response is feeble; there's none after death. There *is* compression in a plant when it is hurt, but it is so little that we are most often unable to see it. An instrument will amplify this compression and record it as the plant's script. The only hurdle for this is the extremely low intensity of the plant's response, one that the instrument is often unable to script—its blade comes to a stop. To circumvent this, I was successful in inventing a flat-planed instrument. If two violins are tuned to exactly the same sur, if a string in one of them is stroked, the string in the other will also create a jhankar. In the Plant-Script instrument, the iron wires inside and outside it are tuned to the same sur. Imagine this—that both the wires tremble hundred times per second. If the external wire is played, the internal wire will move a hundred times, and the blade will draw a hundred dots. This is how the constant friction with the blade can be avoided. The transcript will record even the finest movement of the plant; this is because the difference between one dot and the next is only a second.[19]

The 'torulipi' or plant script was to be based on a record of a plant's responses to different kinds of stimuli; in most of these essays, we find Bose referring to the plants as *brikkhoshishu*, or plant-infant. In 'Udbhider Jonmo O Mrityu' ('The Birth and Death of Plants'), he writes, 'Infants do not have teeth; they only drink milk. Plants too do not have teeth—that is why they can only partake of liquid and air.' A few sentences later, he returns to the image: 'Leaves have many tiny mouths. Seen closely with a microscope, all these mouths reveal tiny lips. When they no longer need food, the lips close.' The metaphor occurs repeatedly throughout his work: 'The seed hides under the earth for a long time. Months go by. Spring follows winter. Then the rains start—a day of rain. There is no need to hide anymore. It is as if someone is calling the child from outside, "Don't sleep anymore, climb out now, you'll see the light of the sun."' And: 'Have you seen a seedling sprout out of the earth? It seems like a child is raising its tiny head to watch a new world with wonder.' And: 'Rejecting the darkness of the marginalized forests, the plant-child lifts its head.'[20]

As a metaphor, this would mean little had it not driven his curiosity to actually articulate a language of plants. In another essay, we see Bose defending his ambition to understand plant linguistics—if I may call it that—by referring to the plant-child equivalence:

Do plants say anything? Many will say, What kind of a question is this? Have plants ever spoken? Can man express himself clearly? And what he cannot express, is it not language? We have a child—he cannot speak clearly; the few words that come out of him are so half-formed and even broken that it is impossible for anyone to understand their meaning. But we can understand everything that our child says. Not just that though. There are many things that our little boy does not say aloud in words; his eyes, the movements of his face and hands, the shaking of his head—he speaks through these gestures, we understand that language as well, but others don't. One day a pigeon from a neighboring house came and sat on our house—it then began cooing and grunting at the top of its voice. Our little boy was thus introduced to the pigeon; he soon began imitating the pigeon's *doob doob*. How does the pigeon call? As soon as we asked him this, he would imitate the bird's call ...

Returning home one day, I found the little boy with fever; a severe headache had made him lie limp on the bed. The naughty boy who prances around the house restlessly all day was now struggling to even open his eyes. I sat by his bed and ran my fingers through his hair. Recognizing me from my touch, he opened his eyes with a lot of effort and looked at me. He then made the pigeon-sound. I heard many things in his pigeon-call. I understood that the little boy was saying, 'You've come to see the little boy? The little boy loves you a lot.' I understood several other things, things that I wouldn't be able to express in words.

If you ask me how I could hear so many things in that pigeon call, there is only one answer—it is because I love the little boy. You have seen that by looking at her son's face a mother understands what he wants. Often there is no need for words. If one observes from love, many qualities are revealed, one is able to hear many things.[21]

In his presidential address at the Literary Conference in Mymensing in April 1911, which would later be published as 'Literature and Science', Bose deliberates on the 'caste system' in academia, the relationship between poetry and science, and the 'invisible' and the 'unvoiced', the first being light, the second being living forms whose language we do not understand. He then turns to communication between plants and humans, and how it is necessary for plants to write their own 'script'. 'It is comparatively easy to make a rebellious child obey; to extort answers from plants is indeed a problem!' The words that follow are borne of guilt, confessions of 'various acts of cruelty' he has enacted in his research. 'I have from time to time perpetrated on unoffending plants, in order to compel them to give me answers. For this purpose, I have devised various forms of torment—pinches simple and revolving, pricks with needles, and burns with acids. But let this pass. I now understand that replies so forced are unnatural, and of no value. Evidence so obtained is not to be trusted.'[22] This is the voice not of a scientist but of a parent—one who realizes, in retrospect, the guilt of having had their way.

It is hard to say, even when propelled by great investigative energy such as what possessed me, where Bose's emotional vocabulary, of plants as children of those without offspring, might have come from. The writer Dakkhinranjan Majumdar had collected grandmothers' tales from villages and provinces in Bengal in the late nineteenth century and published them in 1907 with a preface by Rabindranath Tagore: 'Sadly, this bag of mouth-watering tales is being supplanted by imports from England', Tagore writes. 'The worst sufferers are the children . . . Can a newborn baby who is fed barley water instead of nourishing mother's milk ever grow into a healthy child?'[23] (It's the same anxiety about language we hear in Bose's thoughts about the use of Bangla in scientific argument; the child–mother metaphor is not an accident.) In these tales of kings and queens, good and evil, and fantastic kingdoms, runs a common motif. The queen—the woman—must bear a child, and, for this, different cures are invoked: worship, fasts, sacrifices, donations, rituals, austerity, piety, and, when everything else fails, a trust in the miraculous power of plants. A wandering yogi, passing through the kingdom of the childless king, would leave a root, a tuber, or some leaf for his many wives to grind into a paste and then share among themselves. Then the miracle would happen: the queens would all get pregnant. There are many variations on what followed after this: sometimes the women bear animals instead of humans, sometimes the newborns are kidnapped or smuggled out of the palace by jealous queens, and so on.

We find the same preoccupation in Tagore's own work. Bose, whom Tagore refers to as his 'first friend', often visited the Tagore household. He taught Tagore's son, Rathindranath, to trace turtle footprints and search for their eggs. 'He would make all of us dig pits in the sand and with wet towels round our heads lie down in them to sub-bathe', Rathindranath recalls.[24] It was a friendship rich with the exchange of ideas: Tagore would read a new short story to Bose, and Bose would share the results from a new plant experiment. Rathindranath continues:

Jagadish Chandra was at this time making experiments to compare the reactions on the Living and Non-living to different kinds of stimuli. He believed the results he had obtained with the help of the delicate instruments he had invented would revolutionize the current conceptions held by the scientists regarding the nature of life . . . When Jagadish was satisfied that he had obtained sufficient convincing data to acquaint the scientific would of his discoveries, he wanted to go to England to give actual demonstrations of his experiments to scientists in order to convince them of the truth of his deductions. Father approached the Maharaja of Tripura and was able to get from him sufficient money not only to enable Jagadish to go abroad but to fit up his laboratory with the equipment that he badly needed.[25]

What were these experiments? Bose writes:

Before declaring the results of the experiment, it is important to dispel the superstition that surrounds plants—whether they are shy or bold, responsive or the opposite. That all plant life responds can be proven with the help of electrical energy. Why is it, then, that only the *Mimosa pudica*, the touch me not, responds with its leaves when other plants do not? To understand this, please think of the muscles on your arm, moving only a part of which one can respond with one's hand. If the muscles on both sides of the arm were to move, then the hand would not be able to move. When a plant is hurt, all its muscles are compressed at the same time—that is why it does not move in any direction. But if a section of its muscles were to be anesthetised with chloroform, then it will be easy to prove the response and movement of plants.[26]

First—to imagine that hurt could be measured requires the imagination of more than a scientist or philosopher. Perhaps that is why Rabindranath called him a 'rishi'. And that hurt could be the index and axis of a script that makes us look at our human languages and scripts in a completely new way.

The difference in time causes a difference in response. In the morning, the numbness of the night overstays, and hence the plant's inertia. Repeated injuries cause this inertia to disappear, and its rate of response begins to increase; it is as if it were a state of awakening. If the plant were given a hot water bath, the inertia will disappear quickly. In the afternoon, the opposite happens: tiredness causes its response to decrease. But if you allow the plant to rest, it gradually recovers from exhaustion. An increase in the impact of the injury will naturally tend to rev up the volume of the response as well, but there is a limit to that. In this, there is little to distinguish plant life from the human. Another surprising thing is that just as we take time to recover from our injuries in winter, so does the plant. What takes fifteen minutes to heal in summer takes more than half an hour in winter.[27]

Jagadish Chandra then comes to the comparative, using the since-animals-have reasoning. His instruments, amateurish as they are, prove that plants have a nervous system of their own:

The impact of injury in an animal's body is transferred through the nerves. The nervous system has a few characteristics: there is an increase in the speed of transmission at various times. Heat and cold affect its speed; electrical energy causes changes in the nervous system as well. As long as electrical energy flows through the nervous system, nothing much happens. But the transmission of this current just before it comes to a stop can cause excitement in one zone and exhaustion in another. The space through which the electrical current passes is suddenly excited. It does not allow for any 'news'—or any new electrical impulse—to pass through the same space immediately. But, once the electrical impulse is stopped, closed paths are reopened, and the nervous system becomes a news carrier once again.

With the help of instruments, it is possible to prove and measure, in the finest detail, how nerves behave in a tree. The speed at which stimulus travels in a tree is much slower than how it travels in a frog; but it is faster than it is in lower animals. Heat causes the nervous system in a plant to double its response time. When electricity is given to the tree, it causes excitement to one part of a tree and exhaustion in another. Electric current causes the push in its nervous system to stop. After having conducted all possible tests and experiments about the nervous system, I have been able to prove that there is no difference between the nervous system of plants and other living creatures.[28]

Prakash Narain Tandon, in his essay 'Jagadish Chandra Bose and Plant Neurobiology', tells us that new research in the plant sciences corroborates Jagadish Chandra's intuitive beliefs. 'Bose became the first to use the term "Plant Nerve."[29] Though nervous impulse in insectivorous plants was already reported a few years earlier than Bose by Burdon-Sanderson and Darwin, the types of details of the nervous system provided by Bose, in a large number of papers and a series of monographs (Bose, 1906, 1907 and 1926–1929), were not available from any other source.'[30] New research in plant communication and plant electrophysiology has only confirmed Jagadish Chandra's findings. His work has also led to the creation of a new field of enquiry: 'Plant Neurobiology is a newly initiated field of plant biology that aims to understand how plants perceive their circumstances and respond to environment input in an integrated fashion taking into account the combined molecular, chemical and electrical components of intercellular plant signaling'. V. A. Shepherd writes, 'His (Bose's) overall conclusion that plants have an electromechanical pulse, a nervous system, a form of intelligence, and are capable of remembering and learning, was not well received in its time. A century later, some of these concepts have entered the mainstream literature.'[31] Trewavas, in 'Aspects of Plant Intelligence', while noting the difference between plant and animal intelligence quotes from Jagadish Chandra's recording of the behaviour of roots, styles, and leaflets of *Mimosa* to heat, light, and other: 'The importance of time scale photography for this purpose, as first used by Bose, was highlighted.'[32]

Tandon quotes from Charles Darwin—'It is consistent with the doctrine of continuity that in all living things there is something psychic, and if we accept this point of view we must believe that in plants there exists a faint copy of what we know as consciousness in ourselves'[33]—and new research—'The physiological specificity of plants is mediated by internal oscillations of hormones such as auxin and cytokines and/or electricity that is perceived by the roots through the soil. Such signals are known to be highly dynamic in nature and thus individually unique. Such signals can be potentially perceived and monitored both within the plants and outside roots. Accordingly, the perception of "self" is based on resonant amplification of oscillatory signals in the vicinity of other roots of the same plant'. He ends his essay on Jagadish Chandra's contribution to plant neurobiology by asking whether, as the Indian scientist believed, plants could have a sense of 'self'.[34] 'These trees have a life like ours', said Jagadish Chandra, 'they eat and grow . . . face poverty, sorrows and sufferings. This poverty may . . . induce them to steal and rob . . . they help each other, develop friendships, sacrifice their lives for their children'.[35] Tandon writes, 'Having studied a fairly large number of writings of Bose personally, it is not clear to the present author as to the scientific evidence adduced by him (Bose) to arrive at this philosophical statement, but it can certainly serve an inducement to explore the neuroscientific basis for it. May be a century later, this may find scientific confirmation like his studies in the early 1900.'[36] The 'self' is hard to prove through scientific research. That plants have a self of their own kind is something all the plant thinkers in this book will agree upon. 'The intuitions of emotion cannot be established by rigid proof', wrote Jagadish Chandra of the poet, contrasting it with the scientific worker's 'path'. We now know that Jagadish Chandra Bose was both poet and scientist, who was able to prove the intuitions of his emotion about plant behaviour, intelligence, and communication with rigid proof.

When I read Suzanne Simard's work, as in her memoir *Finding the Mother Tree: Discovering the Wisdom of the Forest*, where she proves how the health of forests is dependent on a network of underground tree communication, I think of the lonely scientist in his Calcutta laboratory arriving upon the intuition of such a phenomenon more than a hundred years ago.[37]

δ

Rabindranath, who called Jagadish Chandra his 'prothom bondhu', 'my first friend', wrote a poem for him.[38] In the first stanza we see how the poet saw him—not as a scientist alone, but as someone who was 'rishi', 'savant', and stood 'alone at the deep centre of all things', who knew that in 'sun, moon, flowers, leaves, beasts and birds, dust and stones' was 'the One', and who set out to prove that for the plant world. That is why Jagadish Chandra Bose was not just a botanist but a plant philosopher—he heard their 'wordless melody':

> Young image of what old Rishi of Ind
> Art thou, O Arya savant, Jagadish?
> What unseen hermitage hast thou raised up
> From 'neath the dry dust of this city of stone?
> Amidst the crowd's mad turmoil, whence hast thou
> That peace in which thou in an instant stoodst
> Alone at the deep centre of all things—
> Where dwells the One alone in sun, moon, flowers,
> In leaves, and beasts and birds, and dust and stones,
> —Where still one sleepless Life on its own lap
> Rocks all things with a wordless melody,
> All things that move or that seem motionless![39]

Bose has been recognized in whimsical ways, such as a crater on the moon being named after him, but Bose was systematically discriminated against for most of his career—for his amphibious life as a scientist in the physical and life sciences, his work being derided as idiosyncratic and unscientific; he was not paid the salary that was paid to British professors at Presidency College in Calcutta, for which he refused to draw his salary for a couple of years until he was paid the same amount; his research was often denied funding. The purposive derision of his work and his reputation as a scientist in the West, particularly for being a mad fantasist who imagined plant response and communication, seems amusing now as new research on plant communication by scientists continues to verify the claims and corollaries that Jagadish Chandra Bose made and established in his own manner a hundred years ago.

Notes

1. Bhattacharya and Chakrabarty (2013), p. 387.
2. Bose (1922).
3. *The Electrician* 38, December 1895, quoted in *The Englishman*, January 1986.
4. Mott, cited in New Worlds Encyclopedia (2021).
5. Bose (1896).
6. Bhattacharya and Chakrabarty (2013).
7. Ibid., p. 387.
8. Ibid., p. 388.
9. Ibid., p. 390.
10. Ibid.
11. Ibid., p. 388.
12. Bose (1899). Translation mine.
13. Ibid.
14. Bose (1927).
15. Ibid.
16. Ibid.
17. Bose (1922). Translation mine.
18. Ibid.
19. Ibid.
20. Ibid.
21. Ibid.
22. Ibid.
23. Tagore and Majumdar ([1907] 2021).
24. Tagore (1958).
25. Ibid.
26. Bose (1922).
27. Ibid. Translation mine.
28. Ibid. Translation mine.
29. Tandon (2019).
30. Ibid.
31. Shepherd (2005).
32. Trewavas (2003).
33. Tandon (2019).
34. See Gruntman and Novoplansky (2004).
35. Bose.
36. Tandon (2019).
37. Simard (2021).
38. Bose (1901).
39. Ibid.

Fortunately, trees do not feel thoughtfulness. Fortunately, the dhatura plant does not criticise the kamini tree and say, 'Your flowers have gentleness but no power' nor does the kul tell the jackfruit—'You think you are great, but I give the kushmando a higher position than you'. Bananas don't say 'I promote letters the best at the most inexpensive rate' and the yam doesn't compete by lowering its price for a great arrangement for the letters.

—Tagore

2

Rabindranath Tagore

Rabindranath Tagore's understanding of his own culture—and indeed of his own consciousness—is mediated through a belief in the Indian subcontinent as being a 'vast land of forests', or even a large forest.

> When the first Aryan invaders appeared in India it was a vast land of forests, and the newcomers rapidly took advantage of them. These forests afforded them shelter from the fierce heat of the sun and the ravages of tropical storms, pastures for cattle, fuel for sacrificial fire, and materials for building cottages. And the different Aryan clans with their patriarchal heads settled in the different forest tracts which had some special advantage of natural protection, and food and water in plenty. Thus in India it was in the forests that our civilisation had its birth, and it took a distinct character from this origin and environment.[1]

What does it imply, when one sees an entire civilization as having originated in a forest? What makes it different from a civilization that, for instance, is biblically said to have found its birth in a garden, as the civilizational culture of Rabindranath's colonizer had?

India's literature and culture, of thinking and of living, comes from the culture of the forest. Rabindranath rarely lets go of an opportunity to emphasize this. In 'Religion of the Forest' he contrasts this with European civilization.[2] 'This ideal of perfection preached by the forest-dwellers of ancient India runs through the heart of our classical literature and still dominates our mind. The legends related in our epics cluster under the forest shade bearing all through their narrative the message of the forest dwellers. Our two greatest classical dramas find their background in scenes of the forest hermitage, which are permeated by the association of these sages.'[3] He is linking Kalidasa, Shakuntala, sages, historical and mythical, and forest dwellers with his contemporaries, with himself. It is

Plant Thinkers of Twentieth-Century Bengal. Sumana Roy, Oxford University Press. © Sumana Roy 2024.
DOI: 10.1093/9780198929314.003.0003

an unexpected leap, even a conceit, to ask, to investigate, intellectually and spiritually, what links us, and what survives of the tradition of the forest and of forest thinking in us, in the twentieth century.

Bibhutibhushan, in *Aranyak*, sees the dissonance between forest dwellers and a city person such as himself, the forest and 'Bharatvarsha'. Rabindranath's energy lies in the opposite direction, in seeking continuity. Europe derives its cultural métier from the sea: 'The history of the Northmen of Europe is resonant with the music of the sea. That sea is not merely topographical in its significance but represents certain ideals of life which still guide the history and inspire the creations of that race. In the sea, nature presented herself to those men in her aspect of a danger, a barrier which seemed to be at constant war with the land and its children . . . he fought and won, and the spirit of fight continued in him. This fight he still maintains; it is the fight against disease and poverty, tyranny of matter and of man.'[4] He identifies this spirit of fighting, of taming the untamed, with European culture.

Understanding cultures through the elements, through the opposition of land and water, and through the indulgence of plant life and its related accessories of thinking and living allows Rabindranath to see cultures and collectives without vilifying them. India's culture of leisure, of the necessity of rest, of optimism, of a natural cosmopolitanism that comes from the accommodativeness of the forest, where there is room for everyone, where no one is rejected, and of ananda, a spirit that Rabindranath understands as genetic to this place and its people, is a gift of forest living. '...'in the level tracts of Northern India men found no barrier between their lives and the grand life that permeates the universe. The forest entered into a close relationship with their work and leisure, with their daily necessities and contemplations. They could not think of other surroundings as separate or inimical. So the view of the truth, which these men found, did not make manifest the difference, but rather the unity of all things. They uttered their faith in these words: Yadidam kinch sarvam prana ejati nihsratam (All that is vibrates with life, having come out from life)'.[5] This is a challenge to the European post-Renaissance anthropocentric understanding of life; man is not at the centre—he is, like all other forms of the living, only a manifestation of life, he is merely one of many, none of whom are rejected by the structure of the forest. 'According to the true Indian view, our consciousness of the world, merely as the sum total of things that exist, and as governed by laws, is imperfect. But it is perfect when our consciousness realises all things as spiritually one with it, and therefore capable of giving us joy. For us the highest purpose of this world is not merely living in it, knowing it and making use of it, but realising our own selves in it through expansion of sympathy; *not* alienating ourselves from it and *dominating* it, but *comprehending* and *uniting* it with ourselves in perfect union'.[6]

Rabindranath then proceeds to make a very important declaration—that the classical writers whose poems and plays are set in the forest were writing when the age of the forest was already over. This is our literary tradition then, that makes them our ancestors: in both, in them and in us, the forest is a memory, a biological memory, where it is not nostalgia for forest living that determines literary form alone but where the forest gives ethical and intellectual direction to the worldview. 'When Vikramaditya became king, Ujjayini a great capital, and Kalidasa its poet, the age of India's forest retreats had passed … In Kalidasa's drama, Shakuntala, the hermitage, which dominates the play, overshadowing the king's palace, has the same idea running through it the recognition of the kinship of man with conscious and unconscious creation alike'.[7] What Rabindranath is trying to suggest is quite revolutionary—that no matter whether it is a Sanskrit poet from 1,500 years ago or him, or us, a hundred years later, we are all inevitably latecomers, that 'nature' has been imagined in a prelapsarian way by poets as much as historians. It is revolutionary because it frees us from being throttled by nostalgia and allows us to renew and remake our relationship with the natural world with greater immediacy, without the burden of recreating what is lost or what possibly had no existence outside the human imagination.

A poet of a later age, while describing a hermitage in his Kadambari, tells us of the posture of salutation in the flowering lianas as they bow to the wind; of the sacrifice offered by the trees scattering their blossoms; of the grove resounding with the lessons chanted by the neophytes, and the verses repeated by the parrots, learnt by constantly hearing them; of the wild-fowl enjoying vaishva-deva-bali-pinda (the food offered to the divinity which is in all creatures); of the ducks coming up from the lake for their portion of the grass seed spread in the cottage yards to dry;

and of the deer caressing with their tongues the young hermit boys. It is again the same story. The hermitage shines out, in all our ancient literature, as the place where the chasm between man and the rest of creation has been bridged.[8]

Even as he posits this against the 'passion' and 'fury' of Shakespeare's plays, and how India's classical literature reminds us of the coexistence of everyone and everything and the resultant peace, not chaos but calm, Rabindranath makes us aware of the spirit of indolence seemingly indulged by nature that the classical poets are aiming to create through the gestures and postures of language. 'Posture', 'salutation', 'chanted'—these are as artificial an understanding of nature as is the idea of 'hermitage' itself.

We are given a model of monarchy whose ethos, ethics, and structure are dependent on the king finding their way through a forest: 'King Dilipa, with Queen Sudakshina, has entered upon the life of the forest. The great monarch is busy tending the cattle of the hermitage. Thus the poem opens, amid scenes of simplicity and self-denial.'[9] Rabindranath chooses to read the Ramayana as the human's relationship with the forest, with nature, of interest and curiosity and coexistence:

In the Ramayana, Rama and his companions, in their banishment, had to traverse forest after forest; they had to live in leaf-thatched huts, to sleep on the bare ground. But as their hearts felt their kinship with woodland, hill, and stream, they were not in exile amidst these. Poets, brought up in an atmosphere of different ideals, would have taken this opportunity of depicting in dismal colours the hardship of the forest-life in order to bring out the martyrdom of Ramachandra with all the emphasis of a strong contrast. But, in the Ramayana, we are led to realise the greatness of the hero, not in a fierce struggle with Nature, but in sympathy with it, Sita, the daughter-in-law of a great kingly house, goes along the forest paths. We read:

'She asks Rama about the flowering trees, and shrubs and creepers which she has not seen before. At her request Lakshmana gathers and brings her plants of all kinds, exuberant with flowers, and it delights her heart to see the forest rivers, variegated with their streams and sandy banks, resounding with the call of heron and duck.'[10]

The worship of Ram, the hero and his heroism that has driven the country in the last few decades, the overwhelming human-centredness in the interpretations of the epic, is rejected by Rabindranath for this model of forest living that gives dignity to all its residents. Only such a life will bring 'sachhidananda', pure consciousness, pure bliss, says the poet. Such a view he finds missing in Shakespeare and Milton, for instance, though he registers Shakespeare's unease with kings and their courtly life. In *Paradise Lost* Rabindranath misses the sense of real 'kinship' between humans and animals and plants; the focus on man disturbs him. Comparing literary—and ecological—cultures, he writes: 'Not that India denied the superiority of man, but the test of that superiority lay, according to her, in the comprehensiveness of sympathy, not in the aloofness of absolute distinction'.[11] India's pilgrimage sites, he notices, are in forested hills, 'man is free, not to look upon Nature as a source of supply of his necessities, but to realise his soul beyond himself'.[12] This is Rabindranath's plant philosophy—not the garden, where man is king and controller, but the forest and its natural cosmopolitanism, and it was this that he would try to recreate in Santiniketan, in the gardens of Uttarayan, and in Sriniketan.

δ

The first book is called *Trees of Santiniketan*. The second is in Bangla: *Uttarayaner Bagan O Gachhpala* (The Trees and Gardens of Uttarayan). That there should be books devoted just to this subject should tell us how important plant life was to the experience of Santiniketan. There's a tree on the cover of the first book, a drawing, of something resembling a krishnachura tree, by Surendranath De. Satyendra Kumar Basu, the writer of *Trees of Santiniketan*, who was at Visva Bharati 'in the winter of 1951–52',[13] begins by writing about the subsoil in the place.

The subsoil of Santiniketan is a decomposed grit devoid of vegetable matter, with a thin cover of top soil. Owing to erosion this top soil has been washed off in many places laying bare the subsoil which is then locally known as Khoai. Further weathering has often given rise to gullies ... One presumes that there was a forest cover at one time. What was the original flora? This must be a matter of surmise only. By analogy, it was probably a sal forest of the Bankura type. But the area was denuded of forest long ago, perhaps centuries ago. When Maharshi Devendranath Tagore established Santiniketan the whole area is said to have been devoid of trees of any kind except in the few villages here and there which must have contained the usual type of fruit and bamboo groves etc. We can take it, therefore, that much the greater part of the flora now in Santiniketan and its neighbourhood owes its origin to the hand of man.[14]

Basu is writing this in November 1956, four years after his stay in the university town, from his house in Kalimpong, interestingly called 'Aranyak'. Santiniketan, therefore, was an afforestation project much before that became an ambition or bureaucratic slogan. Debendranath is said to have repaired, nourished, and changed the topsoil of the place. Turning a desert-like place, unimaginable as it seems now, given its association with particular types of plant life, mythologized as they have been, in Rabindranath's songs, into a place that could be called a 'bon', a forest, was a form of unconscious plant activism that would have been from the awareness of the importance of plant life to a meditative existence. It was, after all, meant to be an ashram, a spiritual retreat.

A list of trees, with identifiable characteristics and brief description follows. I name them here, first the Linnean name and then the local name in Bangla, to give a summary of the kind of plant life that abetted Rabindranath's plant consciousness: *Anona squamosa* – Ata; *Anona reticulata* – Nona; *Polyalthia longfolia* – Debdaru; *Flacourtia separia* – Boinchee; *Flacourtia ramontchi*; *Flacourtia cataphracta*; *Mesua ferrea* – Nageswar; *Calophyllum inophyllum* – Punnag; *Shorea robusta* – Sal; *Hibiscus rosa-sinensis* – Jaba; *Thespesia populnea* – Paras; *Bombax malabaricum* – Simul; *Sterculia foetida* – Jangal badam; *Kleinhovia hospital*; *Pterospermum acerifolium* – Muchkunda; *Grewia asiatica* – Phalsa; *Hiptage madablota* – Madhabilata; *Averrhoea carambola* – Kamranga; *Aesie marmelos* – Bael; *Murraya exotica* – Kaminiphool; *Citrus medica* – Lebu; *Citrus decumana* – Batabi Lebu; *Ochna squarrosa* – Basanti (Rabindranath); Ramdhan champa; *Azadirachta indica* – Neem; *Melia azedarach* – Mahaneem; *Swietenia mahagoni* – Mahagony; *Zizyphus jujuba* – Kul; *Ziziphus oenoplia* – Shiakul; *Dodonea viscosa*; *Nephelium litchi* – Lichu;

Nephelium Longana – Ashphal; *Mangifera indica* – Aam; *Buchania latifolia* – Pial; *Odina Wodier* – Jial; *Spondia Mangifera* – Amra; *Anacardium occidentale* – Kaju badam; *Moringa pterygosperma* – Sojina; *Sesbania grandiflora* – Bokphool; *Sesbania aegyptiaca* – Jayanti; *Millettia ovalifolia*; *Erhthrina indica* – Palte madar; *Butea frondoa* – Palas; *Dalbergia Sisoo* – Sisoo; *Pterocarpus indicus*; *Pongamia glabra* – Karanj; *Peltophorum ferrugineum*; *Poinciana regia* – Radhachura; *Caesalpinia pulcherrima* – Krishnachura; *Bauhinia purpurea* – Kanchan; *Bauhinia variegata* – Kanchan; *Saraca indica* – Ashok; *Adanthera pavonine* – Raktachandan; *Acacia arabica* – Babla; *Acacia farnesiana*; *Acacia moniliformis* – Sonajhuri (Rabindranath); Akashmoni; *Albizzia lebbek* – Siris; *Pithecolobium saman* – Rain tree (same habits as the siris tree); *Pithecolobium dulce*; *Gliricidia maculara*; *Tamarindus indica* – tentul; *Cassia fistula* – Sondal; *Cassia renigera; Cassia siamea; Cassia sophera*; *Terminalia catappa* – Badam; *Terminalia belerica* – Bahera; *Terminalia chebula* – Horitoki; *Terminalia arjuna* – Arjun; *Quisqualis indica* – Madhumalati; *Eugenia jambolana* – Jam; *Eugenia malaccensis* – Jamrul; *Psidium guyava* – Peyara; *Eucalyptus citriodora*; *Lagerestroemia flos-regina* – Jarul; *Lagerstroemia indica*; *Lawsonia alba* – Mehendi; *Carica papaya* – penpey; *Passiflora*; *Alangium lamarckii* – Ankorh; *Anthocephalus cadamba* – Kadam; *Adina cordifolia* – Kelikadamba; *Hymenodictyon excelsum*; *Wendlandia exserta; Gardenia florida* – Gandharaj; *Morinda citrifolia* – Ach; *Pavetta indica* – Bon pulak; *Ixora coccinea* – Rangan; *Mimusops elengi* – Bokul; *Bassia latifolia* – Mahua; *Achras sapota* – Safeda; *Diospyros tomentosa* – Kend; *Diospyros montana* – Gobarlochan; *Diospyros embryopteris* – Gab; *Nyctanthes arbortristis* – Shiuli; *Jasminium sambac* – Belphool; *Jasminum auriculatum* – Jui, Juthi; *Jasminum pubescens* – Kunda; *Allamanda cathartica*; *Plumeria acutifolia* – Golok champa; *Plumeria tuberculate; Plumeria rubra; Nerium odorum* – Korobi; *Thivetia nerifolia* – Kolke phul; *Vince rosea* – Nayantara; *Alstonia scholaris* – Chhatim; *Aganosma caryophyllata* – Malatilata; *Holarrhena antidysenterica* – Kurchi; *Wrightia tomentosa* – Dudhi; *Tabernaemontana coronaria* – Tagar; *Cryptostegia grandiflora* – Chabukchharhi; *Calotropis gigantea* – Akanda; *Millingtonia hortensis* – Himjhuri (Rabindranath); Akasneem; *Oroxylum indicum* – Sona; *Kigelia pinnata; Crescentia cujete; Martynia diandra* – Baghnokhi; *Tectona grandis* – Segun; *Gmelina arborea* – Gamari; *Vitex negundo* – Nishkinde; *Duranta Plumieri*; *Clerodendron infortunatum* – Bhant, *Ghentu*; *Hyptis suaveolens* – Bontulsi; *Phyllanthus emblica* – Amlaki; *Phyllanthus reticulatus* – Panjuli, *Pansheora*; *Gelonium multiflorum* – Bon naringa; *Putranvija roxburghii*; *Ricinus communis* – Rerhi, Bharenda; *Jatropha curcas* – Bagbharenda; *Jatropha gossypifolia* – Lalbharenda; *Manihot utilissima* – Simul; *Euphorbia antiquorum* – Trishira monsha; *Ficus bengalensis* – Bot; *Ficus religiosa* – Aswatha; *Focis hispida* – Dumur; *Ficus nemoralis*; *Artocarpus integrifolia* – Kanthal; *Morus indica* – Mulberry; *Streblus asper* – Sheora; *Casuarina equisetifolia* – Jhau; *Borassus flabellifer* – Tal; *Cocos nucifera* – Narikel; *Areca catechu* – Supari; *Phoenix sylvestris* – Khejur; *Pandanus odoratissimus* – Keya. In this slim volume is an appendix of a 'list of trees in Uttarayan not mentioned in the text', compiled by Ram Mohon Dutta, Garden Superintendent of Visva-Bharati: different species of *Magnoliacease, Malvaceae, Steruliaceae, Leguminosea, Myrtaceae, Boragineae, Bignoniaceae, Laurineae,* and *Conefereae*.[15]

Uttarayan-er Bagan O Gachhpala, also a slim book, is written by Debiprasanna Chattopadhyay.[16] He began his life at the university in 1963, a few years after the publication of *Trees of Santiniketan*, and wrote it a few years before his retirement. The trees recorded in it are mostly from the list above. Along with it are a few beautiful pages on creepers and flowering plants, and the birds that stay or live in the trees of Uttarayan.

The presence of trees in Santiniketan was neither an accident nor adornment. *They* were Santiniketan. It was this that was emphasized in *Prakriti Path*,[17] a manual used by school teachers at Patha Bhavan. Edited by Anil Kumar De, who, quite clearly, is only recording a living oral tradition of teaching the life sciences to school children, it is a booklet meant for four age groups: students from second to fifth grade. After an initiation into the life and working of the five senses, students in the second grade are introduced (the Bangla word used is 'porichiti') to the ashram's plant life, its birds and animals, the change of seasons, and the directions of the wind. This cursory introduction, of just making an acquaintance as it were, is followed by learning how to differentiate between leaf, flower, root, trunk, and branch of trees. Various other things are taught, about wind and cloud and the sky, but I shall focus primarily on how plant life became an integral part of the student's life. It was important to Rabindranath, whose writing draws from flux, particularly the movement of seasons, that students were taught to notice the change in their surroundings as temperatures and humidity and the air changed around them. The longest section in *Prakriti Path* is its appendix—running into more than sixty pages, its primary attention is on the plants and trees of Santiniketan, the different species, their characteristics, flowering and pollination, fruits and medicinal uses, and so on. In this, it seems like an extension of the two books about the trees of Uttarayan and Santiniketan. The empirical is prefaced with the spiritual—Rabindranath's words from 'Banbani' and 'Bawlai' are quoted, with instructions for the teacher to explain the essays in 'sahaj bhasha', simplified or accessible language, with the deduction, 'The impact of these texts on the student's mind will be limitless'.[18] 'Around my room are my dumb friends who, in their love for light, have extended their arms towards the sky. Their call has reached my mind. Their language is the ancient language of living creatures, its gestures reach the soul; it stirs the forgotten histories of thousands of years; that stirring of the mind is in the language of plants—it doesn't have any clear meaning, but in it is the humming of different eras and generations. "Aetoshoibanandashyo Matrani" I see in branches of flowers and fruits; in it I taste freedom, I hear the soul of the wide world unite with the pure and limitless'.[19]

Mahasweta Devi, in her memoir *Our Santiniketan*, writes about her first impression of the place as a young student. 'On the upper walls of the front veranda . . . there were frescos. A girl picking flowers strewn on the ground—that's the only image I can recall',[20] and, later, at night, 'the date palm resembled a petni'.[21] She interprets the Sanskrit phrase 'Where the world resides in one nest',[22] Rabindranath's ambition for Visva Bharati, to include various species of trees. Two long chapters in her memoir are devoted to the trees of Santiniketan alone.

[Y]ou saw the tender green malati vine. I don't know if you all have seen the malati flower. In the rainy season, tender white malati flowers would blossom. Few flowers have such a sweet fragrance.

And then you got to class. Look at the way things were set up in Santiniketan! You attended class, and alongside, squirrels descended from the trees to listen to the lessons. These days, we constantly hear words like 'attentiveness' and 'work culture', but long ago, I had learnt to identify the creatures who remain constantly busy with their work...

I recall something of the language and intonation of the shlokas from the Upanishads that we chanted daily...

Ya oshadhisu

Yo vanaspatisu

Tasmai devaya namo namah

Calm, profound words of prayer. Their tones inspired awe in my heart. I would gaze at the trees. They were indeed vanaspati, divinities of the forest.

Santiniketan taught us to respect nature, and to love it.[23]

Mahasweta Devi reminds us of Aldous Huxley's words about Rabindranath, that his 'major legacy lies in his thoughts on child education'.[24] It wasn't Rabindranath alone—the teachers he had managed to coax and inspire to come and teach in Santiniketan were no less extraordinary in their pedagogic vision, in their belief that knowledge would come only from experience.

Our Nature Study classes were compulsory. Just imagine! . . . Tejeschandra Sen was our Nature study teacher. To the right of the Mandir stood his extraordinary house 'Taldhwaj', 'House with a Palmyra Flag'. Why such a name? Built around a tal tree, it was a round cottage with triangular rooms made of clay. A thatched roof overhead. That was Tejes-da's home.

Tejes-da taught us to recognise plants and trees.

'Treading on the grass, do you realise that in a few days' time, silkworms will appear here?' he would tell us 'Do you know how many butterflies will be seen?'[25]

Mahasweta Devi writes about the education that they were given on site as it were not from books but from cohabitation, being with other beings, realizing that 'being' was both noun and verb. 'From an array of diverse plants—bel, shiuli, karabi, kalke, sal, ishermul, akanda, atasi—what a variety of cocoons we'd harvest! We grew quite competitive about the variety of trees from which we managed to procure cocoons.'[26]

'Look, all these things have medicinal properties,' Tejes-da would in-form us. 'All these plants and trees, shrubs and bushes, all the grasses that you see—were any of them created without a purpose, randomly? What invaluable qualities they possess!'

'Come on, taste some of these things!' he'd urge. 'Try some baheda! Savour the amlaki! No disease will invade your body ever again.' . . .

We referred to amrul as 'sour-leaf'. How lovely those leaves! Like clubs in a suit of cards. You'd pluck and eat them at will.

And as for amlaki, it figures in song after song, story after story. Everything about raw amlaki, from its own flesh down to its seeds, has curative value for a hundred thousand ailments. We'd shake the tree and devour the amlaki. Chewing, we'd feel a bitter taste in our mouths. Then we'd gulp water, and it would taste fine, rather sweet.[27]

In this memoir of her life as a child and young adult, Mahasweta Devi recounts the trees so obsessively that it occasionally seems that she might have set out to write about them alone. Not only does she write about her life with them, or what her teachers taught them, but their histories and mythologies—it reminds us of our conditioning in the limited per-imeter of human history. She mentions the 'ancient chhatim tree', from the 'Chhatimtola . . . adorned by Debendranath's bedi, the platform where he prayed', 'bent and gnarled with age'[28]—the holes in it were supposed to be bones of dacoits. But it is not ghosts alone that she remembers: 'Those deities who reside in medicinal plants and trees—the ones we addressed in our evening prayers—I salute all of them. I don't know about gods and goddesses. But as for trees, or any form of vegetation, they all serve the needs of this earth, after all. So, when I gaze at trees, I feel that all's well with the world'.[29] '"Whatever Nature creates has some form of value." Tejes-da's words remain etched in my memory to this day. "That's why, whenever I see plants or trees, I immediately wonder: What purpose do they serve?"'[30] She recounts the many tongue twisters, they were inevit-ably about plant life—'babla gachhey baagh uthechhey (a tiger climbed the babla tree)'; 'kancha pepe paka pepe (raw papaya ripe papaya)'[31]—and learning to identify different species of plant life—'anantamul, akanda, chhatim, hibiscus, banyan, bakul, need, and dhatura'[32]—and the role of earthworms. Such was their fluency in the natural world that 'running about, we'd recite an entire alphabet of plant life . . .'.

> A-a-a!
> Ashok aparajita anantamul!
> Aa-aa-aa!
> Akanda akashnim amlaki!' . . .
> It taught us to love the entire universe.'[33]

Another chapter on trees follows. It's called 'More Trees'. She begins by saying that the neem trees would be offended if she didn't give a 'proper account' of them.[34] After naming its different varieties, 'akash neem, mahaneem and ghora neem', she mentions the 'jambuvana', jamun grove, near Kala Bhavana, the giant banyan near Ghantaghar, the bell tower, the kul shrubs near the rail tracks, a guava tree in Protima Devi's garden, the 'banapulak' ('rapture of the forest'), a name 'given by Rabindranath to the tree that grew to the left of the path to Uttarayan'.[35] Notice that she remembers and identifies these places by the trees that grew near them. This is the opposite of 'plant blindness'—this is because of the experiential pedagogy of Santiniketan, where plants are remembered, with their life histories, as much as people.

It is the same for the Hindi writer Shivani, who was sent to Santiniketan along with her sibling. Both Mahasweta and Shivani are writing about their childhoods decades after their time in Visva-Bharati—it is all the more striking, therefore, that it is plant life that annotates their memories of the place. Writing about Gurupalli, for instance, Shivani remembers, 'The cottages stood like dolls' houses in a row framed by tall palm trees and fragrant malatilata creepers.'[36] It is the trees that frame her memory of the ashram classes: 'The Ashram offered a number of interesting locations for holding classes. Our teachers had the option of holding a class under the shade of a perfumed creeper, or in an arbour of the Lata Kunj. There was the horseshoe-shaped bower of flowers, or the dark and verdant Amrakunj (the Mango Grove).'[37] At one point she mentions the ashram being like a 'joint family',[38] bound not by blood but by love, a family that includes trees as much as it does humans. So natural is this attachment that students make their own ink and dyes from flowers in the gardens and forests. Shivani writes of a time when 'the Bengali magazine *Desh* published a letter by Tagore where he mentions how his beloved student Jayanti had collected haridra, khadir, palash and burunsh to extract vegetable colours for his paintings.'[39]

δ

Locals used to call Santiniketan 'Bagan', garden. This was because Rabindranath's father, Maharshi Debendranath, had transformed this treeless and uninhabited land of twenty bighas, its topsoil of pebble and stones, into fine arable land, so that it gradually began to fill up with mango, jam, jackfruit, horitoki, coconut, sal, tal, debdaru, bakul, kadamba, and other shade-giving trees. Debiprasanna Chattopadhyay, recounting this in *Uttarayan-er Bagan O Gachhpala*, reminds us of how the idea of the garden was ingrained in the idea of Santiniketan right from its inception. In 1863, Debendranath, having bought the land from the zamindar of Raipur, began turning it into a place for sadhana, a meditational space. By 1901, as Chattopadhyay reminds us, the *Unity and Minister* magazine was characterizing the place as 'Pilgrimage of Santiniketan and Bolpur'.[40] In the same report is the history of both the garden and its first gardener:

It is a noteworthy fact that the gardener by name Ramdas, who laid the Santiniketan Garden, had at first been to the employment of Raja Rammohun Roy who took him to England and after the death of the Master, he returned to India and was engaged by the Burdwan Maharaj to his famous 'Golapbug' Garden. The Maharshi whose taste in these matters is princely, had engaged this man for doing good work.[41]

It was Rabindranath, not his father, who came to live permanently in Santiniketan in 1901. And it was Rabindranath at whose insistence his son Rathindranath went to study the agricultural sciences in the United States. Chattopadhyay believes that it was after Rathindranath's return, and Rabindranath's consequent move to Uttarayan, the name given to the four houses that he lived in, that the gardens of the place began to acquire their unique personality. 'Konark' was the first house in Uttarayan, then came 'Shyamali', 'Punascho', and 'Udichi'. The gardens began to change with the addition of more houses. Rabindranath was not coming to this with a blank slate—there was a history to his fascination for gardens: his sister-in-law Kadambini's garden in Jorasanko; Chhatubabu's garden in 'Prabhat Sangeet'; Shahibagh and Anna Tarkhare's garden in Ahmedabad; Moran Saheb's garden in Chandannagore; the rose gardens of Gazipur; and, later, the rose garden in his own Shilaidaha. Besides these were the gardens he had imagined, while reading the European poets and also in his own poems, such as those in *Purabi*.[42]

Debiprasanna Chattopadhyay shares with us excerpts from letters that Rabindranath wrote to his people in Santiniketan, asking about the gardens and certain trees in them when he was away. This one is to Mira Debi in 1933 from Bombay:

> My madhumalati has been well-nourished at last. From now on, do not forget to bring down her temperature with your bath water ...
>
> Tell them to plant neem, sirish and other trees on either side of the lane in front of my room; it is okay to plant a couple of jackfruit trees as well—besides that pomello trees. The spire of the temple that has been broken—get that put in one corner of my garden, and let a jhumkolata creeper climb on it.[43]

Again to Mira Debi from Aden: instructions to have a boulevard done during the monsoons; to plant mahua, chhatim, and other trees. And then the most affectionate words: 'The swetmonilata opposite the neelmonilata in my Konark house is looking for shelter—ask for a good arrangement for this to be made, for it to climb up.'[44] In 1940, a year before his death, from Mungpoo, he writes to Sachhidanana Roy, an employee of his university: 'Look after the garden very well. Plant a few chameli trees close to each other so that the chameli grove can justify the name "Chamelia". I love tall trees, but not when they are very close to the house. Remember the sajina tree—it flowers during winter but doesn't take very long to grow. Mahaneem, shimul take root in that soil easily ... Cows don't eat raktakarabi, but the flowers look glorious; both the white and red karabi would look good beside each other. The smell of lemon flowers is a favourite of mine, try to keep a little space for it. There is wealth in the flowers of the chalta tree, in jamrul; I like the golapjam for its flowers .

. . A few gandharaj will be good as well. The trees that I do not love are the chhatim and the kadam.'[45] About three months later, he writes to his daughter again: 'There is rasa in the soil now because of the rains. If you want a garden all around the house, now is the time. How are my trees in Konark? They pull at my heart.'[46] His letters are full of these queries— about plants as much as about humans. Writing to Pratima Debi in July 1924, he says, 'Your potted bakul tree was used for the brikkhoropon (tree planting) ceremony. I cannot imagine a tree with a better fortune than it. Lovely girls, wearing their best clothes and blowing the conch, brought the bakul tree to the yajna-khetra. Shastri mahashoy recited a few slokas. I read out six of my poems. With sandalwood paste and gar-lands and incense sticks and frankincense the bakul tree was welcomed. Now it is doing well.'[47]

A poet knows the value of a name, that it implies respect and affection. And hence his unease and sadness for the nameless flowers: 'Flowers bloom on branches of plants, that is its shelter. Humans give them a place in their mind by naming them. There are many flowers in our country that have not been given a place in the minds of men. This neglect of flowers is not to be seen in any other country. Maybe they have names, but they are not well-known. A few flowers have become well-known only through the power of their fragrance—in other words, in spite of the indifference of men to their appearance, they have been compelled to acknowledge their presence because of their fragrance. There are regular invitations to them in our literature. I know some of their names, but I'm not acquainted with them, and have made no effort to know them either. I've been familiar with the names of juthi, jati, sheuti in our kavya. I'm happy when they help in rhythm and rhyme-endings, but what the flower jati is, or what sheuti is, I do not have the enthusiasm to even ask someone. Jati is the flower chameli—I've found that out after a lot of investigation, but about the flower sheuthi I still haven't found an answer, not even after asking many.'[48] Rabindranath is talking about the growing indifference of the modern man to flowers—it is also, of course, a slight dig at both poets and scholars, those who know the world only through books, neglecting not just the natural world but also experience. As someone who had renamed some flowers himself ('madhumalati' as 'madhumanjari', a 'deshaj' flower as 'bonpulak', 'ramdhoonchapa' as 'basanti', 'ghoraneem' as 'himjhuri'), a form of colonialism as that is, he is aware of how names reveal histories—the first sightings and encounters of the human with unfamiliar species is revealed in them. When I was typing the names of the trees of Santiniketan according to the Linnean system, I felt disengaged from the plants—they could have been the names of planets I don't know or molecules I have little knowledge of, an artificial and colonized nomenclature that, in sight of a mythic universal, ignores the specificities of local history. Rabindranath himself is guilty of this. 'Langol phool', a forest flower that is a favourite of Santhals in the region, Chattopadhyay informs us, he renamed as 'agnishikha', the yellow and red, resembling a flame of fire itself. But 'langol phool', a flower that resembles a 'plough', has another history in it—a history of a people dependent on the plough. He does not forget to make a case for these plants and trees ignored by gardeners and horticulturists. In a letter to his daughter-in-law Pratima Debi, he writes, 'This garden will not be for your *civilised* flowers; here there will be ordinary trees such as myself'.[49] (He uses the word 'civilized' in English; the rest of the sentence is in Bangla.) Apart from cacti, there were other thorny plants that he liked—one of these, brought from Tripura, he named 'Kata Nageshwar'. He was fond of plants that did not need a lot of attention from humans—it is possible that he wanted them to retain their independence.

It is pertinent to ask what made Uttarayan's garden unique, particularly because there have been many remarkable gardens in India. Debiprasanna Chattopadhyay explains: 'no matter what the season, it felt like that nature had expressed itself with care in this garden'; 'the coming together—"milan"—of many international species of plant life'; 'it is as if there is no plant that can be rejected, they are all kings'.[50] They are all kings—was it from this where his song had come, 'Amra shobai raja amader ei rajar rajottey', we are all kings in this kingdom. Was it this that distinguished the plant kingdom from the human world, that everyone was king?

It is common knowledge that Rathindranath Tagore, the poet's son, an agriculturist trained at Illinois, was responsible for the internationalism of these garden spaces in Uttarayan and the rest of Santiniketan. Kalidasa's descriptions of gardens, Vaishnav literature, Buddhist architecture, Mughal gardens, Sinhalese and Dravidian culture, along with an understanding of the architecture of gardens in Japan and Europe, fed

Rathindranath's imagination.[51] Rathindranath writes: 'The Mughal em-
perors were as much scientists as they were artists. We learn from their
autobiographies their curiosity about plant life, about creepers and animals. They were not content in building the Taj Mahal alone. They were
restless to create a beautiful environment everywhere. When I think of
gardens I think of the Mughal dynasty'.[52] He then goes on to characterize
the different influences on Uttarayan: the 'English' garden, which, he
thinks, should have the appearance of a 'park'; the 'Italian' garden, more
formal, with manicured trees on their side of pathways, the influence of
the human visible everywhere, in its art and design; the 'Japanese' garden,
almost minimalist, like its art, able to create beauty even in small spaces.
He brings this knowledge into his experiments, both as botanist, agricultural scientist, and artist. The Italian influence, for instance, can be seen
in the rows of debdaru and eucalyptus on the side of the pathway as one
enters Uttarayan. And soon after, keeping 'Bichitra' on the left, under the
shadow of its adjacent sishu, neem, gooseberry, madar, and shirish trees,
a 'gachh-ghar', a 'plant house'. Flowers from different climates, and indeed
brought from different countries, stand and sway beside each other, un-
aware of their nationalities. In these gardens, as in the other tree spaces
of Santiniketan, we find plant thinking given body and space, not kept
limited to thought, to metaphor or philosophy. Shyamali, the mud house,
Gandhi's favourite, was shaded by mango, jamun, tamarind, wood apple,
and eucalyptus trees. In front of it was the 'tawgor', a common plant in
Bengal, adding to its homeliness, as it were. Near Punoscho and Udichi
were plants with variegated leaves, collected and brought from travels all
over the world, by the Tagores but also gifts from visitors and students.
The Japanese-influenced garden behind Udayan, the landscaping, the
drooping bottlebrush tree, fed by a waterbody, the variegated leaves, almost like migratory birds, along with tropical trees, the mango, litchi,
guava, jamrul, and starfruit, created such an extraordinary experience
that the art critic Stella Kamrisch was led to say that 'Rathindranath
Tagore knows flowers by his love for them and by science. He is a biolo-
gist by training. He is also the architect of his garden in Santiniketan.
To its luxuriant harmony he has brought plants from many parts of the
earth and from the undergrowth of the Indian jungle. He has made them
all thrive together each in the soul it requires. He cares for them, knows

and paints them. With loving science he draws the firm logic of their patterns and gives them the space and ground on which they breathe their fragrance'.[53]

Rabindranath's plant thinking, internationalist as it was, in his adoption of plant life from elsewhere and everywhere into Santiniketan, was also, as we can see now, colonialist. In an essay on food discourses in his writing and the Thakurbari kitchen, I tried to show the dissonance between his theory and practice, how the menu in their house was decidedly Bengali.[54] I find the same thing in his attitude towards gardens.

> Tired of the elaborately planned flower-beds, the gardener proceeds with grim determination to set up everywhere artificial rocks avoiding natural inspiration of rhythm in deference to a fashion of tyranny which itself is a tyranny of fashion. The same herd instinct is followed in a cult of rebellion as it was in the cult of conformity and the defiance, which is a mere counteraction of obedience, also shows obedience in a defiant fashion. Fanaticism of virility produces a brawny athleticism meant for a circus and not the natural chivalry which is modest but invincible, claiming its sovereign seat of honour in all arts.[55]

For all his advocacy and practice of garden spaces, his writing, particularly his fiction, reveals his attitude towards them. In *Nashtaneer* (The Broken Nest), *Dui Bon* (The Two Sisters), and *Malancha* (The Arbour), three of his novellas, for instance, we encounter garden spaces. There are other similarities between them—in all three novellas we meet childless women, all three women are interested in or obsessed with gardens, and somehow the garden becomes a site of extramarital relationships. In *The Broken Nests*, Charulata discovers her romantic feelings for her brother-in-law, Amal, while discussing the 'garden of their dreams'.[56] Amal, who has ambitions as a writer, is like Rabindranath when it comes to imagining the garden. Though we are told that 'to dub the plot of land that lay behind Bhupati's house a garden would be an exaggeration',[57] there are plans and diagrams and maps and estimates to conjure it into being. Charulata's husband Bhupati is uninterested in the garden—the plan is to surprise him so that 'he would think they had used Alladin's lamp to transplant an entire garden from Japan'.[58] There is also a difference between the two quasi-lovers in their botanical imagination: the woman is an internationalist, the man is more of a local patriot. 'The plan was to get seeds from Mauritius, of sandalwood from Karnat, and of cinnamon from Ceylon, but when Amal proposed replacing them with seeds of everyday Indian and English plant from the local market, Charu looked glum'.[59] The relationship doesn't flower, neither does the garden.

The two sisters in *The Two Sisters* are introduced right at the beginning of the novella through metaphors of the natural world. 'There are two kinds of women, or so I've heard some pundits say. One is mostly maternal. The other is the lover. If you liken them to the season, the mother is the monsoon. She lets her gifts flow freely from the sky; bestows water, nurtures crops, quells the heat, dispels aridity, fulfils all wanting. The lover is spring. Her mysteries run deep, her magic is bewitching. Her vivacity makes the blood tingle, entering the very core of one's being and bringing the expectant body to life'.[60] The second kind of woman, Urmimala in this story, the younger sister of the childless Sharmila, is 'like a slim tendril in motion, shaking at the slightest of breezes'.[61] A few pages later, when she's frustrated by her fiancé's bookishness and lack of liveliness, we see that 'Urmi was like a tree clinging to the earth but deprived of light, its leaves robbed of colour'.[62]

It is in *Malancha* (The Arbour) that we see this opposition between two kinds of women, the childless wife and the other, playful and attractive, adjacent to the family. Neerja, unwell like Sharmila in *Two Sisters*, worries about her garden endlessly. 'That day Neeraja couldn't help but recall an image from the past. It wasn't all that long ago, but still it felt like history; from aeons ago, from across a vast continent. An ancient neem tree stood on the western side of the garden. It had had a partner in a similar tree, but that one had decayed and died a long time ago; they had chopped its trunk up into even pieces and made a small table from it. This was where they had had their morning cup of tea, sunlight filtering through the green boughs'.[63] The garden, with a neem tree losing its 'partner' to 'decay', is almost like a metaphor for the marriage Neeraja is in. She and her husband Aditya take a lot of pride—and joy—in showing their friends and visitors around their garden, but it is not just love but a strange sense of possession that marks her relationship with the garden. 'As if the garden would have dried up without her'.[64] It's a marriage whose arc is marked by flowers: he always brings her flowers in the morning; 'For the first time he forgot my regular morning flowers';[65] 'Aditya always left a hand-picked flower by his wife's bedside ... And now Aditya had chosen to send the day's special flower with Sarala'.[66] Neeraja tests Sarala's knowledge of flowers, their names, and when she feels convinced that her garden would be destroyed 'under the new regime', she feels that 'she had been banished from the very garden—so near and yet so far—that had claimed her heart, the heart of the childless mother'.[67] This she reads and aligns with her marriage, for once upon a time her husband would say to her, 'In ancient times trees used to flower at the touch of women's feet, flowers used to bloom at a taste of the shower from their lips; my garden has returned to that era of Kalidasa'.[68]

If his wife is this ancient garden, for Aditya, Sarala is the forest: 'we were just a couple of savages living under the shadow of the forest, forgetting ourselves'.[69] In Rabindranath's world, the forest is primeval, the garden bears the impress of human control. His preference is quite clearly for the former. For Aditya, his wife *is* the garden: 'Since we've been married, I have come to realise that your garden is as precious to you as your heart; I considered the garden no different from myself ever since. Or else I'd have quarrelled bitterly with your garden and I'd never have been able to bear it. It would have been my rival in love. You know how I have merged it within myself. How I have become one with it'.[70] Neerja is uneasy with this equivalence: 'Are you telling me that my garden should be on a sickbed just because I am?'[71] And yet, she is unable to see her marriage—and her husband—as anything besides the garden, all three that need her nurturing and attention: 'I'm telling you now, I give you my word, I'll look after all the flowers and plants and trees in your garden, even better than I used to earlier'.[72]

Whether the relation between the childlessness of these women and their deep, even obsessive, affection for plant life came to Rabindranath from his friendship with Jagadish Chandra Bose can only be the subject of speculation. Jagadish Chandra and his wife Abala did not have biological children of their own. The scientist often referred to plants, particularly saplings and seedlings, as infants and children.

We learn from Rathindranath's memoir about Jagadish Chandra's frequent visits to their house, not just in Calcutta and Santiniketan but also in Shilaidaha. He taught the little boy Rathi to trace footprints of turtles, find their eggs, or 'he would make all of us dig pits in the sand and with wet towels round our heads lie down in them to sub-bathe'.[73] Even at that young age, he noticed that 'the attachment of the scientist and the poet was much more than just friendship'.[74] Rathindranath writes about Jagadish Chandra visiting them every weekend, his father reading a new short story to the scientist, the stories that would become *Galpaguchchha*, and the scientist discussing his own experiments and ideas with them. It is only natural that Rabindranath's own ideas of plant life would have been annotated by these discussions.

> Jagadish Chandra was at this time making experiments to compare the reactions on the Living and Non-living to different kinds of stimuli. He believed the results he had obtained with the help of the delicate instruments he had invented would revolutionise the current conceptions held by the scientists regarding the nature of life. He had received great encouragement from Sister Nivedita in pursuing this line of research. Father was also much interested. When Jagadish was satisfied that he had obtained sufficient convincing data to acquaint the scientific would of his discoveries he wanted to go to England to give actual demonstrations of his experiments to scientists in order to convince them of the truth of his deductions. Father approached the Maharaja of Tripura and was able to get from him sufficient money not only to enable Jagadish to go abroad but to fit up his laboratory with the equipment that he badly needed.[75]

What we see here is not just a network of cooperation that enabled artistic and scientific experimentation, but a belief in the importance of each other's work. The need to carry one's work to Europe, the need for validation, plays out in both their lives. The responses of the establishment to their work were also not dissimilar. Jagadish Chandra was attacked by American scientists for turning science into folktale. 'It must be our duty to stop the mixing of exact science research with the nice, wonderful fantasies. We want to have fairytale books and science books; but we don't want that the popular literature becomes a hybrid between the two'.[76] Rabindranath was criticized as ruthlessly. Here, for instance, is Bertrand Russell, after attending a lecture titled 'The Realization of Brahma', in 1913: 'It was unmitigated rubbish—cut and dried conventional stuff about the river becoming one with Brahma ... The man is sincere and earnest, but merely rattling old dry bones'.[77] The responses are conventional and expected, racist and condescending, but also revelatory in being uneducated and closed to any other tradition besides the one that had conditioned them—the European.

From Rathindranath we also learn about other visitors and their suggestions on gardening and agriculture—the poet and dramatist Dwijendra Lal Roy was one of them. D. L. Roy had begun his career as an agriculturist—he was one of four scholars sent by the British government to England, and was now Deputy Magistrate. Rathindranath narrates, with humour and affection, an anecdote about this: 'When D. L. Roy used to visit us at Shelidah, years of administrative drudgery must have made his knowledge of agriculture somewhat rusty. But seeing that Father was laying out an extensive garden he became enthusiastic and suggested the planting of potatoes in a plot. At that time the cultivation of potatoes was almost unknown in Bengal. Father had a plot made ready and waited for instructions. These came in due course along with some seeds. The directions were meticulously followed, ignoring the protests of the gardener, an experienced farmer. The harvest however was no more than the weight of the seeds planted. Father was careful never again to seek agricultural advice from his friend. He would rather hear him sing and recite poems'.[78] I share this hilarious episode to show how the experimental nature—and playfulness—of the times manifested itself as much in writing as it did in gardening and agriculture. It is only to emphasize, again, that our literary history is coeval with our ecological history.

δ

The needs of my work took me on long distances from village to village, from Selidaha to Patisar, by rivers, large and small, and across 'beels' and in this way, I saw all the sides of village life. I was filled with eagerness to understand the villagers' daily routine and the varied pageant of their lives. I, the town-bred, had been received into the lap of rural loveliness and I began joyfully to satisfy my curiosity. Gradually, the sorrow and poverty of the villagers became clear to me, and I began to grow restless to do something about it. It seemed to me a very shameful thing that I should spend my days as a landlord, concerned only with money-making and engrossed with my own profit and loss. From that time forward, I continually endeavoured to find out how the villagers' minds could be aroused, so that they could themselves accept the responsibility for their own lives. If we merely offer them help from outside, it would be harmful to them. The critical question was to ask how they could be stirred to life. I was haunted by that thought and decided to act on it.[79]

'Village life' is a phrase that Rabindranath uses from time to time—to describe a place and manner of living as much as a condition. It is also true that his empathy makes him imagine it to be a place lacking in what he considers to be essential to the human life: ananda. 'It is hard to imagine a life as cheerless as in our rural areas', he says in his address to the Visva-Bharati Sammilani, an essay we find in *Palli Prakriti*.[80] The word 'cheerless' occurs multiple times in his talks and essays about villagers, whose world he sees 'fast degenerating into serfdom, compelled to offer to the ungrateful towns cheerless and unintelligent labour for work'.[81] That is why he has set up Sriniketan: 'The object of the institute is to bring back life in its incompleteness to the villages, making them self-reliant and self-respectful, acquainted with the cultural tradition of their own country and competent to make efficient use of the modern resources for the improvement of their physical, intellectual and economic condition'.[82] I've been harping on the entanglement between literary history and ecological history—notice how Rabindranath's insistence on 'bringing back life' to its villages comes from the same space as his desire to collect folktales and child rhymes from them. It wasn't a Gandhian understanding of village as an unadulterated space, but a more empirical understanding of the archive, a living archive that had not yet been swallowed by European colonialism.

Rabindranath was going to use Sriniketan as an experiment to see if he could bring the village and the city closer—he also wanted to reverse the direction of knowledge from the city to the village to one more democratic, where both could learn from each other. Even as he hoped that experience and experiment with the Sriniketan model might help to understand the village better, he was aware of the limitations of his experiment: 'I alone cannot take responsibility for the whole of India . . . Fulfill this idea in a few villages only, and I will say that these few villages are my India. And only if that is done, will India be truly ours. The scale of our enterprise will never be a matter of pride to us but let us hope its truth will be.'[83] His experience of the villages wasn't new, of course. The Tagores owned large agricultural estates in Orissa and Bengal (and also in what is now Bangladesh). The youngest son had been put in charge of the Birahimpur estates at Shilaidaha. It was the enchanting landscape that became his first real teacher: from the Padma houseboat he would observe the life of humans and animals and plants all alone, as if trying to learn a new language. This language was the language that Wordsworth had learnt from the solitary reaper and the mad mother and the idiot boy; it was the language of the daffodils and the yew tree. An unconscious internalization of this rhythm gave to their individual languages, modern English in Wordsworth's case, modern Bangla in Rabindranath's, a language that changed their literatures and themselves. 'Not a village, not a human being, not a tree, not a blade of grass'[84]—this experience of isolation that he writes about from Shilaidaha in 1889, how could that not have polished his language and its rhythm, this finding a way to speak to oneself or to those outside human languages?

In 'Swadeshi Samaj', his essay of 1905, Rabindranath asked the youth, particularly those who had been educated in the country's towns and cities, to help improve the quality of village life.[85] A year later, he sent his son Rathindranath, along with three other young men, to study agriculture and dairy farming at the University of Illinois, Urbana-Champaign—they returned to Santiniketan and its neighbouring villages to share their learning with the villagers. Rabindranath had, in the meantime, bought a few bighas of land near Surul, where John Cheap, the East India Company's Commercial Resident for the district of Birbhum, had lived for nearly four decades, from 1787 to 1828. From there he sent large supplies of silk and cotton fabric, worth thousands of pound sterling, to the Company. It wasn't hard for Rabindranath to see that this had once been a prosperous region whose natural and human resources had been drained by the colonialists. Rabindranath bought the property, along with the kuthi, called the Cheap Kuthi, after its former owner—once a mansion with an orchard and a garden, it was in ruins by the time he bought it. For a decade after its purchase, he struggled to find people to turn it into what he thought should make the 'Surul farm' a model for villages in the district. But hurdles continued to appear—for it was also the decade when Rabindranath, after his winning the Nobel Prize for literature, would begin to face attacks from writers and philosophers in

England; the digging caused by the district's first railway line had affected the health of its residents—besides malaria and cholera, people had suffered from general poor health.

It was in 1921, when Rabindranath was in the United States, delivering talks about Visva-Bharati, while trying to gather funds for it, that he would meet someone who would help Sriniketan to come into being. This person was an Englishman, a student of agriculture at Cornell University. L. K. Elmhirst could stay in Sriniketan only for two years, but he continued to support it in various ways long distance. His wife Dorothy Whitney Straight made an endowment of Rs. 32,000, which was of foundational help to the establishment of Sriniketan. Rabindranath, as we see in his letters to Elmhirst, requested and hoped for the same things for Sriniketan as he did from his own writing: 'All the time when Sriniketan has been struggling to grow into form, I was intently wishing that it should not only have a shape, but also light, so that it might transcend its immediate limits of time, space and special purpose'.[86]

Sriniketan's most difficult problem was its soil. In 1923, in his lecture 'The Robbery of the Soil and Rural Reconstruction', given in Calcutta, Elmhirst complained that the soil in the villages had been continuously drained of its health. The villages in Birbhum had suffered because of their proximity to Calcutta, how it had had to cater to the city's growing demand for food, and what Elmhirst called 'the three Ms'—'malaria, monkeys, and mistrust'.[87] Rabindranath, who was presiding over this talk, noted, not for the first time, what he would, in a letter later, call 'the total joylessness' that had crept into village life. The jatra, kathaka, kirtan were gone, he said, and, with it, a way of living. The depletion of the topsoil, the disappearance of 'folk education and folk entertainment',[88] the loss of plant life and joy—these are all related and simultaneous. That is why, in a letter to Atul Sen, a worker on his estate, he wrote,

A note of joy has to be sounded in all your work. Village life has become very dull, the dryness of the heart has to be banished. All welfare work ought to be turned as far as possible into an occasion of festive joy. There should be a tree-planting ceremony every year. I think you will have to give your students a day off sometime at the end of the month of 'Vaisakh' and organise a picnic in a forest coupled with a tree-planting ceremony. If a festive element is introduced on the day in which a new work is started . . . a religious appearance will be imparted to all your social activities. Another thing should be borne in mind. It will do a lot of good to the villager if he can be induced to take to the hobby of cultivating flowers. A few 'bel' or a few rose plants, if grown in the yard of every cottage, will make the villages look beautiful. *Let us not forget the cultivation of beauty has become a very great necessity in our country.*[89]

This investment in beauty and the unquantifiable ananda that plant life brings is invoked over and over again in *Sadhana*.

δ

The word 'pata'—leaf in Bangla—occurs in the first poem that Rabindranath Tagore is said to have written in his life. Jawl pawrey pata nawrey, water falls, leaves move. 'Dala' and 'mala'—basket and garland—occur in the first song of the *Gitabitan*. A couple of songs later, possibly the sixth, has these lines:

> Mawra gachher daley daley
> Nachey agoon taley taley
> Fire dances to a beat on the dead branches of trees.

Tagore puts this song in the 'Puja' (Worship) section of the book, his collection of songs. In song after song, we notice a quest—an obsession—with 'sur'. Besides meaning melody, music, song, or even a note, it is also a metaphor here. It is as if the plant world has this sur already; humans have to strive to find it.

What exactly do flowers give us?[90] A flower opens its eyes on a spring morning to see the sun looking at her waking up. A honeybee sings—Where's the honey? Give me, give me honey. The flower says—Here, take it. The breeze whispers in its ears—Flower, you girl, give me your fragrance. The flower cries with joy—Here, take everything, every bit of it. The flower finds its joy in giving everything of itself, and, in that state of ananda, it falls on the leaves. Madhu, honey, and Ananda—these are central to the cosmology of flowers in his world. Sweetness, literal and metaphorical—an internalization of an instinct, almost biological. Every day the flower blooms in your courtyard, why don't you feed it to your mind? Every day people gather in your courtyard, why don't you let this servant sing to you?[91] Song, sur, sweetness. As we read through the songs in *Gitabitan*, we encounter the word 'sur' in song after song. Literally it means note, but in Tagore it is a spiritual word marked with sweetness. Just as plant life always gets the sur right, as we see manifest in flowers, so must the human voice in song.

In 'Phool Photano',[92] Rabindranath posits the limitations of the human will against plant consciousness, the inability of the human to control plants. No, none of you will be able to make a flower bloom, he says; no matter what you say, no matter what you do, whether you lift it up with desperation night and day, whether you injure its stalk, you won't be able to make the flower bloom. Your repeated sightings might make her pale to you, you might tear it or the entire cluster, you might throw it in the dust; it might open its mouth slightly because of all the disturbance you are causing to it, you won't be able to change its colour or rid it of its fragrance. The person who can cause a flower to bloom only looks at it, their two eyes lit, and it seems that the mantra of the fullness of life makes the flower bloom. Their breath makes the flower want to fly, to make wings of its leaves, to float and swerve and fly. Such a person could be god, such a person could be someone who is in tune with the rhythm of the natural world, who lives in tree time and therefore creates no pressure of human life on it. The plant world is—like the world of little children—outside human control, and is therefore a giver of shanta rasa. It is not hard to spot that his belief in unpremeditated art comes from the same space, the uncontrollability of the plant world as analogous to the uncontrollability of creative energy, of dreams, of sleep. 'Literature as an art offers us the mystery which is in its unity . . . No one knows how it exceeds all its parts, transcends its laws, and communicates with the person.'[93]

Rabindranath reserves his attention for smaller flowers.[94] I only make garlands of very small flowers, those which are quick to dry. Even when they do, there is no sadness, I will pluck it for my soul—for those who live in the darkness, in harsh prisons, if this garland brings them a moment's happiness, so that they can forget the pain of cruel bondages. These tiny flowers, their fragrance brings freedom, respite, and hope—in these tiny flowers is the generosity of the sea breeze, when I see them I think of the big world and the large sky. In his world, flowers are shy, often apologetic, but always grateful, their memory of being earth-born never leaving them. In this song from Chandalika,[95] we feel the gratitude of flowers who are overwhelmed for being born as flowers, grateful for their life on earth, for being chosen to serve the gods in their temples. We've been born in dust, forgive us for that, for there is no dust in my soul. In another,[96] the blossoming of flowers in the forest, even when there is little chance of being appreciated, becomes a lesson for the human heart—the flowers have bloomed in the forest, should we still misunderstand each other, should we continue to feel abhiman?

Then there are his poems and songs addressed to particular flowers. The shiuli is one such flower.[97] Shiuli flower, what kind of maya—or mistake—makes it possible for you to collect the fragrance of the night, of forest shade, of dew, of desire and restlessness, and give it to us in a language outside agriculture, combining everything with your absent-mindedness? The return to a favourite trope—a world outside human domination, a life of the night, secretive, contrasted with the openness of daylit hours, noisy, without hum.

There are also the roses in his songs.[98] The roses are in bloom, be careful of the thorns. There are the champa and shefali too—share what's on your mind with them. The bee says, No, not with them, I will share only with the rose; if, for that, I might have to burn for telling them, I will burn from the thorns as well.

What does it mean to be a flower? There is the glamour of flowers, one that attracts all pollinators, humans as much as insects. But what exactly does it mean to be a flower? So many had come to plant life to escape the transactional economy that drives relationships, an unending give-and-take that is the mark of the social, living outside which would make an outsider, and bring with it a trail of adjectives: 'one-sided', 'narcissistic', 'self-centred', and so on. It is because Rabindranath can imagine the human as flower or leaf or plant or tree that he can see the limitations of the human self and what it might mean if one could import the ethics of plant life to the situation of being human. 'Supposing I became a champa flower,' says a child playfully to his mother.[99] In The Gardener, a child gives flowers to an aged man—he likens her to the flowers she's brought him: 'You are blind even as the flowers are.'[100]

In a well-known short story that he wrote to help the students in his newly established school to appreciate the planting of trees and their care as well as to help them imagine this world of plant otherness, Bawlai, after whom the story is named, is the narrator's nephew who behaves like a tree. The narrator points out their similarities: the little boy sits silently like trees, exhibiting no curiosity for new places. He responds to the heat and the rain like trees do. In the month of Magh, he became a mango tree; in Phalgun, he behaved like a flowering sal tree in spring. When he saw flowers being plucked or stones thrown at the gooseberry tree for fruit, Bawlai felt the pain in his body as if he were those trees. A motherless child who was being raised by his uncle and aunt, it hurt Bawlai to see his uncle weeding his garden of plants that he did not like or need. Once, having managed to save a silk cotton tree from his uncle, he nurtured it until it grew quite tall. Bawlai was eventually put in a school in Shimla so that he could get an education before he was sent to England. Many years later, he wrote a letter to his aunt asking for a photograph of the simul tree. His uncle had got it cut only a few days before the letter arrived. His childless aunt was heartbroken—ever since he'd been taken away by his father, she had looked at the simul tree and imagined it as Bawlai.[101]

Even imagining the tree as human, as a foster son, had not prevented a man from cutting it down.

δ

If you ask me to draw some particular tree, and I am no artist, I try to copy every detail, lest I should lose the peculiarity of the tree, forgetting that the peculiarity is not the personality. But when the true artist comes, he overlooks all details and gets into the essential characterization . . . When he looks on a tree, he sees it as unique, not as the botanist who generalizes and classifies. It is the function of the artist to particularize that one tree. How does he do it? Not through the peculiarity which is the discord of the unique, but through the personality which is harmony. Therefore he has to find out the inner concordance of that one thing with its outer surroundings of all things.[102]

In these words are congealed Rabindranath Tagore's plant philosophy.

Notes

1. Tagore, *Sadhana*, p. 3.
2. Tagore, 'The Religion of the Forest'.
3. Ibid.
4. Ibid.
5. Ibid.
6. Ibid. Emphases mine.
7. Ibid.
8. Ibid.
9. Ibid.
10. Ibid.
11. Ibid.
12. Ibid.
13. Basu (1957), p. i.
14. Ibid., p. iv.
15. Appendix, 'List of trees in Uttarayan not mentioned in the text', compiled by Ram Mohon Dutta, Garden Superintendent of Visva-Bharati.
16. Chattopadhyay (1979).
17. Kumar De.
18. Ibid., 29.
19. Tagore, 'Banbani', introduction. Translation mine.
20. Devi (2021), p. 27.
21. Ibid., p. 29.
22. Ibid., p. 27.
23. Ibid., pp. 27–30.
24. Ibid., p. 32.
25. Ibid., p. 33.
26. Ibid., p. 36.
27. Ibid., pp. 36–37.
28. Ibid., p. 38.
29. Ibid., p. 39.
30. Ibid., p. 40.
31. Ibid., p. 41.
32. Ibid.
33. Ibid., p. 42.
34. Ibid., p. 43.
35. Ibid., pp. 43–45.
36. Shivani (2021), p. 22.
37. Ibid., p. 32.
38. Ibid., p. 56.
39. Ibid., p. 150.
40. Chattopadhyay (1979), p. 11.
41. Ibid., p. 12.
42. Ibid., p. 13.
43. Ibid., p. 14. Translation mine.
44. Ibid.
45. Ibid., p. 15.
46. Ibid.
47. Ibid., p. 16.
48. Ibid., p. 17.
49. Ibid., p. 19.
50. Ibid., p. 20.
51. Tagore (1958).
52. Ibid., p. 21. Translation mine.
53. Kamrisch, 1952, pp. 26–27.

54. Roy (2012).
55. Tagore (1963).
56. Tagore (2010), p. 6.
57. Ibid.
58. Ibid., p. 7.
59. Ibid.
60. Tagore (2010), p. 75.
61. Ibid., p. 95.
62. Ibid., p. 117
63. Ibid., p. 140.
64. Ibid., p. 145.
65. Ibid., p. 48.
66. Ibid., p. 149.
67. Ibid., p. 151.
68. Ibid., p. 157.
69. Ibid., p. 165.
70. Ibid., p. 168.
71. Ibid., p. 195.
72. Ibid., p. 197.
73. Tagore (1958), p. 24.
74. Ibid., p. 25.
75. Ibid.
76. Gerta Von Ubisch, cited in Rajinder Singh (2009).
77. Cited in Dutta and Robinson (2009), p. 177.
78. Tagore (1958), p. 23.
79. Tagore (1943), p. 433.
80. Gupta (2022), p. 2.
81. Ibid., p. 10.
82. Ibid.
83. Ibid., p. 116.
84. Ibid., p. 21.
85. Tagore (1905).
86. Dasgupta (1962), p. xiii.
87. Elmhirst (1975).
88. Dasgupta (1962), p. 50.
89. Ibid., p. 51.
90. Tagore, 'Basanto probhate ek malatir phul', *Tagore web*.
91. Tagore, 'Nutya tomar je phul phote', *Tagore web*.
92. Tagore, 'Phul photano', *Tagore web*.
93. Ibid.
94. Tagore, 'Chhoto phul', *Tagore web*.
95. Tagore, 'Phul bale dhanya ami', *Tagore web*.
96. Tagore, 'Bane eman phul', *Tagore web*.
97. Tagore, 'Shiuli phul shiuli', *Tagore web*.
98. Tagore, 'Golap phul phutiye achhe', *Tagore web*.
99. Tagore, 'The Champa Flower', *Tagore web*.
100. Tagore, *The Gardener*.
101. Ibid.
102. Tagore (1963), p. 38.

I feel that flowers, rivers, the skies, stars, the child . . . are all sacred texts. One experiences the wonders of eternal play through
and in them. Wherever the One may reside is naturally a temple,
not stone monuments alone! As I was on my way here, I saw
kumud flowers blossoming in Chorpara Lake; that, too, is a
temple . . . The One is everywhere: vanaspatau bhuvriti nirjhare
va kuley samudrasya sarittatey va . . . in the trees and plants, in
waterfalls, in the seas

—Bandyopadhyay

3

Bibhutibhushan Bandyopadhyay

The first page of Bibhutibhushan Bandyopadhyay's novel *Ichhamati* begins with a revolutionary formulation of history. Both 'history' and its Bangla equivalent 'itihasa' are etymologically derived from a shared investment in the human: story or narrative of a person's life; from 'asti', meaning 'he is'. Bibhutibhushan changes both the subject and the frame.

> Take a boat from Morighata or Bajitpur right up to Chanduria ghat, and you shall see the bright red flowers of the poltey and madar trees on either bank, the aquatic foliage of the bonneyburo, the radiance of the yellow flowers of the wild titpalla creeper and the floating leaves of topa-pana; sometimes, along a high bank, you will spy shrubs of uluti-bachda and bainchi in the dhadow of ancient banyan and pipal trees, the nesting holes of river-mynahs, and everywhere the pleasing spread of creepers and all manner of greens . . . On occasion you may sight a vulture sitting atop one of the crisscrossed branches of a tall silk-cotton tree in a stillness suggesting a higher state of spiritual realisation—like a wash painting done by a Chinese artist . . .
>
> When the moonlight falls on the green grassy fields that have sprung up on the sandbanks where white clusters of akanda flowers blossom in the summer, and the mild breeze from the river sways the golden laburnum along the banks, travellers journeying along the river will sight the remnants of old ruined homes now covered with a profusion of wild akanda . . . As you pass by these ruins of homes you will dream of bygone days, of a mother and her son, of a brother and a sister, whose lives were once entwined with these living signs of habitation.
>
> From one century to another many are the unwritten histories of joy and sorrow that lie on their breasts, like the tracery of lines of water in the rains . . . Their voices, their stories, are the real history of our nation.[1]

Plant Thinkers of Twentieth-Century Bengal. Sumana Roy, Oxford University Press. © Sumana Roy 2024.
DOI: 10.1093/9780198929314.003.0004

The history of plant life, records of its settlement on land as well as its death and evacuation from these spaces, a census of plants and trees—all these constitute our national history, not only the life of kings, queens, and the famous. Bibhutibhushan is writing this in a novel published in 1950, the year India becomes a republic and gives to itself its constitution, and decades before the formation of the Subaltern Collective. Seventy-five years later, these words read like a preamble to an imagined India, of what might have been had this understanding of national history been institutionalized. What we have instead is only a generational memory of plants whose names one must memorize but whose life and life cycles we know little about. Bibhutibhushan is documenting plant life with the kind of intimacy that Kalidasa does in *Ritusamhara*, both aware of the passing of a world that would henceforth be recoverable only second-hand. Only names will have to do from now on, unless they are allowed fundamental rights, like those who are given space in history.

A recurring thought in Bibhutibhushan is the gap between human and natural history, one that has only grown wider since his time. Barring a few, the residents of Nischindipur, the village where his novel *Pather Panchali* is mostly set, are mostly poor—the children, Opu and his sister Durga, for instance, are always hungry, always scavenging for food among forests and orchards owned by the wealthy; their mother has to sell her utensils to buy a little rice so that her children do not starve; the girl Durga is beaten for stealing a few mangoes. But plant life in the village is abundantly rich. Bibhutibhushan smuggles in this awareness in his fiction, both novels and short stories, from time to time. In this passage, for instance, he makes us experience the inexplicable delight the human takes in the colour of flowers:

> Even in the faint light of the evening, the rest of the field gleamed. Yellow laburnums were scattered all over the field, and every tree was in full blossom. Circles of wild woodrose sprouted everywhere, creating little havens of cool darkness within them. Jewel-blue bluebells bloomed on vines wrapped around trees, peeking out from under the thick foliage to glitter in the sun. Spiky amaranth, blue-pea, and numerous other wildflowers grew in thick bushes all over the field, carpeting the field in bright colours.[2]

The sentence that follows this is a political critique, not necessarily in just the tradition of what man has made of man, but of an alternative history, a possible history that might have been had humans been like plants:

> Everything glittered and glowed. *There was no sign of poverty or of middle-class miserliness anywhere. Nature had upturned her bowl of plenty upon the land like an empress bestowing largess . . .* and the little boy could not tear his eyes away. His world, so far, had been rather a narrow one, limited to his home, his friend Nyara's house, their neighbour Ranu Didi's place, and those parts of the neighbourhood that were close to their remote little house. This evening—with its woods, rabbits, indigo ruins, and the misty, boundless field of bright colours—was a revelation to him. In his heart, he was certain that he had stumbled upon the gateway to a magical land.[3]

'Misty' and 'magical' versus 'middle-class miserliness'. The colour of the world, even when it is just 'indigo ruins', contrasted with the dark and, often, damp inside of the small, dilapidated houses of the poor. Poverty belongs to the human world alone, a function of its social structures. If only we were trees . . .

That is why Bibhutibhushan cleverly places this paragraph, with its opening sentence, right after the one above: 'Meanwhile, Nobin Palit was holding forth on the profits he had reaped by planting sweet potatoes on a northern plot of the indigo field.'[4] Not only is this a mocking of the idea of 'profit'—the preserve of a very few, one half of a binary, the polar opposite of which produced the poor, a word or category that people like Opu and his family would never understand or experience—it is significant that Bibhutibhushan sets up the colourful world against the dark earth that produces potatoes.

The difference between the natural and the human social world is held up metaphorically, as if to gently point out the inadequacies of the latter—not just the lacks but the more fundamental, the ethical, the way humans memorialize or forget, and how institutional memory is opportunistic and, almost without exception, linked to power. We are taken to the gravestone of a 'toddler', Edwin Lermore, 'Only son of John and Mrs Lermore', who lived from 13 May 1857 to 27 April 1860.[5] Bibhutibhushan reproduces the inscription on the tombstone in the text. The paragraph in which this occurs begins thus: 'The bungalow, while it stood, had indeed been large. Now, however, its remains sprawled across the land, like a grotesque monster lying in wait'.[6] The ruins of the 'neel kuthi', a generic name for bungalows on indigo plantations of the time, once owned by the Englishman Lermore, is in ruins, abandoned and forgotten, 'a grotesque monster'. But 'one of the wild yellow laburnums grew right by the grave, shading the child's resting place with its branches and leaves. When strong winds blew in from the river's bend at Two-and-a-Half Point, it showered the grave and headstone with golden petals. History may have forgotten the life and death of the little foreign child, but the land has not forgotten one of its own. He has become part of Contentment (Nischindipur), and his unsung memory lives on in its trees, its grass, and its wildflowers'.[7]

Bibhutibhushan's new definition of what constitutes national and public history, an urge we see on the first page of *Ichhamati*, returns as I read these words. Intergenerational memory, that we now recognize as intrinsic to the working of history, both public and private, often lost from humans, it survives and flowers through plants. What is being given to us is, therefore, an interspecies intergenerational memory ecosystem— where plants seem to carry the memory not just of their biological ancestors but also of those who were neighbours to their ancestors. How else is one to explain Bibhutibhushan's assertion that human history has forgotten the dead child but not the land and its plants?

In *Ichhamati*, a historical consciousness is proposed where human history can only be imagined amidst and against the background of plant life: 'You and I will nurture and leave behind a lineage in the soil of this very village: I can see how in this very bamboo grove of ours, five generations will live on'.[8] That is why the novel closes as it opens, with an abundance of plant life:

Generations of leaves, bushes and creepers have come to life in every bend of the Ichhamati, in every fork of its forests . . . a jungle of kakjhonga, koonchkanta-nata and bonmorich, innumerable wild flowers . . . We have seen the beautiful violet-purple of the bonsim flowers flood the riverbanks every year at the end of rains . . . In time, the thickets of kash too make way for thickets of sheora, then come the sodali trees—and then, innumerable creepers of pumpkin, kantabash, wild chalta. Creepers of gulancha, of matar, the small and the big goaley blossom and thrive in turn.[9]

Humans have grown older, died, the little boy has grown up, the Englishmen have died or left the Neelkuthi, Neelkuthi itself has changed hands, but the plants and the trees seem to have remained the same; they are certainly at the same place. That is why the first and last few pages of the novel are almost an echo of each other—not mirror images, but related as our shadows are related, by continuity and inevitability. And that is also why Bibhutibhushan mentions the reclaiming of the abandoned indigo plantations, which are a metaphor of human control, by older native plant life. 'As soon as indigo cultivation stopped on both banks of Panchpota village, the profusion of bonnyeburo, pituli, gamar and tittiraj trees grew rapidly into a jungle.'[10] In this is a moral for the human, a vision for the earth after human extinction. Hence the overbearing recurrence of the near-Shakespearean opposition of human mortality, the short period of human life, when contrasted with what sustains it—the plant world.

δ

Bibhutibhushan Bandyopadhyay was born in a village—Bengal's Muratipur—in the last decade of the nineteenth century. Both these facts would have been insignificant had they not had the kind of impact they did on the writer: he would return to non-metropolitan life, particularly village life and forest living, in his writing all his life; arriving at the end of the nineteenth century, after the Brahmo Samaj and its impact on daily life, culture, and literature, particularly its emphasis on Upanishadic thought, he would combine both his temperament for village living with the intellectual climate around him in the most fluent and sophisticated way. A part of this inheritance came to him from his father, Mahananda Bandyopadhyay, who, though he died young, initiated him into the world of the Puranas, music, the Upanishads, and storytelling. This was the first of many deaths—some of his siblings, and his first wife, to whom his novel *Aranyak* is dedicated, would die very young—in the early years of his life that would leave a deep impact on him, one visible in the moving paragraphs about human mortality, and one, if one can surmise such things at all, that nudged him towards privileging experience over the written archive and valuing the living philosophy of ananda. Going to school and college was difficult because of the economic circumstances of the family, and it wasn't very much better after Bibhutibhushan had got his degree from Calcutta's Ripon College either. He would have to take up various kinds of jobs, the first of which was as a private tutor, a job that he would return to off and on to sustain the family because of the meagre salary he earned otherwise. He lived in what in Calcutta was called the 'mess', a kind of boarding house where rooms were shared and meals often cooked together, an informal institution that made it possible for outsiders in the city to live in it, whether they were college students or office goers. School teaching, not just in Calcutta and its suburbs but in various parts of Bengal; managing an estate of forests in Bihar's Bhagalpur district, supervising parts of it being turned into agricultural land. These two jobs gave him most of the stories and people he would write about in his fifty-six-year-long life.

δ

The unit of distance in South Asia is, often, time: 'How far is this place from there?' might beget the response 'fifteen minutes'. The unit of time in Nischindipur is not second or minute or day or decade. Time is measured through plant life: 'Many springs have decorated the village trees since then, and many winters have stripped them bare. The Chokrobortis' open field has become the Mukhujjes' dense orchard, and now even that orchard is considered ancient'; 'Brojo Chokroborti's house used to be behind this forlorn little house, inside that now-overgrown bamboo grove'. Bibhutibhushan measures human settlement and, indeed, the world through what I understand as 'tree time'.[11] Religious ceremonies and rituals are structured not in calendar days but through the appearance and disappearance of flowers and fruits: 'On the evening of Saraswati Puja, a few men ... had undertaken the ceremonial search for the elusive blue jay'.[12]

Time also does something else—it allows nouns and names to accommodate more than their original meaning and intention. The box of spices, for instance, is called by a name that makes it slightly anachronistic: 'The flower-bowl had long since been relegated to being a spice-holder, remaining a "flower bowl" only in name'.[13] What happens when such a thing happens, when the name of a flower or a plant is no longer able to retain its original intention? Bibhutibhushan is not leading us towards dead language but towards something deeper, such as the mantra, whose sound, as when flowers, leaves, and grass are repeatedly summoned in Hindu worship, is able to carry greater resonance, both of time and history, than its first meanings. The 'flower bowl' in Shorobojaya's kitchen, no longer a flower bowl but a spice holder, has a history similar to the occurrence of 'bilapatra', bel or Bengal quince leaves, necessary for worship, and once as ubiquitous as grass. There's also 'pushpanjali', a manner of worshipping with flowers. When it rains very hard, the children in *Pather Panchali* repeat a rhyme to chase away the storm: 'Currants on citrus leaves, I say,/ O Rainfall, go away'.[14] There are also the curses: 'Let those vermin never taste their stolen fruit. Let them end up under the milkwood pine before that coconut is cooked'.[15] In these expressions, and not in tomes alone, is our history.

Just as it is in the architecture of living spaces, how certain varieties of plant life become 'boundary walls', some given centre stage, some allowed inside the house, others not. 'Once her children were out of the house, Shorbojoya lit the evening lamp and took it out to the holy basil plant in the courtyard. She draped the loose end of her sari around her neck in supplication, and folded her hands in front of the plant.'[16] Once a familiar sight even in India's semi-urban spaces, this daily ritual, symbolic as it is, of showing light to the darkness and welcoming those returning home, is on the verge of extinction with the disappearance of courtyard spaces from buildings and the loose attachment to the circadian rhythm. To those familiar with this everyday practice, it might seem like just a record of an event. But it isn't. When the family, after the death of the daughter, moves to Kashi, they find themselves in one damp dark room. In spite of it being a Hindu pilgrimage town, there is no space for a tulsi mancha in their living space. The holy basil, often worshipped as an avatar of the goddess Lakshmi, has two varieties—Rama tulsi and Shyama tulsi, the latter, with its dark purple leaves, identified with Krishna, the colour of his skin. Both are known for their medicinal and disinfection properties. The small temple-like structure used to house the basil plant is often called the Tulsi Vrindavan—this nomenclature is a cultural memory of the relationship between Krishna and the tulsi plant. 'Vrinda' in Vrindavan is tulsi, the holy basil; Vrindavan, a forest of tulsi plants. It is also a reminder of the gentle percolation of Vaishnavite thought and theology into Bengali life— the Vaishnava devotees can often be identified by a string of tulsi beads around their neck. Folklore, often coming from the Vedas, and prayers and mantras, such as one which describes the Brahma and other gods in its branches, the Ganga running through its roots, the Vedas in its lower stems, indulged a belief in the tulsi plant as being integral to the existence of a house as much as, say, its roof. Perhaps because—as I once heard it being described to me in a village in northern Bengal—it was thought to be a bridge between heaven and earth, its position in the courtyard and its status in the architectural divisions of living spaces became quasi-dogmatic. That tulsi leaves could purify people (as water from the Ganga was supposed to do) perhaps came from a shift from the metaphorical to the literal—its character as disinfectant of germs to purification of people an undeniable casteist extrapolation.

When Opu is unable to walk, 'Amala made a paste of miracle-leaves to put on the wound'.[17] Occasionally I watch a YouTube channel called Villfood. 'You must always keep the banana stem lying, not upright—that keeps it fresh.' 'If you're suffering from body ache, eating the leaves of kakhrol plant will help you.' An 86-year-old woman lives with her son and daughter-in-law, their children and grandchildren in a village in Birbhum, gathering fruits and leaves from neighbouring forests, harvesting the produce from her garden with her grandsons, watering tulsi and neem plants, often repeating wisdom that has come to her from her mother and grandmother. When I read Bibhutibhushan, I have the same sense—of what our history and knowledge systems might have been had our education systems not continued to be colonized, long after Indian independence. That colonization also instils fear—not in Pushparani, the 86-year-old grandmother, older than Indira Thakuran in *Pather Panchali*, but in writers and scholars who want older and ecologically sustainable ways of living and the oral archives around them to be recovered. So blindly colonized are our scholars, particularly those that are away from forests and villages, that they often characterize these archives as belonging to a right-wing politics. The mischaracterization continues, the plants and plant thinking gradually become extinct.

The modernist obsession with time, its intestines and the human's inability to understand or control it, and the desire to see it, if possibly whole, in its entirety, as if it were a material thing, manifests itself in Bibhutibhushan as it does in most of the plant thinkers in this book. 'A wilderness of moonseed vine would hang from the young night jasmine tree, making it look positively ancient from a distance.'[18] Trees are seen by Bibhutibhushan, Jibanananda, and Rabindranath as archives of time— bark, trunk, branches, so what if the leaves and flowers and fruits have fallen and others taken their place? As if indulged by a conditioning in the Buddhist belief that though plants and trees die in a forest, something is added and something taken away, so that the forest continues to remain a forest, it becomes possible for them to see—as Beth Moon does in her photographs of some of the most ancient trees in the world today— aged trees as an archive of time. Not clocks and calendars for them, but trees.[19] Plant life—as metaphor—allows them to also understand time in a relative manner: though the jasmine tree is 'young', it looks 'ancient', just as though seasonal flowers look very young and almost permanently teenager-like, they are closer to death than a tree of many decades or possible centuries. This sense of death, of the difference in the availability of time to different species of the plant kingdom, brings in a new—or perhaps old?—understanding of time.

δ

The title of Bibhutibhushan's novel *Aranyak* comes from the *Brihadaranyaka Upanishad*, the book of the forests in the Vedas, its 'story' from the writer's long stay in the forests of Bhagalpur. That this young writer— was turning to the Upanishads to make sense of his experience is a significant move, particularly when one reads his work as modernist. Just as the British modernists found themselves looking to ancestral literary traditions—as James Joyce did in *Ulysses*, T. S. Eliot in *The Waste Land* and 'Tradition and the Individual Talent' or to premodern spaces,— D. H. Lawrence in *Mornings in Mexico*, W. B. Yeats in 'Sailing to Byzantium', Matisse to Turkey, or Picasso to Africa—Bibhutibhushan turns to the space of the forest, just as it is on the verge of being colonized, and the Upanishadic imagination to write what is now called 'autofiction', perhaps even—for there never is a dearth of such categories today—'environmental autofiction'.

A college graduate, without a job or parental and financial support, Bibhutibhushan had to leave Calcutta for Bihar to become an assistant manager in an agricultural estate. The protagonist—who's also the narrator—of his novel does the same. The diary records of the former transform to become the voice of the latter. We know from *Smriti-r Rekha* that Bibhutibhushan was reading Conrad's novels in Bhagalpur, and one can only speculate how that narrative of colonialism would have affected his understanding of his own role as a colonizer, turning the forests into profit-making agricultural land.[20] As Rimli Bhattacharya, the translator of *Aranyak*, notes, 'The destruction of the forest is a necessary prelude in the Adiparva of the Mahabharata: Khandava vana is consumed by fire to provide a clearing for Indraprastha whose urbane magnificence is only the site of further dissension.'[21] She also notices that 'the two most frequent adjectives used in *Aranyak* are "janamanabheen" (bereft of human beings) and "bonyo" (from Sanskrit Vanya) which has been variously rendered in English as rude, rustic, wild, savage and uncivilized. An "unpeopled" forest is conceived as a lack, the very definition of "people" excluding tribals, beasts and birds, spirits and all other creatures of the imagination who inhabit it.'[22] The idea of 'bonnyo' occurs both in *Aranyak* and *Ichhamati*. Bibhutibhushan's use of the word is readymade, used to name more than to characterize pejoratively. Bibhutibhushan's understanding of the forest is cosmopolitan, not exclusionary—humans have as much a right to it as other living beings. The transition from jungle to forest is obvious— what we have today is a 'Forest Department' and a 'Forest Development Officer', not a 'Jungle Department' or a 'Jungle Development Officer'. For Bibhutibhushan, the human's residency in the forest would seem natural, coming, as it would have, from being conditioned to the reasoning of our epics—both the idea of vanwas, exile, and vanaprastha, retirement. This intuitive understanding would have led him towards the opposite—that living spaces, whether village or city, belonged to plants and animals as much as humans. Equity was not in equal distribution of living spaces for humans but in equal access for every species.

Satyacharan, a Calcuttan, is able to see the limits of his textbook education when he is lost in the forest or when he meets the forest residents, who have the benefit of their inherited political and medicinal systems. In the Prologue, which turns the rest of the novel into a reminiscence, we see the difference: Satyacharan, 'sitting on the Maidan' in Calcutta, notices that 'near me was an almond tree',[23] he thinks 'of the forestlands of Lobtulia-baihar or Ajmabad'—the solitary tree versus the 'dense forest, blood-red with flowering palash'.[24] The first is the present, his location in history; the second has the calm and beauty of a dream, 'dreamt in the half-awake slumber of a holiday evening'.[25] Evening, with its gentle light, daydreaming—all these are the gifts of a forest. Nearly a hundred years after the experiences which led to this book, one feels like Satyacharan in the city—the forested lands, once accessible to most, will soon exist only in a dream, only in memory. That is the prescience of the form of the Prologue.

Satya recounts the horror and his own complicity in its destruction— these are the moments when he becomes Everyman, all of us: ' the sal forests have been set on fire to clear the land . . . By my hand was destroyed an unfettered playground of nature. I know too, that for this act the forest gods will never forgive me'.[26] And then, in Ancient Mariner-manner, he begins telling his story: 'I have heard that to confess a crime in one's own words lightens somewhat the burden of the crime. Therefore, this story'.[27] As I write this, I wonder what good my writing about these plant thinkers would do to plants—what good has Bibhutibhushan's writing done for the forests the protagonist of his novel destroyed?

δ

It is interesting to note Satya's first impression of the landscape, and how he notices the absence of the human. Every time I have read these paragraphs, I have wondered about the opposite—whether humans notice the absence of plant and animal life in cities. Sarbojoya, in *Pather Panchali*, does, but do we? After a night on the train from the city, Satya writes: 'I noticed that the terrain had changed in the meantime, and nature too, had taken on a different guise: no fields or cultivated land to be seen and very little evidence of human habitation—only forests, big and small, dense in some places and sparse in others. Occasionally, there were stretches of open land, but it was all virgin land'.[28] 'Virgin land'—a city-dweller's phrase, as if land was ever virgin, and its virginity marked only by man's absence on it, like a woman's body is. Aldous Huxley would, at around the same time that Bibhutibhushan was writing his novels, write about how nature, particularly plant life in the tropics, was being romanticized for our consumption. The Bengali writer, though, was doing quite the opposite. Satya misses city life and its pleasures; he does not really care for this life in the forest. He complains about being 'lonely', that he 'could not understand well the speech of the local people, could not figure out a method of work . . . The people . . . were as good as barbarians . . . Those first ten days were excruciating. Ever so often, I felt that having a job was of no use; it was far better to stay on half-starving in Calcutta than stifle to death here . . . This was not the life for me'.[29] That is why he's not convinced when Goshto-babu, who was from Bengal's Bardhaman district, tells him, 'The jungle will get inside of you. By and by, you won't be able to bear any kind of disturbance or put up with crowds. That's what has happened to me. Just this last month I had to go to Mugher for a court case, and all I could worry about was when I'd be able to get away'.[30] It is a feeling that is familiar to many of us—a feeling of viraha when away, the urge to get back, perhaps like what a parent feels for a child left alone at home, an inexplicable and unquantifiable attraction, like our bodies experience when up in the air, the urge to return to earth. It is this urge that manifests itself in the Prologue to the book, when Satya, sitting in Calcutta's Maidan, thinks of his time in the forest. Bibhutibhushan returns to this repeatedly in his writing—the indescribability and unquantifiability of the effect of the elements and of plant life, of the untamed and even the wild, on the human. He is repeatedly invoking an informal and continuous pedagogy, one outside the linguistic—for the language of words is exclusionary, and does not allow us to be educated by the so-called non-human. He is pressing for an education by the elements and plant life, and stressing on self-discovery as being as important as the discovery of others and by others.

Gradually the forest compels Satya to question the idea of who or what constitutes the category of the civilized: 'It seemed to me that people in Bengal had become much too civilized in comparison'.[31] As the novel progresses, and we encounter a knowledge system produced by experience, the fingerprints of trial and error still visible in its history of experimentation, we begin to see the emptiness of a bookish and lifeless pedagogy that teaches us very little, almost nothing about our lives and where we live. Bibhutibhushan gives us a spiritual ecology, an understanding of life in its various roop, forms. It takes Satya time to get to this experience:

I would not be able to return to the hurly burly of Calcutta forsaking the vast tracts of forestland, the fresh fragrance of the sun-scorched

earth and the freedom and the liberation they represent. This was not
a sentiment that came upon me all of a sudden. Nature in the wild appeared before my enraptured and inexperienced eyes in myriad forms,
her beauty unveiled . . . the searing afternoon in the guise of a mad
Bhairavi . . . and, on moonless nights appeared the immense form of
Kali, wielding the flaming blade that was Orion, the radiance extending
into space.[32]

Realizations such as these, that connect our thoughts to those of our
ancestors, who, under the spell of fear and darkness, and perhaps other
things, imagined a woman with four or ten arms, or have called the sound
of wind through bamboo groves music, make us question both the idea
of civilization and development. 'It was only here, in these lonely forests,
that one had the opportunity to meditate on and be amazed by every
little thing: it was the ambience which drew out such fine sensations. If
I were to speak the truth, I would say that it is only since I have come
here that I have learnt how to meditate on things . . . I had never before
enjoyed my own mind in this manner'.[33] We think of critical thinking as
only an engagement with the thoughts and ideas of others, not as self-
argumentation or meditation on one's mind, on one's self: 'The vision
I had never known existed inside me was opening up now like a flower,
and thoughts I had never imagined now inhabited my world'.[34]

δ

A word about the moonlight in the forest, which is distinguished from
moonlight elsewhere: 'I have felt that while I was in Bengal I had not
known that moonlight could be so exquisite, that it could evoke such fear
and detachment—the only word for which would be udaas . . . Beauty of
this sort comes alive only under the wide-open skies, in silence and loneliness, with the undulating forests stretching as far as the horizon. Such
a moonlit night has to be experienced at least once a lifetime; he who
has not seen it will never know one of the most exquisite wonders of our
earth'.[35] The word 'udaas' appears often. Like 'maya' and 'leela', the word
is almost untranslatable, the reason the translator, Rimli Bhattacharya,
leaves it in Bangla. Low, melancholic, perhaps even depressed, these
might be equivalent meanings, but it's also much more—udaas is also

interiority, a meditative mood that indulges understanding through detachment. It also allows a sense of history of the kind that does not come to us through textbooks:

> The forest and hills had been thus for many centuries. So must this forest have been when the Aryans had crossed the Khyber long ago and had entered the land of the five rivers; when Buddha had silently left his home at night ... on that night, long ago, the mountain peaks must have laughed as they do on this moonlit night ... An so it was, when the poet Valmiki, immersed in composing his epic Ramayana in his hut by the Tamasa river must have started to find that the day was gone ... So had it been when Chandragupta ... when Chaitanyadev and the sankirtan in the home of Sribas ... through all these episodes of history the peak and the forest of Mahalikharoop had stood exactly thus. Who had inhabited these forests in those distant times? Not too far away from the jungle, I had ... seen an old woman who could have been anything between eighty to ninety years old ... the absolute embodiment of the poet Bharatchandra's rendering of Ma Annapurna as an ancient and decrepit woman. Now, I suddenly remembered the old woman—she was a symbol of the civilisation of the forest ... Thousand of years ago, they had been capturing birds with their gummy traps and their sat-nali in the same manner as they did not.[36]

Time and again, Bibhutibhushan challenges the mainstream idea of history, one that is almost picaresque, following man and nothing else. The forests challenge that notion, as does the woman of the forest, nameless and changeless for centuries. In paragraphs that follow this one, he criticizes the idea of progress, 'the Parthenon, the Taj Mahal, the Cologne cathedral ... the aeroplane, ship, railway, wireless, electricity', while 'the natives of Papua New Guinea and the ancient aborigines of Australia, and the Mundas, Kols, Nagas, and Kukis of India have not moved on in these five thousand years'.[37] Bibhutibhushan rejects the monumental and architectural sense of history for the fleeting, for flux, for the present. Civilization, progress, development—all of these seem empty and inconsequential categories when they are considered against the education given by the forest, not just empirical and scientific information that came through the folk knowledge system, but something unquantifiable, that Satya can only liken to 'epiphany'.[38] We talk about intersectionality often—it is one thing to theorize it, quite another to feel it: 'It is almost as if one can match the heartbeat of every plant and tree with one's own'.[39] This is theory as kavya was philosophy, not the way texts illustrate theories. Bibhutibhushan is giving us a plant theory through his fiction.

While Satya clears the forest for agricultural land, there is Jugalprasad, carrying 'all kinds of seeds' with him and planting them in 'not his own land, but dense forestland'.[40] 'The man was spending his own time and money in order to beautify huge areas of forestland where he had no claim over any piece of land. All this work, with no selfish motive. A strange fellow!'[41] Two world views—Satya, his name meaning 'truth', Jugalprasad, the prefix suggesting twins, a couple, a double, 'jugal', as if capable of accommodating divergent philosophies. Satya is induced—inspired—to start planting seeds of wildflowers and plants in the forest even as he gets parts of it cleared. This doubleness seems ingrained in the character of the forest's cosmopolitanism so that there can be an ashram inside the forest even as another part is being burnt. Not only ashram, forests also have their own kings, and their own political systems. 'The leader of the Santal Revolt is still alive—he is the present Raja. His name is Dobru Panna Birbardi. He is very old and very poor, but all the indigenous people of the land give him the respect due to a king. He's still regarded as a king, although he doesn't have a kingdom anymore.'[42] It seems like an oxymoron in our world—and in Bibhutibhushan's, with George V ruling over the British Empire—that kings could be poor at all. Raja Dobru Panna's wealth is his natural nobility and the riches of his memory, of his valour: 'These forests and the hills, all the earth, was once our kingdom. I have fought against the Company when I was young. Now I am many years old. We lost our battle. Now there is nothing left.'[43] That they, and their politics, derive from the forest itself is emphasized in many ways: the king's grandson 'had a body like a young sal tree, muscular and supple'; farmland 'is forbidden to our race'.[44]

There is both past and present in these words, both history and prescience—'sadhana', not of the human, but of nature itself, not of human years, but of centuries and millennia. The forest, therefore, brings us face to face with different kinds of time—the Taj Mahal, which he mentions critically, took a few decades to build, but the forest? 'It had taken hundreds of years of fervent meditation, of sadhana, to create Narhabaihar;

nature had fashioned it lovingly with her own hands . . . And in their place, what would one be gaining? Thatched houses, unbelievably ugly . . . banners flying above temples to Hanuman, an abundance of phanisama scrub, snuff and tobacco, epidemics of cholera and small-pox. Forests, primeval and ancient, forgive me.'[45] 'My distant employers do not care for the landscape: all they understand are taxes and revenue money.'[46]

And then the prediction, which has sadly come true, in a way theory does not necessarily often: 'Perhaps a time would come when men would no more be able to see forests: all they would see would be fields of crops, or the chimneys of jute and cotton mills. They would come then to this secluded forestland, as though on a pilgrimage. For those people, yet to come, let the forest stay pristine, undisturbed.'[47]

δ

'Almost all the gentlemen of the village owned some parcels of lands—fruit of their ancestors' machinations and labour.'[48] Note Bibhutibhushan's choice of metaphor: 'fruit'. This is not just idiomatic usage. He continues with the metaphor, so that instead of saying that one of Horihor's cousins owned acres of land, he says, 'Awnnoda Roy had been enjoying the un-disputed ownership of his mango and jackfruit orchards all these years.'[49] What Bibhutibhushan borrows—or it might be innate to him—from plant life is an understanding of land and ownership. A plant occupies land as long as it is alive—its descendants, by virtue of pollination or other means of reproduction, find root elsewhere, in other locations. The idea of inheritance, as it has been buttressed by laws that now define the human social world, is foreign to the plant world. It is this intuition that drives Bibhutibhushan's ethics. An extension of this is the question of the modern man—for whom does the plant produce its fruit? Durga 'steals' a few mangoes from a tree that does not 'belong' to her family. More im-portantly, she clarifies that she did not 'pluck' them off the mango tree— she had only collected a few fallen fruits. Once severed, do its fruits still belong to the tree, do they belong to the owner of the land on which the tree stands, do they belong to those who find it? In Shorbojoya's words is implicit such a philosophy: ' There's really no proof that those mangoes are from your trees, Auntie. They could be from anywhere. And even if they were from your trees, they're fallen buds, anyway. So unripe that they're almost inedible. What difference does it make if a child picks them up for fun?'[50] The aunt, to whom these words are addressed, is unable to process what seems to her conditioning an outrageous statement, one that breaks her belief in land and ownership: 'And then the mother says to me (here she mimicked Shorbojoya with extreme exaggeration), "The blossoms don't have your name on it, how dare you accuse us of stealing?" Imagine! The nerve!'[51] Opu, Durga's little brother, becomes conditioned to this philosophy immediately: 'the third-eldest granny could say what she liked, but picking fallen buds wasn't stealing. His sister didn't steal a thing from the Mukhujjes, and that was a fact.'[52]

Horihor, when he discovers the harassment that his daughter Durga had to endure for 'stealing' a couple of unripe fallen mangoes, remembers his begging and pleading to his uncle to not lease it: 'That orchard is all my children have . . . Areca nut, mango trees, black plum—you have two large orchards to meet your every need.'[53] 'The land was ours before we were the land's', wrote Robert Frost in 'The Gift Outright.'[54] Horihor sees not land but its produce—his is not the temperament, therefore, of the zamindar, the landlord, but of a child seeking delight. 'Sweetness, in particular, entranced them. Their family couldn't afford to buy them human-made sweets, so they went hunting in the woods for the abundant natural sweetness of fruits—from the humblest berries to the regal mangoes', writes Bibhutibhushan about the children Opu and Durga.[55] The same could be said of their father, of almost everyone deprived of 'sweetness' by social structures. The plant world remains their only source of such taste. The land for Horihor—and for the children and Bibhutibhushan—is valuable; it is precious because it is the producer of sweetness. Sweetness is almost central to his world—Bibhutibhushan might be unconsciously importing this from the Upanishads. He is giving us a cosmos that is based on 'madhu vidya'. Dadichi, in explaining it, comes to rest on a metaphor of plant life: sun is honey, heaven a bent bamboo, the Rig Veda the flower, and so on. While it is based on the secret and almost mystical learning passed from a teacher to a student, it is predicated on the idea of the Vedas being nectar. In Mantra 9 of the Rig Veda Sukta, Rishi Kakshivana says—'The bee desirous of honey sang songs of praise for you'. Madhu is also Soma, ambrosia, the taste of the deepest spiritual truth. Bibhutibhushan's characters seek sweetness (the use of 'mishti', sweetness, for an unexpected range of things, from a human face to the character of the breeze, is unlike its equivalent in any other language, and perhaps derives from this tradition of thinking) and find it everywhere, particularly in plants: 'the abundant natural sweetness of fruits', 'the humblest berries', and so on. Bhabani, the seeker-householder in *Ichhamati*, is welcomed with this spread by Jagadamba, the wife of his brother-in-law. The surfeit of sweetness—a reminder of the procession of a variety of sweet food served to gods in Bengal—is obvious: 'On this evening a spread was laid out for him of high-quality palm candy, sprouts, little balls of coconut sweets, other sweet delicacies like chandrapuli, khirer chanch, crunchy feni batasha, date-palm syrup, along with a bowl of thickened milk'.[56] This material manifestation is propelled by a spiritual instinct for sweetness, to find it everywhere, because Brahman is everywhere, because Brahman is sweet, and, as Bhattanayaka once said, because Brahman is inside one's mouth. For it is not the human alone that seeks sweetness: 'A nightbird, probably come to drink the honey from the jiuli tree, cried out from the nearby bamboo thicket'.[57]

Ancestry, as seen through land, is something that he remains ambivalent about. When Neeren, one of his cousin's sons, visits the village, Dibu Bhotchaj asks the young man, who's studying to be a lawyer in Calcutta, 'Did you go towards the fields for a walk today? This is the land of your ancestors, you know'.[58] Neeren's lack of interest in the revenue earned from the land owned by his father's land is a contrast to Opu dreaming about returning to his village towards the end of the novel. 'The land of your ancestors' is an ambiguous phrase—Bibhutibhushan's critique is of ownership, his commendation is of attachment. Legal ownership is not a guarantee of affection or knowledge about the land. That will come from experience, from cohabitation. It's a model of plant thinking that is the axis of his philosophy, that Rabindranath sought to include through his *Prakriti Path*, and one that is lacking in pedagogy today.

> 'Wild potato fruits? Are they good to eat? How does one eat them?'
> Durga was surprised. How could such a learned, bespectacled man not know about wild potatoes? Even a child of five knew about them![59]

The girl's attachment for the land is for what stands or lies on them— the trees and the streets: 'Durga has lately been feeling more attached to the village than usual. A sense of impending loss made her want to cling harder to these trees and to the familiar village lanes'.[60]

In *Ichhamati*, we see the effect of the Permanent Settlement Act of 1793, about how landholding changed the economic life of people. Its effect was also to instil a manner of violence in relation to land: 'Rajaram had nevertheless forcibly marked out plots for indigo on Panchu Sheikh's land, and on land belonging to Panchu Sheikh's father-in-law, Bipin Gaji, as well as that of Nobu Gaji.'[61] 'The amin's work was to fiddle with Ram's land and make it appear to be part of Shyam's, falsify measurements and to acquire and mark out—by any means—the best land for indigo farming. The raiyats were afraid of him and so they bribed him. Rajaram had a share in the bribes.'[62] This history, of being robbed of land and its produce, survives as intergenerational trauma in Bengal to this day. There is the simultaneous violation of land caused by the plantationecene: 'The raiyats had been summoned and asked to explain why they wouldn't grow indigo.'[63]

δ

Bibhutibhushan's maps of places, if they were to exist, would not have manmade borders, nor would they have blue and pink colours. His cartography is sensory. That is why when Opu, in *Pather Panchali*, imagines having to leave Nischindipur, it is the trees in the village he thinks of: 'Opu had never left the village. Not once, since the day he was born. The canopy of the old medlar, the Goswamis' garden, the large elephant-apple tree . . . the acacia trees dotting the fields would be heavy with blossoms, yellow against the bright blue sky . . . A wilderness of moonseed vine would hang from the young jasmine tree, making it look positively ancient from a distance.'[64] Later, in Kashi, Opu's mother, Sarbajaya, when walking through the pilgrimage town's famous ghats, remembers their village—what was a place or a street without trees in it, she wonders. 'What sort of a place is it? They tell me that there are no trees in Calcutta: have they cut down all the trees there?' a girl asks in *Aranyak*.[65] Reading Bibhutibhushan, particularly the world of Nischindipur, it feels that if a place were to be analogous to a person, then its birthmark would be its plant life.

We are, of course, reading of a time when trees, and not buildings, used to be signposts. It was them that one would mention while giving directions to a place, and trees themselves would give names to locations, as we see in names like Aamtala, Neemtala, 'tala' being the suffix, meaning 'under' (under the mango or neem tree), Jalpaiguri ('guri' being the suffix, meaning 'root'; a settlement near an Indian olive tree), and so on. 'The matriarch of one of the other Roy households saw the old woman drift past the large drumstick tree.'[66] Sentences such as this one keep occurring in *Pather Panchali*—it is a world where humans and their movements are seen—and often measured—against the background of trees. This intuitive awareness of trees as being central to their cosmology—and not just background—finds its way into metaphorical sayings and idioms. Shorbojoya is screaming at Durga: 'God knows what filth crawled into my womb that I had you for a daughter! I wish I could take you to the milkwood pine and leave you there!'[67] The 'milkwood pine' is not just the name of another tree. And hence—'Opu froze. The milkwood pine marked the village crematorium. Did his mother just say she wanted his didi dead?'[68]

δ

Under a tree. This phrase—this space—has a long spiritual history in the Indian subcontinent: of the Buddha, Nanak, and various other sages and folk saints. Let us look at a few instances of people sitting under trees in Bibhutibhushan. The 'shady banyan' under which Nalu Pal dozes off,[69] the Englishman Grant 'under the Ingleesh tree in this terrible afternoon sun',[70] Rajaram 'under . . . an Indian cork tree',[71] Bhabani, in order to get away from the 'stifling' 'indoors' of his home, where 'there was no sense of freedom', sits under a banyan tree.[72]

> It was a huge banyan whose branches had come down going deep into the soil, transforming themselves into pillar-like slender trunks. Beneath the shady banyan was the peace of solitude . . . Bhabani had found his way to this tree on earlier occasions and had observed the birds. Small clusters of sandhyamoni flowers bloomed at the foot of the tree. Bhabani looked around before he sat down. He needed a lonely spot . . . On this late afternoon he sat down to meditate by a flowering sandhyamoni creeper.[73]
>
> Shade, solitude, meditation, and discourse—these are the gifts of sitting under a tree. 'You would find at least a couple of fifty-year-old chhanra trees with solid trunks, and delightful resting spaces beneath the trees'.[74]

Bhabani preferred to sit by the broad river beneath the shadow of a juggidumur fig tree on silent solitary afternoons. He was getting by, wasn't he? Life was all too brief; why should he get caught up in that mess. He was fine, the way it was going.[75]

It is the mental repose, perhaps possible only under a tree, of watching the world—life—passing by as one sits, tree-like, to one place. It is the vantage point of the observer, both of the world and of one-self, like the tree's attachment to its shadow, real but also fleeting, that has made the tree a favoured site by most of the Indian subcontinent's spiritual thinkers. Having travelled, like many wandering saints and mendicants, through places, pursuing sages and saints in his search for knowledge, Bhabani knew the limits of the philosophy of the road, of the 'path', the road, as it were. He was, at last, able to see and seek the opposite—where the body could rest so that the mind could move more than it had been able to. He had found the tree like Gautama had. In this riverbank of the Ichhamati, though, there was not one but many trees. From under one of these Bhabani found something he hadn't in his long life: 'Never in his life had he come across such a cool and shady place. Bainchi, bamboo, neem, laburnum, roda, kunch creepers and all kinds of wild bushes filled the countryside. At all times of the day you heard birdsong—mynahs, magpie-robins, babblers and bou-katha-kou. With every season came new flowers, not a month went without some new blossoms—dhundhul, radhalata, keya, mango blossoms, bilwa-pushpa, suo, bonchatka, nata-kata flowers, all growing wild amidst thorny bushes'.[76] The 'cool and shady place' is, of course, both literal and metaphorical—imagine this, then, as Bhabani's office. An of-fice without walls, where plants and birds are colleagues and collabor-ators in one's quest—Brahman is in all three, plant, bird, Bhabani, it is in everything. Bibhutibhushan privileges 'experience' as the ultimate site for spiritual existence—not books, not words, not chants alone, but this, this immersion in life.

I do not use 'office' casually—its etymology also means 'divine ser-vice'. It is in his office, under the trees, that Bhabani engages in discus-sions about Brahman and Vedanta, and Nyaya and Mimansa: 'Towards evening, the guru-brothers were seated beneath the juggidumur tree by the Ichhamati'.[77] Under the tree, too, they debate the two schools of thought, both without names—that of the seeking wanderer versus the sitting seeker.

'In that case why did you spend so much time going on pilgrimages as a wandering ascetic? . . . '

'I believed that all desires had been destroyed, then realised that they remained. Better then to exhaust them. Let me put it in Sukdev's words: "Go to the forest only when you have renounced all desires. But not while you still have them." Besides, who has told you that one may not reach out to bhagwan whilst still a householder?'[78]

Two things are being highlighted here: that one may find god not necessarily because one has renounced the householder's life but in it—that Brahman is in every being and experience; that by sitting under a tree, it is possible that one becomes a bit like the tree itself: a part of us still while another half moves, observing and deep, deep because a tree strikes roots, a wanderer is like air.

'In a field adjoining the bundh, beneath a date palm tree, lived Ramkanai Chakraborty *Kobiraj*, the local doctor of herbs, practitioner of ayurveda'.[79] Living on a spartan diet—'all summer long he lived on a bit of cooked rice and fried laburnum flowers'[80]—he treats his people, the suffering and the poor, those who do not have a cowrie to pay him. Living under a tree, Bibhutibhushan seems to emphasize implicitly, stokes and indulges the essential virtues, particularly when one compares them to the cruel and selfish life of those who live amidst riches, such as the residents of Neelkuthi. When Ramkanai is appointed as the kabiraj of Neelkuthi, he struggles to find sleep there: 'The lime shed of the Neelkuthi wasn't exactly the most comfortable of places for a good sleep'.[81]

And so, even after a person's body has left the place, he is remembered—he has become attached to the tree, like its shadow is, off and on. That is why Bhabani says, 'But I feel that my gurudev is still alive and deep in meditation beneath that gooseberry tree'.[82]

And there's Grantsaheb's Banyan in *Aranyak*, the legacy of whose name Satya is unable to decipher—sitting or standing under it he experiences 'loneliness' of two kinds: missing the city, 'not a creature by my side,'[83] but also a kind of aloneness more elemental, where 'the loneliness of

the forestland sat upon my breast like a stone,'[84] a loneliness that is independent of the number of humans beside us, one that is produced by the
landscape and plant life itself. For a moment, Bibhutibhushan indulges
the notion that it could be the aloneness of the king: 'At such times I felt
that I had never before seen such sights as nature had to offer me here.
All of this belonged to me; as far as one could see, I was the sole human
being, as though there was no one to come and break my quietude beneath the peaceful evening sky'.[85] This feeling of kingship is not of 'I am
the monarch of all I survey', not one of power but of no one to interrupt
or distract.

δ

When the young Neeren, his imagination tickled by his sister-in-law
to think of Durga as a prospective bride, first looks at the girl's face, he
thinks—'he thought he had never seen such beautiful, expressive eyes before . . . The tranquility in their depths reminded him of a secluded copse
of medlars—fragrant and peaceful'.[86] Durga is 'always at someone's orchard or garden'.[87] 'The orchards and woodlands of the village were her
whole life. She knew which berries were the sweetest, whose orchard had
the sweetest plums, and which bush of berries ripened first each season'.[88]
The reader knows that Durga doesn't go to school, nor does she have the
benefit of being educated by her father the way her brother is. What, then,
of this extra-scholastic learning? In writing Durga, Bibhutibhushan gives
us a person who has learnt the secrets of other species and of the land, not
from books, not from science, not necessarily from folklore alone, but
whose wisdom is a function of experience, of intimacy, of a life lived almost like trees and grass, and, unfortunately, often also being treated like
them, with indifference or violence. His characterization of the young
girl as being in tune with her surroundings, part of a network of inter-
dependence, links her to an ancestry of female proto-environmentalists,
such as the women of the first Chipko movement in eighteenth-century
Rajasthan, among several others. Bibhutibhushan is hinting towards a
distinction that would solidify much more after *Pather Panchali*—the
university-educated environmentalist and a person like Durga, a con-
tainer of folk wisdom of the kind Robin Wall Kimmerer writes about
in relation to her people of the Potawatomi Nation. The loss of people

like Durga—simultaneous with the loss of land and landscapes that produced women like her—and the concurrent professionalization of the field of environmental studies, which has often been exclusionary, going, as it has, for academia-driven eligibility, is perhaps foreshadowed by Bibhutibhushan through her untimely death.

'You look just like a tribal girl', her mother tells her, contrasting her with 'neighbourhood girls' who 'are lighting lamps and praying to Shib Thakur for good husbands'.[89] What Shorbojoya implies, through her use of a readymade word like 'tribal', is a person who is of the forest, reared by it, and, thus, almost like it, as a tree is of the forest. When he and his mother can't find Durga, and Opu asks Runudi about her whereabouts, she says, 'Have you checked beneath the medlar tree?'.[90] Another time, when Durga goes missing, her mother consoles Opu thus: 'Don't cry. She's probably hiding in someone's orchard'.[91]

When the children return drenched after a storm, their mother describes them as if they were from the plant world: 'You two look like a bowl of soaked rice';[92] 'her children's beautiful, rain-washed faces looked like the buds of newly blossomed jasmine'.[93]

Opu is unable to spend time at the house in Kashi. This is because, 'much like a sapling, his body and mind turned towards sunlight and open spaces. He was raised in such spaces, amidst the sun, rain and wind. The rejuvenating greenness of Nischindipur's fields, woodlands and sunbathed rivers had surrounded him all his life'.[94] He was like a plant who 'felt strangled in the damp darkness of the rooms'.[95]

They are the plant-humans in Bibhutibhushan's world.

δ

The little boy Opu drags home a bamboo, telling his father that it will make 'good pens'.[96] Shorbojoya asks Durga to get a few 'white fever-vines' so that she can make her son Opu a thin fever-vine broth.[97] Even fences to protect plants from thieves are made of plants, often of thorny branches. Is that all that plants give? Surrounded as we are by the bureaucracy of transactionality—we must plant more trees because they give us oxygen and so on—Bibhutibhushan reminds us of what trees actually give us.

There was a large peepul tree a short way away from the Roys' house. One could only see the top of it if one stood on the raised veranda outside and craned one's neck. Opu loved staring at the tree-top. The enormous height of the tree, and the mysteries hidden inside the dense canopy made him think of magical, faraway lands . . . The idea of distance, in general, enchanted him . . . the misty indigo field he had seen as a child . . . all of it made him think of the nebulous adventures that were happening at that very moment, in lands that lay just beyond the average human's reach. With a little effort, he could imagine himself as part of those adventures, far away from this mundane village, with no known way of returning home.[98]

Towards the end of the novel, as we see Opu grow passionately interested in books, in reading and writing, we see the nouns that engage him: the titles of books, the characters in them, the faraway lands that trigger his literary wanderlust. Before that, though—before the nouns, before the words, in a pre-literacy spirit, there is Opu's staring at the tree-top of the peepul; there is no possible articulation of what that seeing gives him—can the devotee say what the sighting of an idol of god in a temple gives them, after all?—but it does, as much to a child as to an adult. Searching for language, Bibhutibhushan uses the words 'magical' and 'mysterious' to characterize the spiritual freedom of plant life often. The microcosm of 'the dense canopy' and the 'enormous height of the tree' surely give something to the little boy. Perhaps it is the inability to find a more materialist and quantitative vocabulary to measure the impact of this experience, of this kind of darshan, that is responsible for the kind of loss we feel today. As lovers and poets have experienced the moon and then tried to articulate its effect in words, always knowing that no matter how honest and sophisticated their expression, it will always be short of the coagulation of experience, so with the effect of the peepul tree on Opu—its impact is as unquantifiable as love. 'Opu had never witnessed the beauty of springtime in Bengal on such a vast scale before. Through the blazing afternoon to the moonlit night, he had absorbed the majesty of the changing landscape . . . In his future life as an artist, it was the memory of this day that he turned to again and again for inspiration and sweet tranquillity.'[99]

One often wonders about the relation between flowers and worship, on why they should be necessary to worship at all. Occasionally, Bibhutibhushan allows us a flash into what could be one of the many possible reasons for this. The first of this is the moralistic, the with-thorns-will-come-flowers adage. 'On his way back from his morning dip in the *Ichhamati*, Ramkanai Kobiraj discovered some lovely nak-joaley flowers that had bloomed atop the bushes bordering the river. They would be good for offering in his puja. He was greatly tempted to pick them. He was delayed coming back to his hut, as he had to make his way through thorny bushes to get the flowers.'[100] There is almost a subterranean tradition of writing about the difficulty of procuring flowers for puja, one that gets more humorous as the genre enters urban spaces where plant life is scarce and flower gathering extremely competitive—Shirsendu Mukhopadhyay devotes an entire novella to this in *Phoolchor*, for instance.[101] But there's also something else, an entry into a spiritual world made possible through the collection of flowers, the near-meditative practice of stringing them into a garland, the withdrawal from worldliness and a consequent experience outside social language. Bibhutibhushan tries to write about it, and, realizing his failure to hold the mystical in words, lets it snap into a near-biological expression:

> It was his daily practice to have a bath before he sat down to worship his little Radha Krishna a doll-like image crafted by a village potter . . . He loved arranging nak-joaley flowers around the icon, making sandalwood paste and anointing the feet, lighting a couple of incense sticks before it . . . If left undisturbed, he would be lost in worship for a long time. At times he would quietly weep. With a shy gesture he would wipe away his tears.[102]

One cannot say whether god created the flowers or the flowers were created for god.

δ

Bibhutibhushan's plant philosophy derives from everyday rituals as much as it does from instinct and analysis of life experience and its analogous relationship with plant behaviour.

Durga was in a corner of the inner courtyard, bullied by her mother into performing the punyipukur ritual. A small square hole had been dug beneath the papaya tree and filled with water to signify the 'Pond of Virtue'. The chickpeas and green peas that she had scattered around it had begun to sprout. Durga was standing over this 'pond' and flying through the rites as quickly as she dared . . . She turned her back to her pond of virtue, folded her palms and chanted the 'mantra', which was really just a verse.

Pond of Virtue, garland of flower,
Who worships at this noon hour?
I, Leelabotee, that is who.[103]

A 'pond of virtue' is one of the many rituals that bring water and land and plant life into purposive play with spirituality, an initiation into living with the elements, and a little girl's adventure into gardening, into creating life through the simple act of soaking seeds and 'scattering' them, coaxing life out of the dormant. One cannot forget something integral to this though: it is the sense of play that attends these rituals, so that they do not seem like a chore, as bureaucratic events around planting saplings by both governmental and non-governmental institutions feel like today. It is this invocation of joy—ananda—that Bibhutibhushan records in chronicling life in this seemingly unremarkable village. There's also something subtle that he machinates through the form of his telling here. From the playful installation of the 'Pond of Virtue' he takes us— and the children Opu and Durga—to a real pond. This movement from microcosm of an idealized world, a world of performative 'virtue', to a pond where the search for water chestnuts comes with risks and the un- expected, is held through the belief in 'play', as everything being 'khyala', sport, a game, entertainment, joy-giving.

Immediately after the ritual of the pond, she tells her brother, 'Let's go. Bhoda's mother said that the pond at the fort is full of ripe water chest- nuts.'[104] From one play to another. When they reach the pond and discover that all the water chestnuts have been taken away, they allow themselves to be distracted by what is available to them at the moment: berries, water lilies, and eventually unripe water chestnuts, 'still too raw', with 'no milk inside yet'.[105] The children, realizing the ad hoc nature of life, behave with the ethics of pollinators: anything will do, anything available in the present moment. This is the ethics of plant life too—the migration from the doll-like ritual of a pond to a real one, from playfulness to the danger of being stuck in the sticky mud of the pond is, in the human social world, a natural trajectory from the child to the adult sphere. In Bibhutibhushan, though, this is not a journey of size, whether of pond or human, but one founded on the idea of iteration, so that the two ponds, and the plant life they harbour inside them and in their neighbourhood, are part of a family of the living, both important and necessary, independent of the size of their occupation of land.

Bibhutibhushan takes care to emphasize the relation between plants and play. That joy comes to these children from the plant world, even when they are scavenging other's people's orchards. Toys cannot be purchased by their poor parents, it is supplied to them by the natural world. 'Durga was much more familiar with the woods and gardens, and knew of more plants than he did. Together, they brought back a very respectable variety of stock for the shop: custard apple leaves to be sold as betel leaves, inedible brown fruit to be sold as potatoes, petals of the honeysuckle to be sold as fish, little ivy gourds as regular gourd, unripe snake gourd as ripe cowpea, clumps of soil as raw sea salt'.[106] In the plant world, something was inevitably like the other, as Durga and Opu's make-believe shop shows us—in this they seem to be intuitively part of a tradition of seeing as the German thinker Jacob Boehme, who saw an echo of things from the plant and other worlds in humans.[107]

Bibhutibhushan is, therefore, altering the idea of play—the adult world is not just miniaturized for the child, as it is in dolls and toy cars; he is encouraging imaginative connections, one deeply rooted in the philosophy of becoming, where every being can be themselves and also more. This is the gift of the plant world—the trees that allow and indulge Opu to be much more than the little boy in Nischindipur. 'Their fresh, evergreen vibrancy coloured every moment of their lives. They knew every bit of this land; its beauty and mysteries filled their young hearts with wonderment and joy. The sweet smell of yellow-nicker blossoms, glimpses of the dancing wagtail . . . the many nameless berries and leaves that the two regularly used in their games . . . all of it made the woods feel like a magical wonderland. Opu couldn't quite explain why, but the smallest things about the woods filled him with a strange, deep happiness.'[108] Without this happiness—ananda—there cannot be love.

The affection for plant life will not come from words, the language of moral instruction, but from this experience. We are propelled by the desire to protect what we love. Even Bibhutibhushan registers the failure of language to record the impact of this experience: 'the glistening brown of the lapwing as it landed on the white morning glory bush, the woven palm-leaf screen, the smell of the freshly turned earth—all of it would fill him with a sense of tranquil happiness that he couldn't describe in words'.[109]

From this sense of happiness and wonder was created the myths and stories—their survival as dependent on the woods and forests that produced them. Hence the significance of play, of the belief in the benevolent energy and protectors of these spaces. 'When the night deepens and the humans sleep, she goes from plant to plant, bringing flowers into blossom and caressing baby birds in their nests. In the final hours of full moon nights, she fills the honeycombs with the sweetness of yellow-nicker and jackfruit flowers . . . All through the night, the misty glow of her soothing beauty pervades the woods. Unnamed fragrances mix with moonlight and silence, creating a pool of mystical repose. Then, as night turns to dawn, she melts into the disappearing darkness'.[110]

Reading this in completely changed circumstances, when not the goddess Bishalakkhi but woodcutters, both amateurs and corporatized, kill plants and trees at night, so that we wake up not to more sweetness but to more barrenness, stories such as these take on a layer of significance. What we call the supernatural today is only a record of loss, of what was once the natural. Pagan mythology—a poor phrase and category, mined by Hollywood movies, for instance—is a record not just of the imagination but also of memory, of our ancestors recording the wonder of life, of the earth, and imagining the forces who could create such strangeness. These mythological figures, such as Opu's Bishalakkhi or a ladybug ('A ladybug was not really an insect. Everyone said it was the god Shudorshon in insect form. It was extraordinary luck to have spotted one'[111]) are carriers of that first experience of sublimity. Today, not creators but destroyers work not only at night but also through the day—they do not generate mysticism but the violence of comic book heroes.

It must have been this innate coexistence between plants and humans that made them such an integral part of our songs, of the 'Vaishnav kirtan' and 'Modhukaner gaan' of course, but also of a semi-classical form such as the tappa. Bidhu-didi in *Ichhamati* sings one:

> Is love merely a world of words, if the heart be
> entwined with one?
> Would the creeper live, if the tree withers
> In which it is entwined?[112]

The creeper is there in Nistarini's song as well:

> My friend, is love only a matter of words,
> When one heart is in the other entwined?
> Will the creeper thrive if the tree dries?
> When one life is threaded with the other?[113]

It is not a coincidence that both women seem to have similar versions of the same thought—and that they think of a creeper on a dead tree.

δ

Freedom comes from the same root as 'friend', someone or something that is dear. When I think of those I feel closest to, those I love, I notice only one thing common among them—they make me feel free. It is possible that it is my conditioning in this understanding of freedom that makes me gravitate so urgently towards what Bibhutibhushan's plant life gives him and the characters in his novels. Idiomatic usage, anthropomorphic as it is, connects freedom to birds, linking, quite obviously, the freedom imagined in flight, the supposed lack of obstructions to movement in the sky, to the experience of freedom. Plants and trees, on the other hand, are stuck to the earth, unable to move. To be able to imagine them as free is quite revolutionary. This understanding of freedom, one that is possible to access even when movement is limited, comes from science as much as it does from the Upanishads—plant and planet; all planetary bodies, including the earth from where and from which we seek freedom, kept in their place because of various forces, are free if we can imagine them as such.

The joy of pure freedom, never before tasted, had made their young blood sing. They had been in no state to stop and ask for directions, in no state to stop and consider the consequences of running wildly into the unknown... his sister had realised that she had lost her way. In their glorious run for freedom through the fields, they had seen no villages to *mark the way*: only paddy fields, marshland and thickets of cane.[114]

The absence of borders, of things that mark divisions, of 'no villages', of the lack of humans and their habitats on the way is what enables this sense of freedom. Two English writers come to mind: John Clare, whose poems and poetic temperament would be deeply affected by the division of land into 'enclosures', the taming of land, its forest and agrarian spaces, into rectangles, how that would affect the sense of freedom; D. H. Lawrence, who wanted to imagine a space that had not been touched by the human. The freedom that Opu and Durga experience is the freedom both to the eye and to the limbs—the eyes meet no obstructions, the species of plants changes, but the visual freedom is that of looking at the sky, only this time experienced through the body, as one imagines birds doing in the sky. It is also the freedom of the unknown, of being unshackled from certainty: to see the impress of the human hand and the human mind is to feel like a dog on a leash. Hence the Bengali modernists' obsession and celebration of the 'nuton', the new: 'At such times, you should feel no less than the famous explorers who charted new lands... When I visit one, I "discover" it—with my mind, my heart, and with all of my senses. I taste of its newness, and I am elated'.[115] Freedom is looseness, looseness that gives grace—the reason even swaying coconut trees and falling flowers look beautiful to the human eye.

Durga's hunger for freedom is what drives her to the wild, to its trees. Bibhutibhushan takes care to mark it visually, through words that divide land, particularly agricultural land: 'She felt like no fence, no rules could hold her back today'.[116] Opu misses what he has in the village only when he has to leave it: 'Opu had been reared in the lap of rural nature... Without him realising it, freedom—in its aspect as untramelled nature—had instilled in him an adoration of the pure and the beautiful. It was a devotion that would blossom within him for the rest of his life'.[117] Freedom as 'untramelled nature'—not agricultural land, with its divisions and 'enclosures', not that unnatural geometry of rhombuses and rectangles that hurt the eye and its desire to flow unchecked. This had given Opu the breadth of curiosity that the humans and the size and shapes of their settlements in the village could not. 'Untramelled'—a rejection of gross individualism, of marking one's territory.

It is less to meet a lover than to experience this freedom that Nistarini, the young woman who is scolded for her disobedience to social mores (and whose name implies salvation), goes to the plant life inside and by the Ichhamati, its 'big yellow flowers of titpalla creeper', 'the jungle of saibable and keya-jhanka', 'the blue flowers of the bonkalmi', 'the little wild purple flowers of chanda-grass'.[118]

> When she saw that the ghat was deserted Nistarini felt a great desire to put her water-pot against her chest and swim in the river. In the fast-running brimming waters of the Ichhamati in the month of Bhadra, even a straw was torn in two in a few moments; people were afraid of bathing during this time for fear of sharks and crocodiles. Nistarini never bothered about any of this; those who have never swim with a water-pot with their chest—what would she tell them of the pleasure! You are swimming, almost borne along by the ebb tide, surrendering yourself to the current and along with you come clusters of floating vegetation—toka-pana, the bright ripe fruits peeping out from the telekucho creeper, the river-mynah cchirping and shrieking from the mossy floating islands that went by you—such bliss! The joy of liberation![119]

It is almost as if Nistarini is a grown-up Durga, not on land but on water. The passages that Bibhutibhushan devotes to Durga and Nistarini's freedom, the need for Bengali women to become independent, linking and likening them, as he does, to the freedom of plant life, have the energy of anthems as much as they do the sap of an otherworldly intimation.

δ

Whether it is the form of the novel *Ichhamati*, without chapter names or even separate chapters, so that every section feels like a temporary stop by the bank of the river, capturing life in flow, a form that reminds us of how the 'stream-of-consciousness' novel, practised by novelists in Europe at that time, had different lives elsewhere, in other cultures, or *Pather Panchali*, which, again, following its title, 'Song of the Road', has the form of a travelogue, the record of a journey to the wonder of the world, or *Aranyak*, which has the form of a forest, unpredictable, as much about getting lost as it is about finding the unexpected, Bibhutibhushan's novels derive their 'roop'—form—from the natural world. That is perhaps why they feel loose and free, their bagginess the comfort of a bed, which takes our shape and accommodates all our bodily postures. None of his novels—or even short fiction—take on the shape of available templates. This might be Kalidasa's gift to him and some of his contemporaries, this access to the natural world, particularly the plant world in a way that is analogous, metaphorical, but also an extension of it. In Bibhutibhushan's case, it perhaps derives from the writer's own 'experience'—not just their subject or content, but the elasticity of his own life, unpredictable in the bends they took: from Calcutta to a forest and back, to the Sunderbans, a riverine life, memories of indigo plantations in his Jessore. This lack of a 'career path', its deviancy from a professionalized life-pattern, gives both freedom and a consequent buoyancy to his writing. The modernist's search for appropriate form therefore became tied to the natural world: beginnings and endings are not about human arrivals and departures, for instance, but are a record of some variation of constancy, whether of plant life or of water. I would say that the temper and trust in such a form—perhaps even deliberate—comes to Bibhutibhushan from the Upanishads, their belief in the presence of the One in every living thing. 'Only the One would be ever unchanging, in the midst of all flux ... Revealing itself in such lovely afternoons, in every flower and fruit, every spring, in the millions of births and deaths, in hope, love and compassion revealed only in faint glimpses ... no religious scripture in the world could say what the One's form was.'[120] 'The fields and the forests were radiant with flowers ... The field, the river, the wild foliage and the greenery, the cycle of seasons, birds, evenings and moonlit nights all had brought to him such exquisite ananda, as though a new Upanishad was being composed within his own heart ... The world was a joyous state of experience—ananda.'[121]

Bibhutibhushan would have extended that, the presence of the One, the brahman, to the living form of the narrative, of its form. As Rimli Bhattacharya, the translator of *Ichhamati*, reminds us,

Bihutibhushan's father was renowned as a kathak-brahman, a reciter of scriptures. He was an unworldly householder, a dreamer and a poet. Apu's father in *Pather Panchali* was cast in his likeness. Late in his life, the author of *Ichhamati*, in repeatedly affirming the joyous

manifestation of the Supreme Being as one who delights in His own creation, was not only recalling his own father—part of an impoverished
brahman literati—whose learning did not extend into colonial forms
of knowledge, but also echoing the Brahma Sutra which refers to 'the
creation of the world as an act of lila, play, the joy of the poet . . . the
Supreme [Being] is described as a kavi, an artist, a maker or creator, not
a mere imitator.'[122]

Bhattacharya points out a couple of significant things. The first
of these is the father's lack of initiation into 'colonial forms of knowledge'. What Bibhutibhushan, a teacher, among other jobs that he held,
wanted to uphold through his writing was a reminder of a robust tradition of learning that had been shamed into a disappearing tradition by
the colonial apparatus. He shows the damage caused by European colonialism in several ways—he calls a few trees 'English trees' all through
Ichhamati, thereby reminding his readers of how the landscape was being
changed by colonial botanists. There is, of course, the indigo plantation, forced on certain areas of Bengal by the British, the cruelty both
on humans and plants, causing impoverishment of both men and the
soil. Following this is abandonment without compunction—land and
life, both plant and human, exist only for commerce. It is, however, not
just the plantationocene that is brought to our attention, to be criticized.
The introduction of 'foreign' trees, seeds, bulbs, and cuttings brought by
European botanists to Calcutta, its neighbouring towns and villages, and
to sanatorium towns, began changing the character of plant vegetation
as well as the quality of soil. (Richard Axelby, just to cite one example, in
his essay 'Calcutta Botanic Garden and the Colonial Re-ordering of the
Indian Environment', explains how the botanical garden near Calcutta
was changed to accommodate and then give hierarchical importance to
migrant plant life.[123]) As great as that damage was, what was worse—and
whose consequences we can see continuing until today—was how it destroyed premodern knowledge systems, so much so that any invocation
of these texts is met with dismissal, as if it were all a symptom of a mindless triumphalist revival of India's 'golden past'. The colonial—and now
colonized—education system wiped away oral learning traditions that
drew from lived experience, so that what is taught in our schools and col-
leges, whether science, mathematics, or even art, derives primarily from

Europe. We are allowed a glimpse of other kinds of learning in the books that are found in Horihor's box, those that Apu spies on, and those that he discovers in Kashi and the school that he later attends, and the oral knowledge system that is passed through sruti, from listening to recitations of the Chandimangal kabyas or discussions about Brahman and Upanishadic thought, or even thoughts about ananda, its provenance and its provinces. These discussions, mediated through Hindu religious texts, engage with philosophical questions as much as they help to understand the circumstances of the material world. The world of folk knowledge, of plants and the seasons, none of which are part of textbooks, was passed on naturally, during the course of daily living.

The Englishman Colesworthy Grant—'not only a painter, but a poet and a writer as well'—had found something in this Bengal.[124] 'Rural Bengal had opened up new vistas before his eyes . . . dazzling laburnum trees dotting an unbroken sweet of fields, the clamour of unknown birds from the flowering bushes, shrubs and trees.'[125] There was a difference between him and the other two Englishmen, who 'did not have the eyes to appreciate the countryside'; 'After all, they were farmers who had come from the villages of Bligh and Faringford from the Western Midlands district of England'.[126] It is ironic, slightly hilarious, but deeply telling that Grant draws a distinction—not just between these two English indigo plantation managers and himself, comparing himself favourably to them, but that he is unconsciously privileging the natural sophistication of the people of 'rural Bengal' over the 'rustic' Europeans. Bibhutibhushan spends a few sentences here, allowing himself to get into Grant's head in a way he doesn't necessarily elsewhere—he wants to emphasize the superiority of his land and its life. That is why Grant wants to 'write about life in the mofussil. About the everyday life of the people who lived here, the wonderful river and the unknown trees and the thick vegetation of the jungle—these were to become pictures in his book. He had already worked out his ideas for the book. It was to be called *Anglo-Indian Life in Rural Bengal*.[127] The 'unknown trees' and 'thick vegetation'—note the adjectives here. Even though it was 'Anglo-Indian Life', the trees and vegetation are important enough for Grant to articulate; the 'unknown' trees denote a landscape that has still not been colonized.

How did the Europeans colonize the land? 'Luxuriant gardens had once been planted on either side. Huge trees, English trees that Robson

Saheb had planted—all of which now made the graveyard heavy with darkness. That one was Robson Saheb's daughter's grave . . . The graveyard was running wild with overgrown bushes and uncut grass. In the heyday of the Neelkuthi you could pick up a drop of red sindur off the graces—so spotless and shining the place was. Who gave a hoot for it now!'[128] Bibhutibhushan is setting up a contrast between the foreign plant life on this soil and how their survival (the 'grave' is a telling metaphor and site here) is dependent on human care and the 'natural' beauty of the village by the river Ichhamati. There's also another—'spotless and shining', a phrase used for the English idea of beauty, is never used for the landscape and its plant life anywhere else. It is almost an indictment, though it is seemingly used to speak of a more favourable time for the colonizer.

δ

Bibhutibhushan uses the word 'Bharatvarsha' to mean more than 'India', more than geographical territory and more than what a concept such as 'nation' can hold. In *Ichhamati*, for instance, that word is inaugurated by 'the scent of fragrant flowers' and 'the green spreading fields of autumn-paddy'.[129]

> This is India, Bharatvarsha . . . Colesworthy Grant mused. He had been wandering all over the country . . . The India that he had glimpsed through Monier Williams's translation of Shakuntalam and in the poetry of Edwin Arnold—for which he had come so far; now at last in all his sojourn he had a sense of a different world, exquisitely beautiful, resonant with poetry—on the banks of a river in this obscure little village in the fading afternoon light. He felt it had been worth all his travelling.[130]

An India imagined through literature, a Bharatvarsha encountered through experience. Grant—and Bibhutibhushan—notes the difference. In this novel, set long before Indian independence, it is not the region, with its geographical marks, that is being invoked. It is a sensibility and a synecdoche—the 'obscure little village' becomes India in a way that maps do not allow, and 'the scent of fragrant flowers' make it possible, for both visitors and residents, to imagine Bharatvarsha. Whether the village or the forest in *Aranyak*, where one of the forest dwellers asks about the location of Bharatvarsha—'Have you heard the name "Bharatvarsha"? Bhanmati indicated by shaking her head that she had not heard of it. She had never travelled beyond Chakmaki-tola. In which direction was Bharatvarsha?'[131]—it seems that Bibhutibhushan is hinting towards the sense of the land being not in its cities. Only in these spaces can one feel 'the nurturing spirit of the earth, goddess Jagadhatri herself'.[132]

δ

'Everything rests on experience', says the narrator of *Ichhamati*, echoing Bhabani Barujje's thoughts.[133] These words, seemingly simple, hold in them Bibhutibhushan Bandyopadhyay's worldview. The directness of encounter, one without the mediation of priests or scholars, brings ananda—this is the real and primary source of education: we will protect what we have come to love. There is also an instinctive groping to name the creator of such ananda, which, he is certain, comes from the natural world and our experience of it. 'There must be a loving mother who lay hidden within cosmic Nature. How else could there exist such boundless love if it were not part of the cosmos? Bhabani had walked along many paths, searched out sadhus and sannyasis in hills and mountains, practised yoga for years; but before this most intimate of bonds between mother and child—all his yoga, his efforts at seeking a cosmic union, had been simply washed away.'[134] Bibhutibhushan's 'mother' is not Abanindranath Tagore's Bharat Mata.[135] This is a figure related neither to any nationalist consciousness nor to a patriarchal worship of the mother. The biological consciousness that makes us gravitate towards the comfort of the mother-child bond is, in fact, at odds with the patriarchal God-the-father template, one that does not really occur to us as we 'experience' the natural world.

> 'Where does he (bhagwan) live?'
> 'There, up there', said Khokon, pointing to the sky.
> 'Where, my son? Above the treetops?'
> 'Yes.'
> 'Do you love him?'
> 'No.' ...
> 'Why don't you love bhagwan?'
> 'Don't know him.'[136]

To be able to love, we must know them. In Bibhutibhushan's world, this applies as much to bhagwan as to plant life. And hence the significance of this model of protection over the bureaucratic and apocalyptic saviour models. 'You cannot love without knowing them, understanding them. Only if your love is based on knowing and understanding, does your love become strong.'[137]

Notes

1. Bandyopadhyay (2018), pp. 1–2.
2. Bandyopadhyay (2019).
3. Ibid. Italics mine.
4. Ibid.
5. Ibid.
6. Ibid.
7. Ibid.
8. Bandyopadhyay (2018), p. 133.
9. Ibid., p. 356.
10. Ibid., p. 357.
11. Roy (2021).
12. Bandyopadhyay (2019).
13. Ibid., p. 110.
14. Ibid.
15. Ibid., p. 125.
16. Ibid., p. 126.
17. Ibid., p. 168.
18. Ibid., p. 158.
19. Moon (2014).
20. Bandyopadhyay (2019).
21. Bandyopadhyay (2017), p. xviii.
22. Bhattacharya, Bandyopadhyay (2017), p. xix.
23. Ibid., p. 1.
24. Ibid., pp. 1–2.
25. Ibid., p. 3.
26. Ibid.
27. Ibid.
28. Ibid., p. 9.
29. Ibid., p. 10.
30. Ibid., p. 11.
31. Ibid., p. 18.
32. Ibid., p. 22.
33. Ibid., p. 32.
34. Ibid., p. 47.
35. Ibid., p. 23.
36. Ibid., p. 83.
37. Ibid., p. 84.
38. Ibid., p. 86.
39. Ibid., p. 104.
40. Ibid., p. 109.
41. Ibid., p. 109–110.
42. Ibid., p. 149–150.

43. Ibid., p. 153.
44. Ibid.
45. Ibid., p. 196.
46. Ibid., p. 213.
47. Ibid., p. 248.
48. Bandyopadhyay (2019), p. 198.
49. Ibid., p. 199.
50. Ibid.
51. Ibid., p. 93.
52. Ibid., p. 97.
53. Ibid., p.116.
54. Frost (1969).
55. Bandyopadhyay (2018), p. 104.
56. Ibid., p. 54.
57. Ibid., p. 69.
58. Bandyopadhyay (2019), p. 203.
59. Ibid., p. 221.
60. Ibid., p. 251.
61. Bandyopadhyay (2018), p. 30.
62. Ibid., p. 33.
63. Ibid., p. 41.
64. Bandyopadhyay (2019), pp. 157–158.
65. Bandyopadhyay (2017), p. 134?
66. Ibid.
67. Bandyopadhyay (2019), p. 99.
68. Ibid.
69. Bandyopadhyay (2019), p. 3.
70. Ibid., p. 15.
71. Ibid.
72. Ibid., p. 23.
73. Ibid., p. 24.
74. Bandyopadhyay (2018), pp. 326–327.
75. Ibid., p. 77.
76. Ibid.
77. Ibid., p. 78.
78. Ibid., pp. 79–80.
79. Ibid., p. 99.
80. Ibid.
81. Ibid., p. 105.
82. Bandyopadhyay (2018), p. 279.
83. Bandyopadhyay (2017), p. 14.
84. Ibid.
85. Ibid., pp. 15–16.
86. Bandyopadhyay (2019), p. 222.
87. Ibid., p. 74.
88. Ibid., p. 90.
89. Ibid.
90. Ibid., p. 97.
91. Ibid., p. 100.
92. Ibid., p. 123.
93. Ibid., p. 124.
94. Ibid., p. 410.
95. Ibid.
96. Ibid., p. 267.
97. Ibid., p. 277.
98. Ibid., p. 78.
99. Ibid., pp. 387–388.

100. Bandyopadhyay (2018), p. 211.
101. Shirsendu Mukhopadhyay, *Phoolchor.*
102. Bandyopadhyay (2018), p. 211.
103. Bandyopadhyay (2019), p. 102.
104. Ibid., p. 103.
105. Ibid., p. 106.
106. Ibid., p. 181.
107. Boehme (2013).
108. Bandyopadhyay (2019), p. 187.
109. Ibid., p. 191.
110. Ibid., p. 197.
111. Ibid., p. 231.
112. Bandyopadhyay (2018), p. 171.
113. Ibid., p. 330.
114. Bandyopadhyay (2019), p. 161. Emphasis mine.
115. Ibid., p. 163.
116. Ibid., p. 229.
117. Ibid., p. 363.
118. Bandyopadhyay (2018), p. 238.
119. Ibid.
120. Ibid., p. 253.
121. Ibid., pp. 255–256.
122. Ibid., p. xvii.
123. Axelby (2011), pp. 150–163.
124. Bandyopadhyay (2018), p. 16.
125. Ibid., p. 16.
126. Ibid., p. 17.
127. Ibid.
128. Ibid., p. 352.
129. Ibid., p. 18.
130. Ibid., pp. 18–19.
131. Ibid., p. 19.
132. Ibid., p. 21.
133. Ibid.
134. Ibid., p. 69.
135. Tagore (1905).
136. Bandyopadhyay (2018), p. 251.
137. Ibid.

4

Jibanananda Das

'Jibananda is a natural poet and a poet of nature.'[1] Buddhadeva Bose used the words 'prakrito kobi' and 'prakritir kobi'—'prokrito' might be translated as 'true', but I have translated it as 'natural' to retain the sense of Bose's original, where the conceit of his sentence is in the wordplay between 'prokrito' and 'prokriti'. Though clever, and even a performance of wit, it is an appropriate characterization of how much Jibanananda's poetry, its 'naturalness', was related to his being a 'poet of nature'.

It is impossible to ignore the obvious point of similarity between the plant thinkers in this book: Rabindranath, Jagadish Chandra, Bibhutibhushan, Jibanananda, and Satyajit—all of them came from families with strong connections to the Brahmo Samaj. That the Upanishadic way of thinking and living, from which much of the Samaj's spiritual philosophy was derived, annotated the way in which one came to think of plants, not just their relationship to the human world, but as and in themselves, led to a naturalized understanding of a multispecies universe where everyone and everything was a citizen.

Clinton B. Seely, perhaps Jibanananda's best-known translator into English, translates 'Shedin E Dharonir', one of his earliest poems, where we have an intimation of his life in a world outside the human:

> Her mother's heart—plump bosom heaved and wept!
> That wished for—longed for son, born of her womb's egg
> Age after age she spread out for him a bed of moss
> Shade of sal and tamal trees!
> She brought new seasons and colors—at the end of Paus nights
> The mystery of Falgun's phagu red powder!
> She poured for him a pitcher of Ganges water on the bank of the
> Vaitarani,
> Stirring the cinders of death, her breasts became moistened

Plant Thinkers of Twentieth-Century Bengal. Sumana Roy, Oxford University Press. © Sumana Roy 2024.
DOI: 10.1093/9780198929314.003.0005

again and again!
She arose adorned in durba grass and rice sheaves,
She who brought woman for man!
The pungent aroma of this earth, ample in spices—
Why then a moment of tears—a moonless night
The thirst of a drunken fly for the distant sky arises in
your chest!
Slowly I closed my eyes—the final light went out at the edge of
a fleeing blue sky,
And the dark world, like a woman just delivered of child,
enveloped me.[2]

The mother, the mother's heart, the grass, the sal trees, the night and
the closed eyes, the dark world—these spaces, soft and tentative, as they
are in the early lives of poets, would solidify into an aesthetic and, more
importantly, a philosophy of the modern man when he is bereft of these.

First, therefore, the mother. In 'Aamar Ma', his essay about his mother,
Jibanananda, after getting the factual details—Kusum Kumari Das, born
in Barisal, studied until the first class, after which she was married off; and
the strength of her will and character, 'she could have easily passed her
university examinations', testifying that she had greater will and strength
than her children; that she was a good wife and mother: 'tolerant, never
lazy but relentless and successful'[3]—moves to his memories of Barisal.[4]
These are, of course, childhood memories, but, as one moves through
them, one becomes aware of how this 'atmosphere' is what he wanted
to recreate in his writing. 'I remember the winter nights of Barisal', he
begins.[5] And then we are suddenly made aware of the cold nights of his
poems and novels, their sur of silence; the faint light of his father's lamp
as the man wrote through the night, the sound of his mother's footsteps,
returning from the kitchen at day-end. There is a beautiful phrase that he
uses for sleep, a subject that he would explore in his writing: 'I wanted
to take revenge on sleep by staying awake'.[6] Those childhood nights in
Barisal—the winter quiet of December and January, the birds on the
coconut trees crying out at every hour, as if with the ghosts of Barisal;
the fear of a neighbour coming to ask for help: someone might have
died, someone afflicted by a fatal illness, the death of a poor person, the
plea of a woman with no one in the world, someone asking for help with

childbirth, all of which would take his mother away from him for she was always eager to respond—would become the world he would try to recreate over and over again when in the city, and how he would return to the town and write his *Rupashi Bangla* poems from there. Reading about Barisal, which, as Clinton B. Seely tells us, 'sits upon a bank of the Kirtan-Khola river on the northern fringe of the Sundarban jungles', his mother's active and selfless support for the needy, the poems he would write from there, I am often reminded of another person from the place[7]—he would have just been born when these poems were recreating a world that the poet was scared of losing after the war: the historian Ranajit Guha. It was Barisal, then, that produced this world of grass and jaam and jackfruit, this idealized and mythicized Bengal, a multispecies and species-fluid democracy, and it was this Barisal that would generate the consciousness that would lead Ranajit Guha to think about 'rebel consciousness' related to the revolt of peasants during the Indian colonial period.[8] Jibananada's mother's words feel particularly relevant when one thinks of Barisal, its living ideal of egalitarianism, when one thinks of Guha and the Subaltern Studies Collective that he founded: 'She asked me to respect and trust the most ordinary person.'[9]

Barisal, small as it might have been, was also where Jibanananda would first read Wordsworth, Shelley, Browning, the Romantic revolutionaries, and also Rabindranath and Vaishnav literature. Jibananada's grandfather was also a writer: 'My grandfather Chandranath Das has written many poems and songs.'[10] And there's his father, about whom the son writes that he was rejecting of 'folk success',[11] whose reading consisted of Charles Darwin, Aldous Huxley, John Stuart Mill, H. G. Wells, Bertrand Russell, and whose literary philosophy, while leaning towards tradition, particularly the tradition of his own culture, Vaishnav, Bankim, Rabindranath, was also curious and welcoming of the Elizabethans and the metaphysical poets, and Tolstoy. 'Indian philosophy and the Upanishads were the most attractive thing in his life', wrote Jibanananda in his essay 'Aamar Baba'.[12]

δ

The sonnet cycle that we now know as *Rupashi Bangla* was published posthumously by Asokananda Das, the poet's brother.[13] Jibanananda is said to have written them in the early 1930s in Barisal. This was after a short stay in Delhi, where he had a teaching job as a professor of English in a college. That it might have been acute homesickness for his Bengal that had propelled the poems becomes apparent from time to time, but that he was writing about Bengal in this manner, of attachment, as if betrothed to this place, seems slightly unexpected because of the form he was choosing to write in—the sonnet, a form recharged in Bengal by Michael Madhusudan Dutt, was understood as a European form, and it's amusing and ironic, even endearing, that both Michael Madhusudan and Jibanananda were choosing it to argue for a kind of superiority: Michael for the Bangla language (as in 'Hey Bongo, bhandarey tabo bibidho ratan') and Jibanananda for the sensory and cultural experience of Bengal, particularly its plant, animal, and riverine life. What is this Bengal, and why was writing about it necessary? Seely explains:

> Possibly because India's attention had turned towards Turkey—as mentioned above—and, by association, to the Middle East, Jibanananda's gaze often fell upon lands far to the west of India. But unlike Nazrul Islam who focused upon the contemporary scene, Jibanananda's interest lay in the ancient period and its civilizations. Egypt's kings and queens, her pyramids and mummies held a special attraction for him throughout his life but particularly during the earlier part of his poetic career. The pyramids were exotic and added a flavor of the esoteric to any poem in which they appeared. But more than that, these timeless structures allowed the poet to traverse eons with one stroke of the pen. Jibanananda, as will be seen later, thought in terms of eons and not in more mundane or human terms of years or even of a lifetime.
>
> The expansiveness—of both time and space—communicated in the above poems was to remain a feature of much of Jibanananda's poetry. He lived in a physical-fanciful world peculiarly his own, a world which he experienced through all his senses augmented by his imagination. His world knew few of the spacial limitations experienced by men who rely too literally upon their physical senses. The skies in Jibanananda's world are broad and immensely deep. They contain palaces of bygone days and distant places. Much later in life Jibanananda tried to bring his vision back to the real, contemporary world but with uneven poetic success. He is at his best when physical space and/or time are merely his

stimulants, not his cinctures. As in "That Day This Earth's", Jibanananda will continue to anthropomorphize nonhuman nature. He will animate the dawn, the stars, the wind, the grass. And he will try to live or relive life through his nonhuman environment.[14]

What he was trying to do was to perhaps imbue a sense of the 'ancient', to give a modern people, without a classical language and history as rich as those that enter his poems, of the Middle East, as Seely mentions, but also various ancient Indian cities, a poetic history of belonging. That is why the smuggling in of 'Natore', an unremarkable place on this list of historic cities, and that is why his necessity to create this lineage through plant life, which would have been here even if man—the 'Bengali'—wasn't.

In the first sonnet in *Rupashi Bangla*, we discover a person who wants to be reborn just so that he can return to 'this Bengal'.[15] What exactly is this Bengal? Nowhere are we given a map or its geographical contours. What we are given, instead, is the sensory experience of this place, one that allows infinite returns and infinite rebirths and infinite species transformations. Jibanananda, for instance, does not want to return as human but as—in this sonnet, for this moment—a bird:

> Again I shall return to the Dhansiri's banks, to this Bengal,
> Not as a man, perhaps, but as a shalik bird, or a white hawk[16]

And then the habitat of this bird amidst the leaves: 'the shade of a jackfruit tree', 'floating on duckweed-scented waters', 'a shimul tree branch', 'on the grass of some home's inner courtyard'.[17] Like infinite lives as an infinite number of species, plant and animal, never man again, an infinite number of homes as well—for this is the gift of Bengal: its infinite plant-homes. In the next sonnet—for how many homes can fourteen lines hold?—are other plant-homes: 'upon a fig tree', 'underneath a big umbrella-looking leaf'; 'piles of leaves / Of jam and banyan, of jackfruit, hijal, and ashvattha, lying still'.[18] It is not just the 'I' who is fortunate enough to dream of so many homes in his future births. 'Behula, too ... had seen countless banyan and ashvattha, by the golden paddy fields ... bhant blossoms wept like ankle bells around her feet'.[19] Behula, from the *Mangal Kavyas*, had seen these trees, the 'I' will see them in his future births as well—'I' will no longer be in human form but a bird, but the trees shall remain trees, and that is the reason Bengal shall remain Bengal.

In the third sonnet is an experience of 'Bengal's heart'—the heart, we soon discover, is a composition of plant life.[20] 'I' remains 'sitting on this very grass' as clouds appear in the sky—because even the abundant plant life is not enough for him, he imagines the clouds as fruits: they are 'kamranga red' (kamranga is starfruit).[21] 'Bengal's calm, compliant, bluish' evening arrives, and it, too, is turned into hybrid plant forms, plant graftings as it were, right after he's seen it as a woman: 'nor had I ever seen / A kiss of hair so rich and full, held so long, tumble onto hijal, jackfruit, jam.'[22] These trees are common—in Bengal and in Jibanananda—and their different colours help to characterize his Bengal, sometimes woman, most often multispecies forms. Even when we see her as a composition in water, it is through plant life: after the 'tender paddy', the 'kalmi water weeds . . . reeds, pond water', 'a young girl's moistened hand, wet from rinsing rice', and then the return to land—'the aromatic mutha grass' and 'the anguished scent of / Tired silence from the banyan's crimson berries'.[23]

The fourth sonnet seems like a continuation of the third.[24] This land of rice eaters, of people who often eat rice three times a day—Jibanananda's sentimental obsession with rice and grass, both from the same family, reveals his affinity for more democratic systems, and those more readily available, in the domestic, in one's surroundings: 'Bengal, amidst her grassy dampness-scented dust, surrounded by Bengalis',[25] the last phrase revealing its ubiquitous presence; 'I've offered up my heart / To Bengali womankind, smooth rice-steamed hands, winnowed paddy in her hair', lines that reveal Bengal's food history, an agrarian rice-dependent culture.[26] This woman, Bengal, wears a sari with a red border—it is a sari made of fruits: 'green mangos, a kamranga, and a kul'.[27] All three fruits are sour—is that the taste of Bengal? It is interesting that Jibanananda curates a sour taste while Bibhutibhushan chooses the sweetness of fruits to characterize Bengal.

'She does not sleep, / Neither does she ever die.'[28] That is how he gives life to his Bengal in the fifth sonnet of the *Rupashi Bangla* cycle. Perhaps she does not die because she remains unchanging and—given his obsession with sleeplessness—awake, always awake for the human, his

eyes and his senses. Perhaps she does not die because she remains unchanging, Jibanananda must use the same metaphors to ensure her unchanging nature: 'She wears a sari made of grass. Her black hair is the
paddy, / Bengal's autumn rice crop'.[29] Besides the grass and the paddy,
there is an addition now—but that, too, is from the domestic and familiar
space: the betel leaf, eating which, as both digestive and palette cleanser,
is common practice and even a social ritual. 'I watch a stand of bluish
betel palms/flutter gently, slowly in the breeze'.[30] Now Bengal's heart is
not made of grass anymore—it has become a different species. 'She takes
into her heart that stand of betel palms'.[31] It is an appropriate metaphor—
betel leaves, which hold a few tiny pieces of those betel nuts, are heart-
shaped. But it is, again, not the 'I' alone which sees Bengal like this. There
have been others before him:

> Srimanta, too, saw as much
> When . . . he . . . returned and witnessed Bengal's betel groves—
> Unexpectedly a deep, an intense blue [32]

The betel groves, and their bluish green, have been mentioned a few times
already—this repetition of phrases, the decision to live in the sonnet, owes
to the form and its invocation of certitude, that there was Srimanta, and now
him, and that, though he might not return in human form again, these betel
groves will still be there. As I write this and look out of the window, the betel
nut trees that framed the skies of my childhood and early adulthood are
gone—I can see just one of them, lanky and lonely, the last survivor.

Bengal is always—and inevitably—a woman. The circumstances of
their meeting is often mentioned, their mating left to history. In human
form, the speaker has spent this lifetime amidst her plant life:

> I was your companion, time and again, meandering among
> banyan, ashvattha trees.
> I strewed paddy and puffed rice many a day in the courtyards . . .
> I watched you . . . in hands dewy and white like banana flower
> petals[33]

Grass, paddy, betel nut—and now banana flower and then 'a body soft
as custard apples' and then a life 'inside that betel tin'.[34] The instalments

of metamorphosis seem never-ending. A botanical catalogue is being given to us—only with more spiritual history and its consequent interiority. This reliance on the plant world as the last refuge of continuity, surrounded as they were by world wars, colonial destruction, the advent of technology, the various avantgarde movements in Europe whose impact they could feel from their provincial outposts, marks the consciousness of all the plant thinkers in this book. Only in plant life, in its manifest seasonal cycles of leaving and returning, is some stability, some certainty:

I've seen basmati paddy, kash catkins swaying, as though erasing, time
And time again, desire's blood, transgressions. From some mys-
      terious mist
Wherein none is born and no one dies, from such a magical
      place emerge
Scarlet sunlight, autumn rice, grass and kash . . .
On this earth's paths I've often stumbled, shed some tears. But
Those geese, that kash, paddy, sunshine, grass come and come again,
      erasing all.[35]

'Magic', 'mystery', 'mist'—the secrets of plant life, mostly invisible, like time itself, and hence their coupling perhaps, how they behave in relation to each other. The grass comes and come again, erasing all . . . As if it were like time made visible, in its infinite instalments.

Jibanananda's Rupashi Bangla, Rabindranath's Shonar Bangla, Dwijendra Lal Roy's Bangla of 'Dhono Dhanney Pushpey Bhawra' (with its 'dhan', paddy, 'pushpo', flowers, and the 'madhu', honey in them)—it was a temperament, anti-colonial and perhaps even slightly ethno-nationalistic, but a Bangla repeatedly imagined through the plant world, a Bengal not marked by borders but by experience, one created by plant life and its rivers. That is why when, many decades later, towards the end of the twentieth century, when Pratyul Mukhopadhyay would sing 'Aami Banglaye gaan gai', a revival of the historical and cultural sense of Bengal, he would say 'Bangla aamar Jibanananda', 'Bangla is my Jibanananda'.[36]

Jibanananda's cosmogony is one that one hadn't encountered in Bangla poetry before. Alokranjan Dasgupta, in his book *Jibanananda*, compares the poet's Bengal to Yeats's Ireland[37]—just as Yeats had to bring the entire perimeter of Irish history and mythology to be able to proceed with his understanding and practice of anima mundi, so too with Jibananda, in whose veins ran the puranic history of Bangladesh, one that allowed him to move towards 'biswa-desh', a world-country, in his poetry.[38] *Rupashi Bangla* is dedicated to 'Bengal and Bengalis', and Dasgupta locates this in Jibananda's turning towards Bengali folklore, mythology, and history as an effect of World War I. Bengal was moving away from 'palli-gramganjo-mela', the 'countryside-village-fair', after the war, and like many of his contemporaries who were trying to create a modern Bangla literature by retaining a connection with an older tradition, Jibananda turned to the puranas, Mangal kavyas, and oral folklore. The village was to be his province—his Bengal. The adjective 'abohoman'—'atmospheric'—in the dedication of this collection is a nod to this intellectual and emotional experience. Alokranjan Dasgupta believes that the Kankabati-Shankhamala-Chandramala-Manikmala archetypes of this world lead naturally to Sabita-Suranjana-Suchetana-Sudarshana in Jibananda. He quotes from a passage from the novel *Jibanpranali* to explain the origins of *Rupashi Bangla*. This is a conversation between two lovers:

'You could have come to Bangladesh.'
'I've become Westernised.'
'It is because of getting acquainted with you that I have recognised
   Bengal's roop. Otherwise I would have been roaming blindly on the
   streets and pathways.'
'You have recognised Bengal—that is because of the glory of your own
   heart. I have no hand in this, Sachin.'[39]

δ

The interest in grass might be an intuitive affinity for the modernist temperament. In a child rhyme, Rabindranath wrote about Anukul-babu who thought that if animals could live by eating grass, man could too, an action that led to disastrous consequences. Jibananda brings more attention to grass than just curiosity and the comedic. In 'Ghash' ('Grass'), a poem in the *Banalata Sen* collection, grass is turned into something epical, an aesthetic that was usually reserved for 'trees'. I'll paraphrase the poem: the world is filled with the soft green light of tender lemon leaves; grass like unripe pomelo—a similar fragrance—the deer are tearing it with their teeth! I, too, feel the desire to drink the fragrance of this grass in glassfuls like green wine, I mix and grope this grass's body—I rub it on my eyes, the wings of grass are my feathers, I am born as grass inside grass, dropping from a dense grass-mother's dark delicious body.[40] It is quite evident that grass is not just grass for him—it is metaphor, it is the poetic, it is also his politics, a natural analogy for the human, to humanitas, to humus, to humility, all related to the soil. It is that smell that he seeks—as if by becoming grass he can find secrets of soil and depths that the human body, with its vertical life, has made him forget. Grass and its light leaves will also allow him levitation, but, more than anything else, it is unbound green that he seeks, its blood that he wants to drink as wine. The fantasy of 'shobuj manush', green man, occupied many of that generation.

'Suranjana, / Today your heart is grass.'[41] What does it mean to have a heart of grass? In 'Merged into the Skies', where these lines occur, limits are being drawn for the woman: Suranjana, 'do not go over there', or do not speak to that young man, or 'Come back to these fields'.[42] It is as if life—this world, this world of space and of time—was composed of grass. Grass, fields of grass, without beginning and end, as infinite as the human heart. It is as if Jibanananda was proposing the rhizome much before Deleuze and Guattari. That is why, even though, in a neighbouring poem, 'Come Back', when he makes the same plea, to 'Come back . . . come back to paths through fallow fields', he seeks the same thing—much as he seeks for her to return to 'a world of mango, nim, and jhau trees', it is as grass, not as tree.[43]

Jibanananda was a professor of English literature, and he often wrote about some of the English and European poets in his fiction and essays. Many critics, including Alokranjan Dasgupta, find the influence of Yeats's metaphor of grass (in *Acre of Grass*, but also present in his other poems) and dead leaves ('Turning, he saw that he had thrust dead leaves / Gathered in silence') on the Bengali poet.[44]

And then there is paddy—grass's relative and, in Jibanananda, sometimes its doppelganger. Paddy *is* Bengal. All the paddies been harvested—the hay lies in the fields; cut leaves broken egg (one isn't sure whether the poet wants us to see the cut leaves as broken eggshells). People sleeping in the fields ... Still there is peace: dark dense grass and grasshoppers; today they cover the taste of thoughts and questions, their darkness.[45] The smell of grass in their chest—the smell of dew in their eyes; tasting it, the paddy fatigues into ripeness ('Abosharer Gaan'). What, then, of Bengal after the harvest of paddy? Is it death?

I do not know of any poet who thought about and wrote about death with as much attachment as Jibanananda did. It wasn't death alone that haunted him—it was the afterlife, the return to this world, a different life-time, a different time, and, most important to him, a life as a different species, that interested him. In 'Kamlalebu', that Clinton B. Seely trans-lates as 'Tangerine' (many of us would probably have gone for the more common word, also because of its similar evocation of colour: 'kamla' is 'orange'), we find the desire—and attendant fear and curiosity—about this interspecies transformation.

> When once I leave this body
> Shall I not come back to the world?
> If only I might return
> Upon a winter's evening
> Taking on the compassionate flesh of a cold tangerine
> At the bedside of some dying acquaintance.[46]

This short poem of six lines is enough to hold a lifetime, or perhaps two. It begins with one death, imagined as it might be, and ends with another. We know almost nothing about the speaking persona's life—we can only allow ourselves to presume a melancholic life of this person who specu-lates about his death. We also notice something common to the moderns, in spite of their various differences and emotional genealogies—the des-peration to return to the earth. Perhaps the plant world is kinder, less harsh than the social world of humans, relationships which Jibanananda struggled to understand as we see in his fiction and in essays about him by his contemporaries. And hence the adjective—'cold' in the human world would be a pejorative; in the body of the fruit it is recommenda-tion: 'taking on the compassionate flesh of a cold tangerine'. The Bangla word Jibanananda uses is 'him'—it has connotations beyond 'cold': frosty, also dew. 'Shital'—a word related to 'him'—is related to shanta and shanti, quiet and peace respectively. A respite after the heat of being human, of 'blood boiling'—what a relief it must be to be cold, without blood, with the cooling orange sap in one's body. At the end is the most unexpected judgement—a plant, its fruit, is more 'compassionate' to a dying human than another human.

Not content with plants that he sees around him and that then populate his poems and his prose, he tries to turn everything else into plants—sometimes it is the wind that he wants as green, at other times, it is red: 'splitting open watermelon winds';[47] water, too, isn't water alone, it is 'scarlet like machka flower petals'.[48] It is the nature of the comparative to invoke difference. In Jibanananda, the comparative is inevitably one that joins species or states of being. It brings in an expansiveness that gives the lyric poem the layers of the epic. Sometimes, this happens not necessarily with the use of the comparative but because of a chosen form—two unrelated thoughts in two unrelated lines begin to annotate each other. In 'The Hunt', from which the comparative above is taken, 'a bed of grass' is mentioned, and, right after it, 'Several human heads, hair neatly parted'.[49] This juxtaposition makes us see the similarity between the human ordering of both human bodies and the plant world: both the bed of grass and the hair on the human head are 'neatly parted', revealing man's desire to control and impose a design. It is possible that Jibanananda is also pointing us to think about possible similarities between hair and grass—both are rhizomatic, after all.

Banalata Sen is the name of his muse, an imaginary woman with a surname that was of Jibanananda's caste, a fact that has been pointed out by several commentators, that the women in his poems inevitably have upper caste surnames, Sen, Sanyal.[50] 'Banalata'—bana is forest, lata is creeper. Abdul Mannan Sayeed tells us about the mention of two other Banalatas in his work: in a poem called 'Hajar bawchhor shudhu khyala kawrey',[51] where there is a Banalata Sen, and in the novel *Karubashona*.[52] There is also 'Shefalika Bose', her name deriving from the flower Shefali, of course.[53] In 'Banalata Sen', possibly the most famous modern Bangla poem, the sailor of a ship, finding his 'rudder broken, far out upon the sea adrift, / Sees the grass-green land of a cinnamon isle'.[54] It is a sensuous image, one that, while moving through the eyes, goes directly to the olfactory: we smell the cinnamon, as we imagine the helpless sailor does in the poem. It is also the smell of land, felt by a homesick person on the sea. What is this cinnamon island doing in this poem about a woman who has been desired, seen, found, lost, and never really understood? Like the sailor on the broken boat who finds hope and comfort at the sighting and smell of the cinnamon isle, the speaker in the poem 'sees' Banalata Sen. It is the human species's comfort in finding plant life, in the world of cinnamon and creepers as solace. I read this poem, particularly today, as an early manifestation of climate change fatigue, of a life of plant deprivation. There must be some relation between cinnamon islands and the women to whom he addresses these poems. For we find one more again, in the poem 'Suchetana': Suchetana, you are a distant island for afternoon stars; there is solitude in the midst of cinnamon forests. It is perhaps the similarities between cinnamon bark and the human skin that trigger these lines: I've seen ship come to our port, I've seen the harvest reach them—these grains are the corpses of innumerable men.[55]

It is not the sacred mythology of the asvattha tree that Jibanananda taps into or even seeks—not for him the lineage of Hindu and Buddhist tales of the tree's enabling of a spiritual consciousness, not for him the history in its etymology (asvattha, literally horse under a tree, reminding us implicitly of trees under which horses and horse-driven carriages would stop); it is only its fixity that moves him. That is why the ashvattha asks slowly:

> Which way are you headed—
> Where do you wish to go?
> We've all been neighbours so long, so very, very close.
> Your sun-stained straw huts, they're standing yet.
> And here you go forsaking home and lands,
> Heading where, what path—I have no idea.
> You've wrapped up your belongings, even the broken bowls,
> that leaky pot.
> Now where are you set on going?[56]

The fixity—Jibanananda's shorthand for certainty—is both in space and in time, the two axes of his understanding of history. Man moves, man dies—in both he makes space, he vacates space, produces emptiness. The ashvattha tree, older than man, has always been there, and to it 'fifty years' 'seems just yesterday'. It remembers human settlements: 'Your grandfathers, fathers, uncles . . . they bought land, built their straw huts'.

'Standing here I watched it all—it seems like just the other day'.[57] What exactly does he mean for us to experience *as* the ashvattha tree? The lack of availability of other 'paths', of 'huts', of 'dreams', all of these digressions accessible only to the human imagination? 'But, no matter where you go, life itself does not change', says the ashvattha tree, as if in not being free to move is to be really free.[58]

In 'A Day Eight Years Ago', the ashvattha tree appears again, almost in a cameo role.[59] A man has been taken to a morgue: 'He'd had the urge to die'.[60] 'Now, lying in the morgue, he sleeps.' Yet he is still on earth—there are mosquitoes around him and flies and 'winged insects'.[61] There is a taste of life around him: 'this taste of life—the scent of ripe grains in an autumn afternoon' that can only be expressed through plant life.[62] Then there is 'the ashvattha limb—Did it not protest?'[63] Though he does not say this anywhere, it seems implicit to me, his question: when humans are burnt with branches of trees, how many die? Just the human or the tree again?

There are others: the 'sundari' tree, invoked in the poems 'Camp' and 'Sundarbaner Galpo',[64] which gives Sundarbans its name, literally 'beautiful forest'; the palash in 'Horinera',[65] from which, as Clinton B Seely reminds us, 'comes shellac as well as a bright red pigment. Though irrelevant to this poem, it is this tree that lent its name to the village near which, in 1757, the Battle of Plassey was fought and won by forces of the British East India Company, marking the beginning of the colonial period in South Asia. ("Plassey" is the Anglicised pronunciation of "palashi", the adjective derived from palash.)'[66] Kolmi greens grow in these poems, and always new rice, the fragrance of the champa comes and goes, declaring day and night, the jackfruit is older than man, branches of the Shirish tree touch afternoon clouds, and the hair of women is as soft as jaam.

Places are remembered for the trees in them: the Western Ghats for 'the coconut palms', the 'palm trees', 'the whitewashed cabins in that coconut grove';[67] mahogany shade,[68] the smell of missing pear;[69] and then the colours that are turned almost otherworldly: the green of guavas and custard apple, both compared to parrot wings, the red of 'morog phool', celosia, and 'mochka'.[70] Not their sights alone, Jibanananda has heard trees speak and sing: 'I've heard the heavenly singing of debdaru trees';[71] he has heard the silence of the plants: 'the trees remain as quiet as deer'[72] or the silence of fallen leaves on grass as if it were a bed;[73] 'the tree of completion is silent about its own progress'.[74] He also knows the minds of those who are almost like trees: 'the debdaru shadow is hesitant'.[75] Why? Exhaustion is articulated not through gestures and language of the human body but through plant life: 'Today at dawn acute exhaustion. / In the afternoon, too ... On the river bank/Upon its brown mud leaves fall. /... On my finger, too—for as long as there is— / A yellow leaf alights'.[76] The falling of leaves, almost a pathetic fallacy, as if one were a tree. Exhaustion and melancholy and afternoon—they appear as plants or their likenesses: 'Long shadows cast by trees / Stretch over Bengal's barren tracts of land'.[77] 'Korun hoyechhey jhaubon', the Tamarix forest is melancholic.[78]

In these poems is the botanical history of provincial Bengal.

δ

What is harvest, and what does it signify to the human cycle of sleep and wakefulness, living and dying? In a poem such as 'Mrityur Aagey',[79] we meet post-harvest fields—is that what the moment after death feels like, as if life was a crop waiting for its seasonal harvest? If that is indeed the logic of this poem, it helps us to understand Jibanananda's conception of life and death and planting and harvesting as cyclical, as reiterations and instalments of the same thing, of the same people, with differences that annotate history, both the history of the world and the species.

> We who've walked deserted fields of stubble on Paush evenings,
> Who've seen upon the fields' far edge soft river women spreading
> Fog flowers—they all, alas, like village girls of days long past;
> We who've seen in darkness the akanda shrub, the dhundul
> Filled with fireflies, seen the moon standing silent vigil at the head of
> Fields already harvested—not lusting for the crops there [80]

The metaphors are all unexpected, as in most of Jibanananda—it is not just the defamiliarization of trees in Bengali neighbourhoods, it is what is, for instance, the non-botanical being turned into plant life: 'fog flowers'. Harvest season has ended, the earth is denuded, one needs more—and more of—plant life to be able to survive. That analogical relationship between harvest and death crawls under every comparative. These are not the 'dhundhul' one eats or uses as a scrub; Jibanananda's dhundhul is 'filled with fireflies'—fireflies, microcosms of fire, the fire of farm stubble, and the fire of death and after. The landscape is Bengal and yet not quite, for it is a Bengal seen right before death, and, therefore, through death. The fields are fields but also more—'greenish winds on Baishakh's farther fields':[81] the winds are green because harvest season has meant the depletion of green, and so, like a transferred epithet, the air must compensate by turning green. 'Thick juices ooze into the bosom of a blue-green custard apple, heavy with desire.'[82] The fruit, as we can see, is no longer fruit—it has been turned into a human: it has a 'bosom'. The fields too have become creatures with eyes in Jibanananda's lyric-epics of interspecies metamorphosis. It is because everything has been granted another life, and because 'there is *another* light',[83] and that is why perhaps even life seeks death, as the fields seek endless cycles of growth and repair, planting and harvesting. The fields seek more, more than themselves, for life is not enough, death might be a surplus: 'The lonely fields, huddled together, staring at their faces reflected in the river.'[84]

What, then, of sowing, in this transforming universe? Sowing, as we know intuitively, is metamorphosis in action—from seed to fruit and, following it, fruit to seed again? Is sowing an investment in life alone?

> Who apprehends the joys
> of life anymore like everyman?
> Where is that relish? And who, hungry for the harvest,
> Has smeared himself with scents of earth . . .
> Who would anymore remain awake upon this earth?[85]

Here it is then—the secret of Jibanananda's interest in the seed, in sowing: the seed is awake, the seed is awake after a period of sleep, the escape from sleep is life. The strange causality helps us to understand why sleeplessness is the one haunting state in his body of work. In this world, as much beyond human control as sleep is, seeds have independent lives, free as they are from human control. Sowing and watering are only aids in creating habitat, in as much as gifting a house can bring good health or a comfortable bed can bring sleep. It is this world that he seeks to understand—for this his comparatives, the mixed metaphors, the mixed species, all new to the Bangla literary imagination. He thinks of the infrastructure of sowing, of life-giving—the 'plough', a counterpoint to the 'sickle' of the harvesting imaginary, and he thinks of time and age. A seed is young, after all. 'The children, or they who come to the sown fields of this world / To give birth—to give birth— / Is not my heart / Like theirs, their heart and head? Is not their mind / Like my mind? / Then why am I so alone? / Yet I am all alone. / Did I not raise my hand to see it hold a peasant's plough? / Have I not drawn water by the pail?'[86] The poem is called 'Sensation', and through its four pages, we grow in different directions of sensations, as life, still invisible inside a seed, would when planted in soil. It is impossible to not wonder whether the seed is as alone as Jibanananda or the speaker in his poem. After the algae and the fish, and dreams and shadows, the metaphor comes to the heart: 'Will it never ever sleep? Will it not enjoy just / Resting calmly?'[87] When I read these lines, I think of the seed as much as I do of the human heart—will it never ever sleep? Will it not enjoy just 'resting calmly'? If they slept, the heart and the seed, life would stop. What he is doing, through this repeated to-and-froing between the plant and human world, is a few things: throwing one into relief through contrast; moving towards an ethics that is based on the interspecies fluidity, one that allows borrowing a politics from plant life; creating a cosmology of modernism, where night and sleeplessness, rotting and aloneness, moves away from Baudelaire's city and its architecture to the tendrils and branches of plant life. 'A spoiled cucumber—chancred pumpkin, / All that came to be within the heart of man / —All that.'[88]

Where are these fields, Jibanananda's fields? Are they in Bengal alone? In 'Vultures',[89] we see 'forsaken birds descend to earth upon Asia's fields for a few moments only . . . and fly to palm trees'.[90] While birds are a very important part of his cosmography, his interest in birds is also in relation to trees—where else will they rest and make homes in? Sometimes, one is mistaken for the other, both in his poems and in his fiction, leaves for things that fly, birds and insects. In 'On City Sidewalks', for instance, the speaker tells the addressee of his poem that 'You'll not mistake a yellowed papaya lead for an unexpected bird', on the 'green grass' are 'soft and green and gorgeous dead dewali bugs'.[91]

δ

'I think that the inspiration for my poetry is the consciousness of indef-
inite time and greying nature. But it is not that the nature in the poems
is always grey . . . What you have called the consciousness of time that is
emitted by gestures of the universe, "consciousness of time as a universal",
that is, for me an essential truth. While on the path to writing poems,
I was compelled to accept this. There is no deviation from this meaning.
But it is possible that there might be new inventions related to meanings
and evaluations of time-consciousness.'[92] Abdul Mannan Sayeed begins
his introduction to the edition of *Banalata Sen* by quoting these words
from Jibanananda. Pradyumna Mitra, in trying to analyse Eastern and
Western literary influences on him, quotes from a passage from T. S. Eliot
that Jibanananda was familiar with, and one, Mitra believes, he might
have endorsed:

> The historical sense involves a perception, not only of the pastness of
> the past, but of its presence; the historical sense compels a man to write
> not merely with his own generation in the bones but with a feeling that
> the whole of the literature of Europe from Homer and within it the
> whole of the literature of his own country has a simultaneous existence
> and composes a simultaneous order.[93]

Mitra is implying that Jibanananda derives his understanding of the
historical sense as much from Bengali literary culture as he does from his
reading of the English poets.[94] Picking out lines from the Bengali poet,
he shows influences, particularly of images and metaphors, of *The Faerie
Queene* and Keats's 'On Grasshopper and the Cricket', Edgar Allan Poe's
'To Helen', of Yeats, and their varied understandings of the relation between history and poetry—itihasa and kavya—in cross-pollination with
his reading and life in Bengal and its history to generate his own 'historical sense'. Taking quest myths and discovery myths from both cultures, as Mitra carefully points out, he imports them to make something
new: seeing the historical sense through plant life and botanical culture.[95]
Masdul Haque, a Bangladeshi critic, even calls this 'bigyan chetona', a scientific consciousness.[96]

Man has lasted long upon this earth;
His shadow cast upon time's tracks
Is yet to dim. But, he stands in the desert
Like a tree, seemingly pointlessly.[97]

Man's life on this earth is what gives him history, but what about the
tree, and why is the man of history being compared to a tree? What does
the tree do? For all the modernists in this book, the counterpoint of
human history seems to be that of plants, of trees, of forests, an intuitive
acknowledgement that plants have been here before the human. Plants,
their first cells, from which life is said to have originated, were there before us—how could they be, as the Europeans believed, less intelligent
than us? The affection for plant life, then, comes from reverence—as it
does for the aged in the family. The tree in the desert is a hardy survivor—
no tree stands 'pointlessly'. In the shape of its roots is a map of water, in
the shape of its branches a map of its history of eating light.

Jibanananda measures time not with a clock but through plant history.
In 'After Twenty Years', another of his well-circulated poems, he writes:

If twenty years from now I should meet her again,
Again, twenty years hence—
Perhaps beside a clump of paddy stalks
In late October—
As the evening crows head home—as the tawny river
Softens in amongst reeds and grasses—through fields.
Or, perhaps there is no longer paddy standing in fields.
No more hustle, no more hurry.[98]

Twenty years is as long or short a unit of time as a thousand years
in 'Banalata Sen' or centuries in *Malloban*—like Wordsworth's 'ten
thousand saw I at a glance', it is an experience instead of a real number
or a count of something. There are other words related to time used
here: 'hurry', a function of time. It is interesting that though the speaker
is thinking of how it would feel to meet this woman twenty years hence,
he is immediately diverted to think not of how they would have changed
but how the world, particularly the plant world, might have changed.

Both possibilities are imagined: 'perhaps beside a clump of paddy stalks'; 'or, perhaps there is no longer paddy standing in the fields'.[99] It is paddy, agricultural produce, a consequence of human control over plant life; it is not a naturally grown tree or forest. This alignment of time, of history, as being made visible through the plant world troubles and energizes all the Bengali moderns here. Reading Jibanananda's poem, not after twenty years, but more, one feels even more unnerved—all the plants in my house or the yard outside are dependent on me for their survival. Can there be any sense of time besides the human in such a world? 'A clump of paddy stalks'—that is all a melancholic lover can imagine, not fullness, not surplus, but a world after harvest. The woman's 'lunar face' might be seen as if it were a blur, through a mist—through 'thin dark branches of the shirish or the jam, / The jhau—the mango',[100] or 'through the alleys shaped by babla branches, / Through the windows formed by the ashvattha',[101] but these come too late in the poem, and what one remembers from it, in spite of the procession of names of plants, is the stubble of paddy on the field, a metaphor for a world where the human has extracted everything it could, until the end, and, because of it, there is this end. 'I have come to the home of human-births because of the pull of the earth, knowing that it would have been better to not have come'.[102]

'In Fields Fertile and Fallow', the speaker wonders about the date: 'Nineteen forty-two, it seems. / But is it really nineteen forty-two?'[103] The uncertainty is as much about time as it is about timekeeping and its apparatus—does it really matter whether it's 1942, because does it matter to the tree that it is 1942? How to measure a human's life then?

He was born; he will die one day.
He had come to the field with the rising sun.[104]

Jibanananda condenses human life into two lines—the beginning and the end, separated by a semicolon, in one line, the line following it holding a lifetime's action and events in it: 'he had come to the field'. That is the definition of human life—he must go to the field, to sow, to harvest, with plough, with sickle, with his body and being. What kind of a field?

Here the earth is rugged . . .
Mere stacks of straw extending for two, three miles,
And even then, not like gold.
Only the sound of sickles drowns out the world's cannons,
Pathetic, meek, homeless.
There are no more promises . . .
Has the cultivator, human being of today, arisen from an amoeba
Through some purposeless expansion
From a comedy of errors in a sea overspread with blue?
Buddhist shrines, the cross, ninety-three, Soviet myths and promises
Are all histories of eras ending.[105]

δ

As I read and reread *Malloban*, a novel said to be based on the circumstances of Das's life, I notice the absence of sunlight. It is a novel of home
as much as it is of sleep. The world outside is not really shown to us—we
are told about the protagonist's regular walk to Lal Dighi, a water body,
and his return from his workplace. But the day—and the life of the
day—is a secondary thing in the novel. Everything—things that happen
come to us through Malloban's mind—here happens after dusk. As I observe this, I cannot help contrasting Malloban's—and Jibananda's—
life to plants. Malloban's name means 'of the garland', and, in this, his
relation with flowers—pollinators—is made evident.[106] The Bengali
poet, like Baudelaire, whose influence marks his poems, is a writer of
darkness. What light is to plant life, darkness is to Jibananda. How,
then, is one to reconcile these opposite urges—to be a plant feeding on
darkness as it were? Then there is sleep, or, to be more specific, sleeplessness. 'I've wanted to sleep again / Inside the breasts of darkness, inside its womb, I've wanted to mix with infinite death'.[107] What happens
to trees at night? Jibananda doesn't really know. That is why he comes
up with contradictory answers. In 'Sharadin Aami',[108] 'light becomes
sleep'.[109] In 'Path Hata',[110] a poem where sleep is the guiding force, the
eyes are downcast and then shut—they are echoed by the trees: golden
brown leaves have flown from the tree. 'I sleep day and night, the
morning breeze, the moving leaves, gooseberry, sal, the falling of silver

rain . . . I had become you'.[111] In 'Kokil', the nights are not the nights we know. For darkness casts shadows—'tall tall restless trees', their 'abundant shadows', the green breeze at night, the kokil awake in the jamrul grove . . . it won't sleep, it doesn't know death, we, too, do not know death.[112]

But the wind does know death: when it comes to a branch of the horitoki tree, it stops suddenly, it dies.[113] Perhaps because he believes that trees don't sleep, he associates deathlessness with both. In the plant world is Jibanananda's cause and cure—the wild yam that stings the throat meets the tiger tamarind that cures us of it. And the world becomes well, temporarily.

Notes

1. Mitra (1983), p. 15. Translation mine.
2. Das, Seely (1976).
3. Guha (2017), p. 63. Translation mine. Kusum Kumari's writing was published by Ramananda Chatterjee, the editor of the *Modern Review*, and a leading member of the Brahmo Samaj.
4. Das, cited in Guha (2017), p. 63.
5. Ibid,
6. Ibid.
7. Seely (1976), p. 1.
8. Guha (1999).
9. Das, cited in Guha (2017), p. 67.
10. Ibid., p. 66.
11. Ibid., p. 68. Translation mine.
12. Ibid., p. 70.
13. Das (2018).
14. Seely (1976), p. 52.
15. Das (2018), p. 95.
16. Ibid.
17. Ibid.
18. Ibid., p. 97.
19. Ibid.
20. Ibid., p. 99.
21. Ibid.
22. Ibid.
23. Ibid.
24. Ibid., p. 101.
25. Ibid.
26. Ibid.
27. Ibid.
28. Ibid., p. 103.
29. Ibid.
30. Ibid.
31. Ibid.
32. Ibid.

33. Ibid., p. 105.
34. Ibid.
35. Ibid., p. 107.
36. Mukhopadhyay, 'Ami Banglay Gaan Gai' (I sing in Bangla).
37. Dasgupta (1995).
38. Ibid., p. 33.
39. Ibid., p. 34. Translation mine.
40. Das (2018), p. 53.
41. Ibid.
42. Ibid.
43. Ibid., p. 55.
44. Dasgupta (1995).
45. Das (2018), 'Dhaan Kata Hoye Gyachhey', p. 54.
46. Das (2019), p. 3.
47. Ibid., p. 33.
48. Ibid., p. 29.
49. Ibid.
50. Arunima Sanyal in Das (2018), 'Buno Haash', p. 36.
51. 'Just Playing for a Hundred Years'.
52. Abdul Mannan Sayeed, p. 11.
53. Das (2018), 'Horinera' (Deer), p. 42.
54. Ibid., p. 47.
55. Ibid., p. 60.
56. Ibid.
57. Ibid., p. 57.
58. Ibid., p. 60.
59. Ibid., p. 59.
60. Ibid.
61. Ibid., p. 61.
62. Ibid.
63. Ibid.
64. Ibid., 'A Tale of the Sundarban Jungles'.
65. Ibid., p. 42.
66. Seely (1976), p. 111.
67. Seely (1976), p. 81.
68. Das (2019), p. 38.
69. Ibid.
70. Ibid., p. 40.
71. Ibid., p. 44.
72. Ibid., p. 50.
73. Ibid., p. 61.
74. Ibid.
75. Ibid., p. 56.
76. Ibid., p. 83.
77. Ibid., p. 85.
78. Ibid., p. 55.
79. Ibid., p. 5.
80. Ibid.
81. Ibid., p. 7.
82. Ibid.
83. Ibid.
84. Ibid.
85. Ibid., p. 11.
86. Ibid., p. 13.
87. Ibid., p. 17.
88. Ibid.
89. Das (2019), p. 71.

90. Ibid., p. 71.
91. Ibid., p. 75.
92. Sayeed (2010), p. 7. Translation mine.
93. Mitra (2000), p. 29.
94. Ibid.
95. Ibid., p. 40.
96. Haque (2011), pp. 22–29.
97. Ibid., p. 35.
98. Das (2019), p. 49.
99. Ibid.
100. Ibid.
101. Ibid.
102. Ibid., p. 60.
103. Ibid., p. 85.
104. Ibid., p. 87.
105. Ibid., pp. 88–89.
106. Das (2022).
107. Das (2018), 'Andhakar', p. 45.
108. Ibid., 'All Day I'.
109. Ibid., p. 547.
110. Ibid., p. 62.
111. Ibid., p. 552.
112. Ibid., p. 568.
113. Ibid., 'Batasher Shobdo Eshey' (The Sound of the Wind), p. 578.

5

Shakti Chattopadhyay

When I read Shakti Chattopadhyay, I have the sense of listening to a tree. The word for leaves and the pages of a book are the same in Bangla—'*paata*'. When I am with Shakti Chattopadhyay, I have an intuitive sense of where that might have come from, and why so many poets have imagined leaves as a tree's poems. 'Does the garden recognise all its plants?' is the title of one of his most famous poems about plant life.[1] I doubt he had any conscious sense of writing about plants, I doubt whether he was even aware when he was a tree and when a human person, such is the fluidity between the two in his lived and imagined life. I worry if the huge garden remembers all its plants, he says; so many birds on so many trees, so many sadnesses, each as tasty as dried fruits in the perfect heat and light. I worry about the philosophy of I-eat-from-the-tree, I-gather-what-falls-on-its-floor, he continues. Someone's come to collect happiness in a giant basket, the fruit that looks ripe and reddish in the light's flame isn't right enough for plucking. And here, at the poem's last stop, the fruit divides the man from the tree—it looks ripe to the man, but the tree knows that it is not ripe enough for plucking. It is a kinship that many of us recognize—one moment we are the flower waiting to seduce a prospective pollinator, the next moment we are the guilty gardener with a pair of scissors in hand.

But before I begin talking about Shakti Chattopadhyay's life as a tree, it'd be proper to look at his life as a human.

Born in November 1933 at around 3:15 in the morning—an inconsequential piece of information that has somehow come to acquire some kind of unknown value for me, as if to question the implication that plants do not work at night—at his maternal grandfather's house in a village called Baharu in pre-independent India, Shakti Chattopadhyay was the second of three children born to Bamanath and Kamla Chattopadhyay. His father, who'd die four years later, in 1937, was, in Shakti's words, a

Plant Thinkers of Twentieth-Century Bengal. Sumana Roy, Oxford University Press. © Sumana Roy 2024.
DOI: 10.1093/9780198929314.003.0006

teacher of the old-fashioned Sanskrit 'toles', semi-school-like units: 'Baba chhilen tulo pandit', my father was a pandit in a tole. (The similarities between our plant thinkers seem obvious, even though they might seem coincidental: the loss of fathers at a young age, in the case of Bibhutibhushan, Shakti, and Satyajit; Shakti and Bibhutibhushan's fathers came from similar intellectual histories—Sanskrit teaching, classical literatures, the Brahminical background.) Bamanath Chattopadhyay came from a family of Sanskrit teachers in Hoogly's Krishnanagar village. His death, unexpected and wrong as it seemed to him, was an event that would never leave the little boy—Shakti's most powerful poems are not just about death and a human's probing into this unknown world, they are also a desire for and an invocation of death. It is also how the world would see his work, so that when Bishnu Pal Chaudhuri would make an English documentary on the poet in 1991, he'd use the title of one of his poems about death—'Cremate Me, O Fire!':[2] 'I can't remember my father very well. But when I have to pass by that life-warring place where a little child had to cremate his father, I am unable to even walk down an adjacent street.'[3] (These poems acquire another dermis after one has read these words by his friend, the poet Sunil Gangopadhyay, on death and Shakti—'Shakti would often say that he'd live longer than me. Given how self-reliant he was, I'd come to accept that as a fact. Shakti will, of course, outlive me in literary history, but that I have to write this in memory of Shakti fills me with great pain—it's one of Time's cruel jokes.'[4]) I sometimes wonder whether this sense of living an orphan's life—with a dead father and an absent mother—was responsible for his identification with plant life. For, among all living beings, isn't it a plant that lives a natural orphan life? Whether from seed or sapling, graft or bulb, there it is, growing alone, without parental and postnatal care.

Shakti's mother had left him with his grandfather and taken her other two children, the oldest and the youngest, with her to her brother's place in Calcutta. His maternal grandfather was a teacher and a homeopathic doctor. It was in this village of Baharu that Shakti developed his unique relationship with plant life. 'I spent my childhood alone in a village—I was self-indulgently imaginative. There's a taste of the rural and the rustic in my poems.'[5] The plants and the ponds, the water and its neighbourhoods, the domestic life of villagers, and perhaps even of plants—it was amidst this that he grew up. What he also grew up with were Sanskrit pandits who'd visit as houseguests. Very early on therefore, Shakti grew up with a sense of language besides the one he'd been born into; there is a curiosity about words and their lives and livelihoods in his writing, particularly his poems. Apart from the education in Sanskrit that came to him almost naturally, by his happening to be in the neighbourhood of the sounds of words in the language, there was something else that would affect little Shakti at this impressionable age—it was his grandfather's recitation of the Gita which left him entranced as a child. There is no religion in Shakti's world, but there is, often, a sense of the awareness of god. Who this god is we're never told or shown, for, in all likelihood, Shakti himself wasn't sure, except that he might be a stranger lurking in the neighbourhood. Sanskrit, its mantras of worship and prayer, and the shlokas of the Gita, would bring to his poetry a psychological conscious-ness of words, their inner workings as it were, even their intestines, and time and again Shakti would create portmanteau words, poetic neolo-gisms and hyphenated words to 'yoke together' (to borrow that phrase from Samuel Johnson) the unpredictable routes of the mind, its digres-sive tendencies. It was also an intuitive residency in that root language (root for Bangla, that is) that might have been responsible for the oral quality of his poetry—in this it is also very Tagorean, in being as effective on the page, yielding to multiple and peculiar planes of reading, as it is as a spoken poem. Shankha Ghosh, in his introduction to the seventh volume of Shakti Chattopadhyay's Collected Poems, called this a style that was 'urban as well as pastoral, grave similes as well as earthy colloquial-isms, elegant as well as vulgar, imperious as well as modest—all manner of expressions burst out of his poetry with a potent but graceful sinu-ousness. Such a breath-taking experience has almost never before been offered by Bengali poetry'.[6]

I mention these biographical details not to produce a linear narrative of his coming into poetry but to place his work amidst the environment that produced it. It is necessary to do this partly because Shakti's work has been largely bypassed by researchers of Bangla literature for being too individualistic—'unique' is a double-edged word, it allows people leeway in cutting further explanation. At the same time one needs to be careful while talking about Shakti's life because, as his poet-friend Sunil Gangopadhyay reminds us in Proshongo Shakti Chattopadhyay, an intro-duction to a collection of writings—primarily reminiscences by family, friends, and fellow poets—it has been a tendency to talk more about the idiosyncrasies of Shakti's life than about the peculiarities of his poetry.[7] The encounter with death at such a young age, the primeval aloneness of a parentless child, the sounds of Sanskrit, a language that is not of the everyday but which carries within it history and mystery, and Baharu, tiny and ignored by a city-besotted civilization, a second-hand paradise filled with forgetful plants and absent-minded water—all of these, in varying degrees and at different times, were responsible for creating a person like Shakti Chattopadhyay.

There was a lack of professional ambition in mofussils and villages like Baharu that is bound to remind us of the self-contained ambitionless lives of what were called the 'rustic characters' in Thomas Hardy's Wessex novels. It was inevitable that Shakti would be touched by the same indifference to worldliness. Related to this lack of worldly ambition was his living in asystemic open boundaries, without parents and a parental home, in a place that was neither completely untouched by urbanity nor severed from naturally growing plant habitats. A student who had done well in his school examinations, he took up commerce and finance as his choice of subjects to study in college—the reason was unequivocally practical: his maternal uncle, to whose house in Calcutta he'd moved to be with his mother and his siblings, had promised him an accounting job in his printing press if he got a degree in the subject. Quite naturally, he soon dropped out.

What followed is, again, an illustration of his rebellion against standardized education—he enrolled to study Bangla literature at Presidency College in Calcutta, but dropped out soon after, in spite of having made friends with classmates and seniors there. Later, after he'd begun writing poetry, and the writer, editor, and academic Buddhadeva Bose—who'd just founded the Department of Comparative Literature at Jadavpur University, and published three of Shakti's poems in *Kobita*, one of the most well-respected Bangla magazines of its time—almost forced him to enrol as a student there, he dropped out again. This peripatetic behaviour would also mark his professional life—he'd work as a journalist, an editor, try his hand at publishing (it is Shakti Chattopadhyay who is largely credited for having introduced the concept of 'Shrestho Kobita', 'Best Poems', 'Collected Poems', in Bangla publishing), a travel writer, a reluctant novelist, an enthusiastic translator, among other undocumented professions, including keeping accounts for a tiny period of time.

The categories 'interdisciplinary' and 'transdisciplinary' did not exist then in the way they do now. Even if they had, they wouldn't have been able to contain a spirit like Shakti's. It wasn't learning he despised but its weird rituals of decorum—the artificiality of mores that attended social life, and that were amplified in the functioning of educational institutions and their rigid systems. In this too I think of his natural allegiance with the plant world, where no such structures exist. And yet the deep learning that forms the axis of his poetic universe comes from a place of inherited learning, an education that began, institutionally, with his admission to the village school at the age of 10. There his primary interests seem to have been in Sanskrit grammar and the taxonomy, habitats, and living habits of plants. As Samir Sengupta, his friend and the editor of his seven volumes of poetry and uncollected prose, reminds us often in his book *Kobi Shakti* (a title that has great resonance in Bangla, that could translate to 'The Poet Shakti' but could also mean 'A Poet's Power'),[8] this learning never left him—it would inform and create his poems about the natural world. Sengupta also mentions another kind of education that Shakti would find a home in, an indoctrination as it were, around the age of 15 when he'd move to his uncle's house in Calcutta and get enrolled in Maharaja Casimbajar Polytechnic School in 1948—that was of the philosophy of Marxism. The friends he'd acquire for life would inevitably be left-leaning, some of them cardholders of the Communist Party of India. This, in retrospect, is not difficult to understand—it wasn't only the theatre groups and associations which were unabashedly Marxist at that time. Most writers, affected not only by Partition and the violence generated by the creation of two independent states but from deeply scarring events like the Bengal famine, lived their lives and their writing by leftist ideologies. This would permeate the greater socio-political consciousness to such a degree that the electoral results of 1977, of the Left parties winning an election through votes for the first time in the world, would seem like a most natural consequence of the viscera of anger and frustration that had been building up amidst the poor, and the new refugees of the 1971 India–Pakistan war.

Shakti would join—and found—the Hungry Generation group before that. The other three founding members were Malay Roy Choudhury, Samir Roy Choudhury, and Debi Roy; poets like Utpal

Basu, Binoy Majumdar, Sandipan Chattopadhyay, Anil Karanjai, and a few others would come to join the movement. Malay Roy Choudhury had taken its name from a phrase from Chaucer, 'In sowre hungry tyme'; Shakti collaborated with them to write the manifesto in 1961, but he'd soon be disillusioned, again. It was the asocial that he'd perhaps sought, the kind one finds in the plant world for example, but after the initial energy of dissent and resistance, the mitochondria of disobedience to conventions, the meetings with artists like Ginsberg, the enthusiasm dampened—the institutionalization of dissent is also a kind of institutionalization, after all. Writing about that time, of the cultural temperament and literary atmosphere of Calcutta, the poet-critic Shankha Ghosh writes, 'This is the time when, in the words of Shakti's self-projection Nirupam, Allen's *Howl* has been translated into Bengali. We've read both the English and Bangla versions. We've read other fragments of poetry besides *Howl*. We've read about them. We've learnt quite a lot about them by now.'[9] Allen Ginsberg has even arrived in Calcutta with his heady poetic techniques and lifestyle, and Shakti and his companions are consorting with him closely. 'We have just the one weapon against this world bound for destruction, and that is our creativity'—a new circle of poets is making waves in America with this credo while *Howl* is being banned in San Francisco on grounds of obscenity.[10] This is the time when a new phrase is about to be coined in Calcutta's literary circles: the Hungry Generation. The Angry Young Men of Britain and the Beat Generation of the US had inevitably appeared in one of Shakti's pieces, but in order to convey the distinctiveness of this particular movement, Shakti had written at the outset: 'The social environment in those countries is one of affluence, they can be Beat or Angry. But we are Hungry. It must be termed a hunger for any form or aesthetic. No form or aesthetic can be left out ... the main thing about this revolution is that it is omnivorous.'[11] Yet, this is also the time when, along with Baudelaire and Rimbaud from the nineteenth century, twentieth-century names such as those of Rilke or Jiménez have also reached the young poets. The first English translation of Jiménez's gentle *Platero and I* has already appeared in 1957, entrancing some in Calcutta soon afterwards.[12]

Ghosh also explains Shakti's moving away from these influences and friendships, both with people and literary movements:

Baudelaire or the Hungry Generation remained only a starting point for Shakti—they could not have become the primary force of his poetry. The imminent revolution with the word 'Hungry' in its name, one that would seek 'to destroy the conspiratorial positioning of material objects', one that would wish to 'dance in ecstasy on the corpse of modernity', was not one with which Shakti would be directly connected, therefore, and his work would soon become unacceptable even to the Hungry poets. Once upon a time he had said: 'Poetry is a sort of private and solitary sexual act for poets. Poetry is deeply unsocial.' But this too was only his preparatory period. During this period, as Shakti himself did not hesitate to acknowledge, he had received an education in 'imagery' and in 'romanticism' from his contemporary Ananda Bagchi, while from Alokeranjan Dasgupta he had learnt 'rhythm, wit, and an apparently liquid Bangla.' And he had invariably mentioned and adopted Jibanananda as the most important poet in the Bengali language. But all of this were the preliminary ingredients used in the process of developing himself consciously. Eventually, Shakti matured himself through a variety of poetry from home and abroad, modern and old, his poetic personality being formed by the pull of the internal lyric, although there was a constant link with Bengal's villages . . . the primary technique Shakti applied at the core of his poetry was the use of melody, the touch of music. That is why one or two lines, sometimes an entire stanza, keep recurring in his poetry with a noticeable distinctiveness, like a refrain. That is why his poetry is often configured like a song, as if only awaiting melody. [13]

I mention Shakti's associations with the Left, the Hungry Generation, and other Bengali poets, both his contemporaries and his predecessors, and his gradual dissociation, at least spiritually, from them, to stress that in spite of his escape routes from the social, from the primarily human world, he had to step back because the protagonists in the play of both Marxism and the Hungry Generation, and indeed his contemporaries, were homo sociologicus. These worlds, and their dramas and cycles of rebellion and violence, were human-centric. In Shakti's mental—and poetic—universe, man was not the centre of the universe. It seems like a prescient philosophy in the almost sudden wake of environmental schooling which aims at reversing man's control over natural forces and a more egalitarian distribution of resources, in tune with population proportion and other forces. Shakti, it must be said, wasn't alone in resisting this post-Renaissance validated urge of putting man at the centre of the universe. It was a subterranean urge common to a few artists of the time. Take a drawing by Nandalal Bose, for instance. It is called *Picnic in Winter*. The date tells us that it's the last day of 1959, the 31st of December, a day Bengalis have turned into a 'picnic day'.

The title of the drawing tells us that it is a picnic—a human event, a social event. Yet, what occupies the frame—the canvas—are blank spaces, presumably a bank of the river Khowai in Bolpur, and trees swaying in the wind. There are three mats, and on them human figures. To confirm their presence and to attest to the title of the drawing are utensils and containers—we imagine the food unconsciously as we imagine blood inside living men on canvases. While its span is almost panoramic, its perspective tells us that we notice the trees over everything else. To be slightly more accurate, we notice the wind in the trees more than we do the trees—it might be the first time we have actually *seen* the wind. Art gives us this gift that life withholds: it allows us to see the wind, as it were. The wind, as you can see, affects each tree unequally, so that while the trees at first form only a cluster in our eyes, we quickly see them as individuals, defending themselves by practising their resistance movements in proportion to the size and length of their bodies. They are not generic, as the humans enjoying the picnic in winter are not. What I want to stress here, by entering this temperament through Nandalal Bose's drawing, is the equitable distribution of canvas space to the human and non-human worlds. Shakti's vision is similar to this, and it is worthwhile, therefore, to remember that he wasn't alone in being ahead of his times, in resisting the centrality of man in our understanding of the environment. Labelled a misfit very early on in his life, it seemed a natural choice—to reject the centrality of the social human.

The human figure is often, therefore, an intrusive presence, even an intruding force, in Shakti's plant world, as interfering as, say, the gardener. That is why when he mentions human figures at all, he shows them as itinerant figures, such as the postman in 'Hemanter Aranyer Postman' ('Postman in the Autumnal Forest').[14] It is perhaps in line with this that Shankha Ghosh, when writing about him after his death, called him 'an urban shepherd'. A limited contact with the social world, a nomadic interaction, would perhaps maintain the balance of something inexplicable and unnameable, a kind of Blakean innocence, in the world. In his writing and in his life we sense this urge and this temptation all the time, an urge to go back to how it once was. This is not really a call for a Roussean back-to-nature, and neither is it an imagined nostalgia for the premodern—this urge exists not so much in time as in space. His philosophical metaphor for this is depth: to dig deep, to go far beneath the topsoil of thought and experience, deeper than human imagination, than human truth, deeper than drills and boring machines, deeper than the plough, as deep as the most curious tree roots can dig. Tree roots create their own paths, for there are no roads inside the earth, no human maps—they travel only for nourishment, for nutrition. They seek wet places, damp worlds that do not scare with loneliness but welcome these scaly curiosities—there is nothing to fear, for water has been here before their arrival, preparing to welcome them. So soil, moist soil, becomes a guesthouse waiting for traveller-roots.

It might be pertinent to mention the influence of Baudelaire—who was brought to Calcutta in Buddhadeva Bose's extraordinary translations—on Shakti. Here is Shankha Ghosh again, recording those moments of introduction and interaction with the French poet:

> Shakti was primary among the young poets who were possessed by Baudelaire's work immediately on arrival. It isn't just that Shakti was to write the dedication to his first book as a eulogy to Baudelaire: 'Beloved, most beautiful of all / who is my dazzling salvation', nor that the title of a Baudelaire poem—'I have called out from the underworld'—would emerge as a poem in that volume ('Calling from the Underworld') and, much later, become the title of one his volumes. More important was the change in the fundamental idea of poetry, the change that Baudelaire had wanted to bring to European poetry, a change that was praised by Rimbaud. When Bose referred to an old ideal of the intoxication of mystery, many seemed to discover a new foundation on which modern poetry might be built. 'The invisible must be seen, the inaudible must be heard.'[15]

Yes, the invisible must be seen, the inaudible must be heard. Art has devoted grossly disproportionate attention to what is visible, and hence its monological attention to the parts of the tree that lie above land. As I've argued in my book *How I Became a Tree*, human art has ignored the root—no art teacher spends any significant energy on teaching their students how to draw roots.[16] Their unknowability, their not needing to take a road already taken, their journey for a four-dimensional depth, as four-dimensional as death—all of these must have appealed to Shakti. Man, dominating by nature, controls the branching of trees above the ground. He has little control over roots. Roots have also managed to remain calibration-neutral, so that no gardener is able to measure roots in the way they measure tree and branch growth. Relationships in this subterranean world do not run to readymade templates but to ad hoc whimsies. And his life, his poetry, was based on slippery whimsies. A good illustration of this would be Shakti's marriage to Minakshi, whom he met in the informal literary gatherings that he attended in Calcutta. There were no declarations of love or plans for the future, and so one day, when Minakshi got to know that Shakti had told several people that they were getting married on 15 August (also Indian Independence Day, of course), she asked him whether he had indeed said such a thing. His response was casual—he had. What if I refuse to marry you? she asked him. 'I'll push you into the Ganga if you don't', he's supposed to have said. Together they'd visit the many forests and jungles of India, some over and over again, and as his wife says, 'Few knew the forests of India as intimately as Shakti did.'[17]

There are two other strains about Shakti's life that are part of the wrinkled halo around him. The first of these has to do with his alcoholism. His drinking habits are captured in photographs and even in Bishnu Pal Chaudhuri's short film, where Shakti is seen to be drinking and singing a Tagore song in an inebriated state, while returning home with his shirt unbuttoned. Shakti himself added to this mythology about alcohol producing his best poetry—without 'moddyo' (alcohol) how could there be 'poddyo' (verse)? (He always used the word 'poddyo' over 'kobita', 'verse' over 'poetry'. 'Kobita' was too distant and elitist for him; the kobi was not an elevated figure, he was of life, and poddyo, like goddyo, came from the same space.) He confessed to writing 'Abani Bari Aachho', without a doubt his most famous poem (it is part of a collection that is said to have sold a record number of copies in Bangla publishing, second only to a few of Tagore's collections of poems), while under the spell of liquor, possibly mohua, a drink made by forest dwellers and tribals. Shakti's poems have always been related to his life, this life, they've been read as confessional poems, as 'autobiographical', to use that stunted cliché, but it is not for secret revelations about his life events that one goes to these poems. One goes to them for some kind of secret wisdom, and perhaps because of the unexplained and unverifiable relation between the abandonment of some kind of social consciousness under the addiction to rhythm in language and the consequent lubricated entry into poetry. (There's a doctoral dissertation waiting to be written about alcoholism and Bengali artists around the time, poets, filmmakers, actors, painters, all of whom considered alcohol as an attendant boy of their muse, or perhaps the muse itself. He's documented not so much his life events as his dreams and desires that sit at the top of the hierarchy of taboos of mid-twentieth-century Bengali middle-class life—drinking, sex, the body, and an anarchic attitude to all of these that formed the subject of his poetry turned it into a kind of teenager's cave where the thrill of the illegitimate and illegal drew many to it. If one allowed oneself to go beyond the superficiality of these things, it wouldn't be difficult to see that the ethics of these poems is one of the plant world.

The other strain is of the person who's impossible to avoid in twentieth-century Bangla literature. As Buddhadeva Bose said of people like himself, who'd come to write after Tagore, 'It was impossible not to imitate Rabindranath; it was impossible to imitate Rabindranath.'[18] Shakti was perhaps as addicted to Rabindra Sangeet as he was to alcohol and the forests of India. Rabindranath was, also, possibly a link for him with the music of the Bauls—Shakti, who considered mysteriousness as possibly the central characteristic of, and indeed requirement from, poetry was taken not just by the mystical quality of Baul song but by the free-spirited lives of these people. They were what he'd have liked to be—he romanticized their lives as being timelessly connected to the village, to the rural, untainted by urbanity and materialism. Shankha Ghosh, in the same introductory essay to the seventh volume of Shakti's *Collected Poems*, writes of Shakti who, for the remainder of his life, remained the same boy of 15 when he first came to Calcutta, confused by urbanity, by the city, as if it were another planet:

A young boy has come from the village to the city which is waiting with wide-open arms to consume him. The boy feels unmoored, for 'those who are heartless, those who do not tell the truth, those who do not have minds as open as flowers, those who always have their fists balled up close to their bodies, those who live amid constant noise and unresolved riots between Hindus and Muslims' are the ones who live in cities, who live in Calcutta—he knows this only too well. Perhaps they are to be found everywhere, these people 'whose hearts hold no love, no affection, no stirring of compassion', without whose valuable advice today's world would stand still. There is no attraction anywhere, no desire that anyone feels. Is this detachment 'urbanity', 'modernity'?[19]

The Bauls, their spiritual energy condensed in Tagore's songs, offered him a momentary stay against confusion. Critics like Kuntal Sengupta have identified phrases and lines and expressions from Tagore, his poems and songs and sentences from his prose writings, that Shakti incorporated into his poems—this Found aesthetic (more Found and less intertextual) perhaps allowed him a temporary habitation in a time, a place, and a sensibility that was more akin to his temperament than the life in which he had to move with his body.

These things, these different but related strains, the mysticism of the Bauls, the spirit of Rabindranath's songs, the search for a new language within Bangla itself, the quest to make the invisible visible—all of these, imbibed from different poets and artists and different traditions, came together in the way he understood and felt the plant world. Did Shakti Chattopadhyay write about plant life and what is called the natural world from the very beginning? The truth is that the extraordinary and intuitive understanding of the non-human world was evident right from his first published poem. Here is Shankha Ghosh's energetic and affectionate record of the arrival of the poet and his first poem:

It must have happened earlier that a magazine had published a brand-new writer, only to see them disappear over a period of time, or perhaps make a mark slowly, without their first published piece creating a sensation. But those who read poetry had no way of ignoring what this new poet had written, for it seemed to leap upon their senses with its entire being. The positions of words within the flowing prose had been turned upside down, the images rising with a deeply sensual force. Nature seemed to be breathing through the entire composition. There wasn't as much surprise in the line 'immaculate vagina concealed in an undergrowth as soft as velvet'—possibly others could have written the same set of words, in the same sequence—as there was when it was followed by the object of the simile: 'Like the feet of a peasant in the monsoon' . . . When we keep reading this poem, which fuses woman and nature, lines such as 'the male in my body touches the heavens', or 'In every limb of my living body is the consort of my love', it becomes clear that a powerful young poet has appeared, with a deep proclivity for demolishing the accepted way of using words and images.[20]

Ghosh is writing about the poem 'The Birth of the Subarnarekha', and right in Shakti's first published poem the poet-critic has identified the primary characteristics of the latter's poetry—the 'deeply sensual force', of course, and this: 'nature seemed to be breathing through the entire composition'.

What did 'nature' or plant life really mean to Shakti? What was he seeking in this other world? Now, Shakti's understanding of poetry was not very different from his understanding of plant life. Like branches and leaves together make a tree, so with fragments of poems making a larger poem. 'Every poet's verse is one long poem—it's just that he writes it in fragments', he wrote.[21] There's also the interconnectedness between roots and branches of trees, canopies above the earth and embracing secondary and tertiary roots beneath it. This is not unlike Shakti's poetics where lines and titles from poems enter one another freely, without ticket: Shakti had written in the introduction to what was almost his last book of poems: 'Although the long poem titled "The Jungle Is in Mourning" features in the book *Here's the Figure in Stone*, I am naming this new book for that old poem.' If we get the line 'The inglorious loneliness of weapons' as a line in a poem in his first poem, it comes to us as the title of a book much later, as does the name 'Calling from the Underworld'. A poem titled 'I'm Happy' will be available long after the book of poems with that name, in the volume titled *Fire of My Reverence*. It's the same story with several other volumes such as *The Flying Throne* and *You Believe in Faith, You Believe in Giraffes Too*.' This habit, of quoting himself, is akin to the natural world—every seed, and consequent sapling, is actually quoting the original (or originary) tree it is coming from, and the likeness of which it'll grow into. All poems originate from the same poet, and so all the lines in the poet's writing are related to one another. There is another thing that occupied Shakti throughout his life. It was the nature of truth. Was truth relative? Were there different truths for social and asocial beings? Was plant truth and person truth and poetic truth the same, or at least similar? 'I blow a gust of untruth into the truth of poetry / the truth of poetry changes in just one day'; or, 'I drag the truth kicking and screaming to the river / To feel the breeze, then slap it across its face'. Truth and its relation to morality confused him—it was a social ailment. The plant world and the poetry world offered a similar refuge. If the plant and the poem offered him a more comforting and comfortable kind of truth, were the poet and the gardener built of the same sense organs? Is this why, in his novel *I am Leaving*, he says that he 'will hang poetry from trees'.[22] Why? Is this his way of protesting, by combining what Robert Frost, in a slightly different tone, called his 'desert places'?[23] For it is not just urbanity that he wants to dismantle but his self-help cure to urbanity too: 'turn the village, the forest, the habitations upside down/all of it, all of it'.

Looking at these various arcs now, it seems inevitable that all these interests and self-investigation, and relationships, both real and speculative, were to lead to his overwhelming identification with plant life. The entry point is from a site where the human and the natural worlds meet, such as the site of the garden. Take this poem about the garden—it's called 'Paata Aar Phooler Gawlpo' ('The Story of Leaves and Flowers').[24]

Leaves are more necessary
than flowers in a garden.
Flowers bloom against the background of leaves,
both bad and good.
But leaves are always awake,
filling up the garden—
for there might be an attack on fruits, on seeds.
If the maternal leaves spread deep into the garden
I feel happy, I stare at the beautiful garden.
The various manifestations of green fill me with envy –
for flowers live as men in society, inside households.[25]

Reading this poem in Cornell University, where I've been revisiting him, has its own rewards—to see leaves gradually take on the colour of flowers this season. I found myself thinking about this poem, almost reciting it to myself in Bangla, while walking by the Botanical Gardens in the evenings. The Ithaca evening sky, as is well documented, is a garden whose flowers cannot be contained on a canvas or whose bagginess cannot be captured by origami. Oftentimes I had the sensation of the sky having left its colours by mistake in the garden the previous evening. These colours, both of the sky and the leaves, are perhaps of no great use to anyone except the aesthete. Or to Shakti Chattopadhyay. We can see his rejection of the garden even when he is inside it—a rejection of human domination, of prettiness, of privileging a human model of beauty over the natural. The likening of the casual glamour of flowers with men, 'men in society, inside households', reminds us of Shakti's rejection of both society and its smallest unit, the family. 'I am unsocial', he declared once, and this poem becomes a metaphorical illustration of that choice. Flowers—their prettiness, even cheap prettiness, cheap because it reminds him of the materialistic investment in the culture of flowers, in bouquets and garlands, wreaths and worship, and pretty because of its need to attract pollinators—are not for him. Flowers, fruits, seeds—the reproductive cycle. Shakti is making a choice outside this cycle by choosing leaves, and yet, by calling leaves 'maternal', he is also suggesting—and indeed creating—an alternative world within the already alternative world of plants. Are leaves security guards protecting flowers and fruits and seeds? Is Shakti suggesting that those who guard and protect a culture are more important than those who create it? For there's the biblical-botanical ring of the first line: 'Leaves are more important than flowers'. Partly true—or even largely true sometimes—because, as is common textbook knowledge, leaves are food factories; and yet, there would be no passing the baton to the next generation for flowering plants if flowers didn't do the seduction dance for pollinators. What could Shakti be suggesting through this cosmography? 'Poetry has no actual objective', he wrote somewhere, and yet it is impossible not to *see* that he's making a case for the background to be foreground—'the flowers bloom against the background of leaves'.[26] It's his politics and his aesthetics—to make the invisible visible, to go back to the Baudelairean dictum he adapted for his needs. Like Nandalal in his

painting, who turns the usual background of trees into almost the subject of his painting, Shakti is doing the same. The margins and the marginalized were the subject of his affection and attention, and it is from
this that his plant philosophy emanates. For who remembers the timid
green leaves in a bouquet? All eyes are on the flowers, the Cinderella of
the bunch. There's also something else, another desire that completes
the poem—the envy for the different manifestations of green. Why is
Shakti envious? He is envious of those who can live outside society, outside its units like the household. That is why he longs to be a leaf.

> For life's woodcutter, as long as there is the weeping willow It's a bad
> time The flower is not greater than the leaf The flower is not better
> than the leaf[27]

If there is a moral in the garden, it is only this—the flower is not
greater than the leaf. This is an instruction for all gardeners. By valuing leaves as much as flowers, weeds as much as trees that are useful
for man, the undisciplined forest space over the office, darkness as
much as light (light without which the plant world wouldn't exist),
rotten fruits as much as edible ones, Shakti is continually advocating
for—and renewing—a world where things are as natural as the plant
world, one without hypocrisy and privilege and elitism. In this poem
for instance, he's exposing the shallowness of gifting flowers on birth-
days. Apart from that, to call himself of the 'winter race', winter that
is cruel to plants, he's also making us think of our non-egalitarian attitude to everything, including the most basic and natural ones, like
the seasons.

> A winter garden next to me on my birthday.
> Saplings near me, no flowers on them.
> The fragrance of madhobilata only in the mornings and evenings
> No other flowers in this garden.
> Fragrant hibiscus in one corner.
> My wife's an expert at decorating the room
> with leaves for my birthday.
> What if there are no beautiful flowers
> I'm of the winter race—in my hands emptiness.[28]

Though he keeps making these choices, his confusion never seems to leave him. Who are these people who care for the tree's produce? He identifies two kinds of people in the poem 'Manush Jebhaabey Dei' ('The Way Man Gives')—the woodcutter, and the worshipper who worships with flowers.

No, not from any forest but from the corner of a house
the woodcutter comes out with an axe on his shoulder.
He hides behind the shirish trees. He hides the axe.
It's because just a little while ago he's committed a murder—
after cutting a weeping willow, astounded, he's turned into stone.
From his hiding place he's watching the anger, the mourning, the
    withering and the loss
the folded face, without will but still in control
This letting go, this leaving home.

This is how man gives away his infant child from his lap,
because it needs to be given, given when there's a storm in the blood.
Because she cannot not give, she tears it from her breast.
Rummaging the garden, she gives flowers for anjali—
the way man offers anjali, with tears and sanyas,
no one does, not beasts, nor birds.[29]

Both the woodcutter and the worshipper are uniquely human figures—they belong to the human kingdom; they could belong nowhere else. For no plant or animal worships with flowers or cuts wood—it is foreign to their ecosystem. What is Shakti trying to do in this poem? Notice the irony of 'give' in the title: the way man gives. Gives? But the poem is about taking. Man is taking wood and flowers—wood, the tree's past, and flowers, its future, respectively—from the tree. What does man give in return? The inaudible answer in the poem—'nothing'—is there in the title, in the verb 'gives', 'The Way Man Gives'. Shakti does not judge this through the barter economy of reciprocity—for someone who wrote about unrequited love the way he did, it seems like a most natural process. The human releasing their infant child into the world, the devotee throwing flowers at their god, the woodcutter cutting off a tree's branches—all of these actions are beyond Newton's third law. There will never be any equal and opposite reaction—this makes me wonder whether Shakti believed—like I do—that all love is non-reciprocal. For love—which is at the heart of Shakti's philosophy of living—is given and received in different currencies, not the same kind of love.

But to return to Shakti's garden and the play of giving and taking. This poem is called 'Aashtey Dao' ('Let It Come').

Shiuli doesn't bloom in my garden on time.
Many other flowers don't bloom there.
Sometimes they bloom but not quite—
they come close to blooming, but still sit far away.
Shiuli doesn't bloom in my garden on time.
Many other things don't bloom,
they don't blossom in my garden.
They uproot themselves and stare at the sky—
Clouds, give me rain, give yourself in abundance, selflessly . . .
Give me rain, let it come, let the waiting-list come before that.[30]

This poem too, it is not difficult to see, is about reciprocity, for 'blooming' is about reciprocity after all, soil, water, air, and luck coming together to produce beauty—this is all the more magical, and even a routine miracle, because we don't notice the raw material that goes on to produce this unexpected beauty. But must a combination of these ingredients always produce the desired results? This inability of the flowers in Shakti's garden to bloom on time, or to bloom at all, seems to be an extension of his philosophy—life, though joyous, mostly joyous, doesn't aim to please; it is not a guarantor of our happiness. All trees—and indeed all humans—do not need to provide us with fruits; or even shade.

In poem after poem, we are given a philosophy of the other in a way that seems so familiar that we feel that we've encountered these thoughts in a past life. It is an alternate life not only because plant life is being posited against the social world but also—and perhaps primarily—because we're being given an imagined life in a language of the social world so that there is no barrier of suspicion when we enter that space. Take 'Gachh Kawtha Bawley' ('Trees Can Speak'), the title of a poem, said in such a matter-of-fact manner, like Jagadish Chandra Bose did about plant writing and the plant script, that we're not even allowed to remember that trees don't speak, even though there are numerous variants of the 'speaking tree' genre in the literature of religious philosophy.[31] The operation is pretty simple—if I were to walk on fours, like a four-legged animal or like an insect, after the initial laughter resulting from surprise, there'd be the inevitable question about intention. There'd gradually be a transfer—however unreal and temporary—from the human world to the world of four-legged animals. This process is necessary to create a practical space of empathy: only if we begin to try and walk on one leg can we perhaps understand why ramps for wheelchairs are necessary in buildings. Shakti employs a similar method in these poems. The philosophy in both my example and in his poems is the same: it is love.

> I sit inside the tree
> Morning and evening—
> I water every tree,
> the tree gives me fruit in return.
> This give-and-take continues in gentle unspoken love.
> Tree and man understand this love, no one else does.
> I sit inside the tree morning and evening.
> Not everyone is a tree, there are weeds too.
> They have to be plucked out with some strength, a little care.
> The trees live happily. To be able to live happily the trees look at them
>   with indifference—
> it hurts to pluck out weeds, they too bear flowers.
> They might not be upper caste,
> like the sunflower or the jasmine,
> but even then,
> they've squatted in our garden with love.
> Without our giving water they're giving us flowers,
> of so many shapes and colours.
> So that trees can thrive and live happily,
> we pluck out weeds.
> I sit inside the tree,
> morning and evening.[32]

Notice the first line—I sit inside the tree. Not only do we know, from rational experience, that trees don't speak, but we are also aware that

humans might sit on its branches, but not really inside a tree. How is one
to sit inside a tree? But we don't pause to doubt this statement of fact because we are pulled by an unsaid promise that owes to the form of the
poem—we will be rewarded by something, some piece of wisdom or experience that we do not yet know we need, and so we read, with greed.
Two castes of plant life are given to us—the upper caste, the jasmine
and sunflower, and the lower caste, the weeds. In an essay called 'Dalit
Plants', I'd written about how gardening—and gardeners—employs a
caste system among plants where weeds are treated like the lowest caste.[33]
They suffer the fate of the powerless and the marginalized (in their case,
literally)—they are uprooted and left to die. Shakti reminds us that weeds
also give us flowers. It might seem odd to see him use flower as argument,
particularly after we've read his thoughts about leaves and flowers in a
poem, but here the reason is obvious: it's one used as the primary axis to
create a sense of equality, one used by activists, and one that someone like
Jagadish Chandra had to use—plants have feelings *too*. Now, if we were to
transplant this space of the garden, where Shakti wants a sense of equality
between trees and weeds, to life, chaotic and complex and uneven, in the
world out there, we will easily see what he is trying to do. Even those
without merit or talent, beauty or wealth, or any of the things that human
society values, they too have as much a right to live and grow, to love and
bear children, as those who come first in class.

The same sense of equality, an organic refusal to privilege any being
over another or any kind of superiority, wherever that imagined sense
of superiority might come from, marks a poem like 'Baganer Keu Noy
Nawshto Phawl' ('Not a Single Fruit in a Garden is Rotten').

Some rotten fruits are rolling on the ground.
Not by themselves, for they cannot roll on their own.
A few ants are dragging them, to throw them into a ditch—
throw, they won't say anything.
They can't speak, there's only their rotten gaze,
to say something just by staring,
saying something rotten by staring.
The pit speaks instead of the fruit!
There's water, water says something—
There's muddy soil, it says something!

Some rotten fruits are rolling on the ground—
bad days are over, so they're rolling on the earth,
a few ants are dragging it, to throw into a ditch—
Not a single fruit in the garden is ever rotten,
it was, only for a day.[34]

What humans call 'rotten'—and in this poem 'rotten' is quite obviously a metaphor, where Shakti is playing on the bagdhara or idiomatic phrase 'nawshto phawl', rotten fruit, not for plants but for humans—is a terribly human ascription. That overripe fruits will begin to rot is the way of nature, but the rules of human consumption—and ingestion—have created this ideology of rottenness. Nothing is rotten in a garden is Shakti's way of saying that nothing is rotten anywhere. (Think of how adverse criticism of the performing arts has become related to the throwing of rotten fruits—rotten tomatoes!) Then there is the conscious rejection of the glorification of the metaphor of 'fruit' and 'fruition'. Wickedly he adds an adjective in front of 'fruit' in poems about fruits: 'rotten'. Many of his poems have similar titles: 'Nawshto Aekta Phawl' ('A Rotten Fruit'), or 'Pawcha Nawshto Phawl Aami' ('I'm a Rotten Fruit'), where he seems to be echoing society's catcalls to him, and where he writes of himself as a wasted, rotten fruit, rolling down with its round body in a world where the fruit is the 'third party', not the tree's, not the seller's, but someone belonging to itself alone, the ultimate possessive case.[35] Though Shakti doesn't really say it, it is implied—fruits are usually round, Dali's perfect shape; when they rot it is the first thing they begin to lose, their roundness, their form. Rottenness is, of course, also related to ripeness. When is a fruit—or a poem—ripe? Why is ripeness 'all'? Shakti is insistent that we understand that ripeness has to do with an idea about completeness that he doesn't understand or believe in. His poems are never sealed tight— lines and phrases move between poems. Seeds move out of fruits to create new life. How could ripeness, with its connotation of an ending, mean anything at all?

The garden is not a thing of beauty but a happy-sad space in which the journey of flowers is not necessarily from bud to flower to fruit to death but one where flowers can travel in all directions. This might sound surreal at first, but what Shakti does is to make the journey from the branches of a tree to the human hand, where it is cradled, smelled, and stoked, seem like a natural progression. This is the trick of the garden, where humans are allowed to become trees and its parts. It is a place with invisible walls that allow privacy at the required moment and openness at the other. The constituents of the garden, for all purposes a human space as much as we might like to believe otherwise, have all become a little like human persons themselves but also vice versa. The similarity between humans and plants is to be seen, for instance, in the way both react to rain. Men might rush to the roof or the courtyard to soak the first showers of the season, but the immobile and dependent houseplants? And so the instructions in the poem 'Tawber Phoolgulo Ke Dao' ('Give It To The Flowerpots'): throw the flower pots from the stairs to the terrace. Let them spread on their hesitant roots and mistakes. How else will they grow a towering personality, firm green, whose only desire or ambition is to stand . . . Let the potted plants, those house plants, drink some rain, let them grow roots in the pot itself, the burnt clay plots have a lifetime's thirst anyway.[36] These instructions by the poet, in casual ellipses, seem to emerge from the plants themselves. Lonely as he was in the spiritual and intellectual world that he inhabited, and acutely aware of being and being labelled a misfit, he did not want to be anyone's voice, but he moved, in transpersonal movements, between the two voices and identities—of plant and plant-empathizer.

The tree is him and he is the tree, on land and also in water. And so, in another poem, titled 'Brikkher Protiti Gronthey' ('In Every Nerve of the Tree'), the lotus roots connect to his chest—'Defeat, the leftover roots of the lotus are on my chest, they only carry the noise of the pond to my ears.'[37] Roots are transmitters—connecting them to the chest (an image that immediately conjures up an image of a man on a hospital bed with wires connecting his chest and abdomen and limbs to stern-looking machines) is Shakti's way of connecting the plant's mind and heart to the human's. This interspecies engineering, reminiscent of fairytales where multispecies existence is not considered odd, and horror films where the surgery's gone awry, is Shakti's 'only connect'. Surely something will emerge out of that conversation? These poems seem like the closest one can get to the alchemy that can turn humans into trees. The garden, and sometimes even the forest, is Chattopadhyay's laboratory for that alchemy—men and women move through them like the wind, like the breeze, even like the storm. And, almost like the butterfly effect, the consequences are inevitably greater than the actions from which they originated. 'Did You Hold Her Hand in the Garden?' is the title of a poem about the garden, and that question about what seems like a tumultuous and extraordinary verb ('hold') holds in it the destiny of the garden space and those who inhabit it.

> Your hand holds in it travel and itinerary . . . Did you hold her hand in
> the garden?[38]

Even the mere proximity to plants can change people, make them forgetful, absent-minded, or do something completely unexpected. It is as if they were not plants but fire, capable of changing things through contagion.

> 'Whom you loved, this is not him This is a new craftsman—' Suddenly
> your path loses its direction near the golden chaapa's tree-room[39]

The waywardness, caused by both humans and plants in the garden space, the sudden loss of direction near the golden chaapa tree, an aberration in behaviour and routine morality, has a bit to do with humans not becoming as plant-like as they should. Plants are never late, why should humans be? This double consciousness, a constant comparative swing between the human and plant worlds, living in a moment of permanent simultaneity, is part of Shakti's living aesthetic. There's a childlikeness in this—seasons arrive on time, why doesn't man?, he asks in one poem.

> Spring comes, the cherries are in bloom in the garden This is the
> time—the bridge has been built If you are late out of habit Animesh
> is nearby[40]

To an outsider to this universe this might seem like a taut and conscious morality, but the garden is neither a classroom nor a church—if anything, it is an escape from morality.

One of my favourite sub-genres among Chattopadhyay's garden poems is where the speaking persona calls out to a passerby or stranger, even a flower thief or poacher, in the garden. 'Who is it?' has never been more philosophical and poetic. As if we ever really know who's out there, in the garden or otherwise, as if the person will ever respond. Does the wind ever respond to such a question when it leans on the window, tired after travelling long distances? The anxiety and curiosity about the presence of an invader in this private-public space gives birth to the matter-of-fact hoarse title of the poem 'Ke Baaganey' ('Who's in the Garden?'). But, as we read, we discover the expectation behind the 'who'.

> The silent corridor lights up
> There's the night-clothed thief
> Who's in the garden?
> Speak, speak, it seems as if all night boats have weathered the storm
>
> The bat's wings
> Living on the weeping willow-lined street
> A l l n i g h t
> There has been no bloodshed yet
> There has been no bloodshed yet
>
> Everyone's come for the festival
> We'll get married
> The moon's lantern moves on this path
> Is it a grand ceremony?
> Sura?
> The searchlight's in the hands of Neempura [41]

'We'll get married'—where but in the garden? The joyous self-assurance of that line, as if the poet needs to say that to himself just to be sure again, turns the garden from its weeping willow-lined street to one charged with the electricity of a 'festival'. The definition of the garden comes in the repetition however: 'There has been no bloodshed yet'. That is why the garden is precious—there are killings in the world, in the desert and in the forest, but who will come to war inside a garden?

And so the only way to escape bloodshed is to let the world turn into a garden, for us to become trees where the only natural violence is the fall of flowers and the nodding acknowledgement of the wind by leaves: 'Every leaf in the forest shakes its head to the wide wind' ('Tumi shudhu nawho tomari aapon!' ['You're Dear Not Only to Yourself']).[42]

Falling is touching, touching the earth, touching other fallen flowers. How else is one to love, tree to tree, human to tree, tree to sky, tree to moon? The pine forest was flooded one night in the month of Magh—this is how love touches our bodies, says Shakti in 'Chhinno Paatar Shajai Tawroni' ('With Severed Leaves I Decorate My Boat').[43] This is how the clay oven wakes up in a free mind. The pine forest is our house, he repeats. The forest as house is no longer metaphor because the poet is now a tree. He looks at the world as a tree would—only one is never sure which tree he is at any given moment. Is the Krishnachura's path naturally red? From a distance the sal stares at it. From the pine tree in the previous poem, he has become the sal in this one. This tree-jumping, sal one moment, krishnachura the next, grass on another page, or just a generic tree in another, this endless inhabitation of selves—as if only humans should be allowed multiple identities!

The garden is, in spite of the presence of plants and animals, a human and social space. Shakti is never really sure what he wants for and from the garden—as in, should there be humans in it? If yes, what is the role of the human? And the related philosophical question—what is a garden without a gardener? Self-doubt accompanies this question. In 'Maalir Ekanto Proyojon' ('A Gardener is Utterly Necessary') he begins by becoming a self-reliant garden: I have trimmed my branches all my life; a gardener is necessary, a gardener is necessary. Life fills on the thorny plants, nothing else. If it was something else, life would have lost. Only sometimes, an enthusiastic branch bends away, to control and return to the routine body, exactly how the moon hides itself behind the clouds.[44] When I read these lines, I wonder whether a garden without a gardener is an orphaned garden, and whether Shakti wasn't able to ever leave his orphaned childhood behind.

The human in the garden is an outsider figure in Shakti's world—a refugee, however temporary, from the social world, he has entered the garden like a bird enters a house or a creeper a window. The garden is not his home though; like a tourist, he desires permanent residency there. Could such a man live permanently in a garden or a forest? Shakti chooses the figure of the postman, one who travels between these worlds, but is also a person who facilitates communication between the plant and the human. The letter, the roots of the lotus attached to the human heart that we encountered in another poem a little while ago—these are tropes of communication. Shakti, like a scientist, is groping for a way, some way that would make plant to human translation possible. In one of his most famous poems, 'Hemonter Awronney Aami Postman' ('I am a Postman in the Autumnal Forest'), he pursues the I-am-a-tree narrative to substitute the clock-running dictatorship of human life with the season-controlled life of trees. I can only paraphrase this impossibly beautiful poem: I have seen many postmen move in the autumnal forest. Their yellow baskets are filled with grass, like the stomachs of lambs. They have found such old letters, these forest postmen. I've seen them digging the earth like cranes do for fish. So impossible and mysterious and alert is their busyness. These are not like our postmen from whose hands letters of our luxuriant love get lost so easily. And so the poem continues, with Shakti criticizing modern life and the disappearance of love-laden letters from it, how we no longer hug, kiss or listen to the music of man.[45]

> The distance between two letters has increased.
> I have not noticed the distance between two trees grow.[46]

This constant feet-in-two-boats, as the censoring Bangla idiom goes, this fluid jumping between being tree and man, looking at something as a man and experiencing it the next moment as a tree, marks Shakti's iterant literary life. The growing distance between letters, that synecdoche for man, and the unchanging proximity between trees, a fact that would make any lover want to love like a tree, also comes in a poem with the self-confessional title 'Tar Dalpaala Aamar Choitonyo' ('In Its Branches My Consciousness').[47] He is instructive without giving instructions. In 'Prokritir Kachhey Phera' ('Returning to Nature'), in spite of Rousseau's ghost sitting in its title, it is a poem about love.[48] Return to nature, the way man eats grass every day. Say something cheap, something healthy. The same way you return to grass, sit inside it, spreading your legs. In heat and greed, make the grass softer and greener, eat salt. But of course the world is already salty. Blood, tears, the calcium in bones—it's non-vegetarian enough. I held my breath as I read that line. It struck me that apart from salt, all our taste additives, sweetness, heat, bitterness, all of these came from plant life. And so the alienating, 'non-vegetarian' saltiness at the end of the poem. I also thought of Jibanananda's ghost in the poem, in the grass, Jibanananda whom Shakti considered to be his strongest influence.

Sometimes he is the postman leaf, sometimes the branch of a pom-egranate tree, sometimes a 'lonely' root. That adjective is from his poem 'Shikawrer Mawto Aeka' ('As Lonely as a Root').[49] The quiet fire inside his head has turned him mad. He is sitting there, having dug a hole, like a wrapt root. Insects, white and smelly, move around him. Only there is no human neighbourhood. All the men have gone to temples and podiums. All of them have some prayer, some opinion. Insects do not have temples and mosques. They do not care for creed or groups. They surround the madman. He is sitting there, having dug a hole, like a wrapt root, all alone.

We have all been witness to aged men turning into trees, but the lone-liness of a root, often explained by botanists to be the equivalent of the human brain, can turn us into depressed, sad, and lonely madmen living in a neighbourhood of ants. In spite of his many choices of flower, leaves, branches, and various kinds of trees, it was the tree root that Shakti Chattopadhyay loved being most. In 'Monay Monay, Gachher Shikorer Shawngey' ('In My Mind, With the Roots of a Tree'), we see this man, whose alcoholic spirit a human house could not contain, finding a home inside a root.[50] In my mind, he begins, I've rolled down a long distance with the tree roots, from where I can see a mridanga-beaten river, one of its banks as strong as sadness. Yellow, the other bank, is guarded by mist. The tree roots and I look through the earth's soft hole—a group of red crabs, their household, their warmth. I can spot Shakti's sly equiva-lence: the root and the mind, both burrowing through holes, landing upon the unexpected.

Roots are, without a doubt, his synecdoche for trees. In 'Ei Shei Shingbhum, Jar Jawngoley Paharey' ('This is Shingbhum, In Whose Jungles and Mountains'), he wants 'to wrap my body with the roots of a tree';[51] in another poem,

> A tree's hunched from the weight of golden thread
> There are stones lying around its root.
> They're lying scattered, some hugging grass—
> as pieces of precious yellow letter-memories.[52]

Stones will always lie around trees—Shakti leaves it to us to decide whether the roots will embrace them or move away from them. In many of this sub-genre of poems there is the contrapuntal urge to make the root visible (and root, therefore, acquires symbolism here—the hidden, the submerged, the underworld, the repressed), but also to become invisible like roots. It couldn't be a coincidence that Shakti Chattopadhyay was thinking about tree roots and grass at around the same time that Deleuze and Guattari were writing about the rhizome and the challenges it posed to hierarchical models in society.

Shakti writes about middle-aged trees and their roots in particular: I have seen the root of a middle-aged tree, seen both its curiosity for life and its forgiving dailiness. The leaves of a middle-aged tree, those who are fond of faces, only they spread out into the silent uninhabited space. The rest stand guard, send shadows below. Were the flowers of a middle-aged tree affectionate always? Or has my coming turned them into willing prisoners of love in this blue flood of love? He wants to be this tree—these trees—but self-doubt arrives frequently. Human habits return, and the differences between plant and person amplify. In 'Chhinnobinno', he writes about the effect of rain on both.[53] Heavy rains have left all the leaves wet. Where's the sun to dry it now? Man knows how to dry himself after getting wet in the rain, but trees? It is a subject he returns to—rain and the tree. Rain washes the dust off leaves, he begins, in another poem, 'Je Kishore Hriday Boshechhey' ('The Youth Who Sits in the Heart'), but would it also be natural if it washed the earth off roots?[54] Rain might wash the dirt off man's skin, then the soul would be rid of dirt too. But men and trees have different lives. Their deaths are different, too. No housefly would circumnavigate over a tree corpse, but a congregation would immediately begin its operation over a dead human's body. The death of a tree is the birth of a metaphor in his world. When a simple tree lies on the banks of the Khowai, that horizontal lying is much more than the death of men ('Jwalanto Rumaal' ['The Burning Handkerchief']).[55]

Just as he sees men as trees, he also wonders why trees sometimes behave like men. 'Gachh Kyano' ('Why Do Trees') is full of these unbalanced curiosities—the ellipses is an illustration of the unknowability of these questions.[56] Here is Shakti: 'Why does a tree speak against the other? I do not know the reason, I don't know why birds fly. Just as I don't know why there are clouds in the sky and flowers have fragrance. I do not know why hair is beautiful. I do not know why trees speak against trees. Trees are not men after all!'[57] The exclamation mark is Shakti's, not mine—we recognize the exasperation with the exclusively human machinery of

rumour and gossip, complaint and accusation. The same resignation re-
curs in poem after poem, as in 'Ekhaney Kobita Peley Gachhey Gachhey
Tangabo' ('If I Find poems Here, I'll Hang It from the Trees'):

> From inside a tree I will resign
> I'll take leave of men and their cities.[58]

In 'Upodruto Ghasher Bhitorey' is a similar if-only-men-were-trees
desire: sitting deep like this inside grass seems nice in this fierce sun, he
begins. Under the sky and not yet, in their shade, this grass is a river-tree,
this bird-music of the wayward wind. It'll scribble some trees inside the
mind. They do not lie, there is no caution about their words. They are not
like men, they are slightly disorganized. That is why I like them more than
one can like oneself. Here it is, sometimes a tree, sometimes grass, and
the overwhelming desire to be them, to not have to speak lies, be cautious.
This precious spontaneity—only being a plant will allow that. But, being
a natural misfit everywhere, he isn't completely at peace being a plant either. Questions return from time, as in 'Ei Neel Shobhyota' ('This Blue
Civilization'): why the difference in the size of trees? For his utopia has
been transferred to the plant world—his dislike, even hatred, of hierarchy
of any kind has made him imagine the plant world as ahierarchical. He is
dismantling hierarchies everywhere. Why do we never make bouquets
out of grass flowers? That thought, I have to confess, has occurred to me
several times, or why we don't make gifts out of the nameless flowers that
grow by the roadside, but never the accompanying thought that follows
this question in the poem 'Duti Kawthaye' ('In Two Words'):

> That is why you haven't even got a bouquet of grass flowers,
> I am the real patriot.[59]

What is patriotism in the world of plants? Is grass the foot soldier
keeping vigil on soil borders for us? Shakti gives us a kinder interpretation of patriotism by relating it to protectiveness—because you care
for the grass, you cannot sever its flowers from its flesh to please another being, another species. His strong feelings about grass inevitably
remind me of Deleuze and Guattari's thoughts on the rhizome, and how
the model of the rhizome was their way of breaking hierarchy. Was it

the temper of the times when Shakti and the French philosophers were writing that made both of them gravitate towards grass?

> I think it's good to sit deep inside grass now,
> in this furious sun,
> to live under the sky is not to really live
> but there's the shadow—grass, river, tree.
> The messy wind, the birdcries—
> they'll sketch some trees inside my mind.
> There are no lies in what they say, no alertness.
> Not like man, they're a bit messy.
> This is their nature—that is why I like them more than one can like!
>
> You'd got so many things. Your hand on your unhappy forehead,
> those eyes inherited from the birth-hour are the tree's face.
> You'd got an upturned black cloud on your way,
> shining coins on your lips—does anything of that still remain?
> A sign-coded blue envelope.
>
> Everything's gone quiet, gone silent, stay inside the grass.[60]

'Stay inside the grass.'

Did Shakti Chattopadhyay succeed in becoming a tree? Did these poems—his laboratory experiments to make that metamorphosis possible—help him to turn into a tree?

> I don't have roots, I have no branches, no leaves
> A deep sadness in my flesh, the flow of wind in my bones
> I have no garden, no soil, no motherland
> Only stone and dust fly in my dreams.
>
> This is me, one man among the world's men.
> A man who had everything once, who has lost everything now—
> Not suddenly but lost it gradually, with stops and pauses, one by one.
> There is really no need to say anything about this
> There is no need to tell anyone about this
> There is no accusation, there is only the gain through loss.[61]

Shakti Chattopadhyay offers an affectionate footnote to this poem: 'To think of man as tree is my favourite desire. Especially to think of myself as a tree. That is my nature. Wherever I go, I gather roots. Branches sprout and grow. Stems and tendrils move in the wind. That kind of tree has no treeness. The sky and the underworld above and below the tree have no dreams, only stone and dust. Even that is restless.'[62] To escape from this restlessness, from the tyranny of human dreams, dreams that live inside human heads and control all other parts of the body, we must turn into trees, trees who know no restlessness, no fever, no fret, no fight. And so the deduction in 'Manusher Moddhey Thhekey' ('Living Amidst Men'): Vanwas, exile in the forest, is better than this living amidst men but not being of men. He then annotates our interpretation with a soulful note: 'One cannot support man anymore. Being a forest resident is better. There is an ethics about the violence of animals. One cannot say the same about the violence of men.'[63]

He was completely childlike in his 'method' of turning into a tree—like entering a cave often changes people in fairytales, he thought that entering into the bodies of trees would help him turn into a tree. And hence his plea to trees, to allow him into their bodies: if I could enter a tree, just once in this life, to hide myself . . . I am ready to do this even for a moment. For just one moment I want to be alone, not water, not wood nor stone. Wood, without offering promises, would make me its own. For so many days now, with this desire, I have gone to the jungle, at night, inside its dark. I've got lost. I've tried to enter the jungle by holding a root's hand—there are roads, but only one traveller. O Tree, take me, even if for a moment, take me please, inside you, where I can see Slow, the gradual and steady growth of life. You are not silent like stones, you are friendly, you have rasa, affection, love, judgment, O Tree, take me inside you, even if for only a moment ('O Gachh, Aamakay Nao', O Tree, Take Me).[64] This urge to enter a tree, to sit inside grass, is almost to discover their phenomenological being, to enter it first through touch (as a character in Margaret Atwood's *Surfacing* does: 'I lean against the tree. I become the tree'[65]), and then, after contagion and mimesis, to allow various layers of entry.

There is a sadness in these poems, a sadness born not only of unfulfilled ambition, in this case the incomplete process of becoming a tree, but of something that is incomprehensible to both man and tree, the tragicomedy of loving in a foreign tongue, as it were. Everything he wants is inside a tree:

> O weeping willows and your expanse—
> I can hear
> the waves breaking inside you,
> the light playing lazy,
> a lonely bell ringing.
> You toy, the light of the cow-dust hour in your eyes
> has moved to the cow-dust-light lit world.
> The universe is singing inside you.
>
> Inside you is the river and its song—
> because you desire it, I run towards it.
> After that you do what you want.
> The bow's aimed at you,
> suddenly I'll send a flock of arrows your way.
>
> All around me is your misty country
> Your silence makes me restless
> On the underside of my feet affectionate kisses,
> you're the home of an unknown wet-wet desire,
> your embrace is one of two clean stony arms.
>
> Your singing, as if from the heavens,
> in which love plays softly,
> the echoing darkness of the dying evening.
> It is like this, at some dark deep hour,
> I've lifted my head to look at the horizon—
> how inside the mouth of the wind
> the ear of corn grows into fullness.[66]

Man exists on the margins of the plant world always, trying to sneak in, pleading to be allowed in to its secretive life, watching flowering and fruition as a morality play coming in instalments, intruder with the ambition to be an insider. The worlds clash, but it is such an everyday phenomenon that it evokes little surprise. In a poem about spending a night in a dakbungalow in Assam's Kaziranga, he writes about this collision be-tween the life of plants and animals in the jungle and men who have come to watch their everyday routine as a spectacle and celebrate that viewing as a carnival, with meat and alcohol and the breaking of routine morals as it were. And how do the plants react? 'The sad smell of cooked flesh brings out water—tears?—from the plants.'[67]

Jagadish Chandra Bose tried to design and create instruments that would record the behaviour of plants. Did they have a unique hand-writing? Convinced that they did, he gave it a poetic name—'Torulipi', the script of plants. The world can only imagine a torulipi, for who has ever seen a tree signing a cheque? When I read Shakti Chattopadhyay I have the sense of having seen a torulipi at last. One morning I woke up having found a Linnaean name for him in my sleep. I struck out 'Shakti Chattopadhyay' from the cover of the last volume of his collected poems and wrote this name: Gachh Shakti. Gachh Shakti, the power of trees; Tree Shakti.

Notes

1. Chattopadhyay, 'Does the Garden Recognise All its Plants?' (2014), p. 35. All quotations from Chattopadhyay's poems are my translations.
2. Chaudhuri, *Cremate Me, O Fire* (movie) (1992).
3. Chattopadhyay (2014).
4. Gangopadhyay (1995).
5. Chattopadhyay (2014).
6. Chattopadhyay (2014), introduction.
7. Gangopadhyay.
8. Sengupta, *Kobi Shakti*.
9. Ghosh, cited in Chattopadhyay (2014), introduction.
10. Ibid.
11. Ibid.
12. Ibid.
13. Ibid.
14. Ibid., 'Hemanter Aranyer Postman' (Postman in the Autumnal Forest), p. 235.
15. Ghosh, cited in Chattopadhyay (2014), introduction.
16. Roy (2017).
17. Chattopadhyay.
18. 'Buddhadeva Bose: Forty Years on' (2014).
19. Ghosh, cited in Chattopadhyay (2014), introduction.
20. Ibid.
21. Ibid.
22. Ibid.
23. Frost (1933).
24. Chattopadhyay (2014), 'Paata Aar Phooler Gawlpo' (The Story of Leaves and Flowers), p. 15.
25. Ibid.

26. Ibid.
27. Ibid., 'Prokritir Kachh Thekey' ('From Close to Nature'), *Padya Samagra*, p. 89.
28. Ibid., 'Sheeter Jatok Aami' ('I'm of the Winter Race').
29. Ibid., 'Manush Jebhaabey Dei' ('The Way Man Gives').
30. Ibid., 'Aashtey Dao' ('Let It Come').
31. Ibid., 'Gachh Kawtha Bawley' ('Trees Can Speak'), p. 206.
32. Ibid.
33. Roy (2014).
34. Chattopadhyay (2014), 'Baganer Keu Noy Nawshto Phawl' ('Not a Single Fruit in a Garden is Rotten').
35. Ibid., 'Nawshto Aekta Phawl' ('A Rotten Fruit'), Vol. 3, p. 56; 'Pawcha Nawshto Phawl Aami' ('I'm a Rotten Fruit'), Vol. 3, p. 58.
36. Ibid., 'Tawber Phoolgulo Ke Dao' ('Give It to the Flowerpots'), Vol. 1, p. 63.
37. Ibid., 'Brikkher Protiti Gronthey' ('In Every Nerve of the Tree'), Vol. 1, p. 68.
38. Ibid., 'Did You Hold Her Hand in the Garden?', Vol. 1, p. 78.
39. Ibid., 'Swarnochaapar Kachhey' ('Near the Swarnochapa Tree'), Vol. 1, p. 79.
40. Ibid., 'Bawshonto Aashey', Vol. 1, p. 89.
41. Ibid., 'Ke Baaganey' ('Who's in the Garden?'), Vol. 1, p. 110.
42. Ibid., 'Tumi shudhu nawho tomari aapon!' ('You're Dear Not Only To Yourself'), Vol. 1, p. 111.
43. Ibid., 'Chhinno Paatar Shajai Tawroni' ('With Severed Leaves I Decorate My Boat', Vol. 1, p. 112.
44. Ibid., 'Maalir Ekanto Proyojon' ('A Gardener is Utterly Necessary'), Vol. 1, p. 112.
45. Ibid., 'Hemonter Awronney Aami Postman' ('I am a Postman in the Autumnal Forest'), Vol. 1, p. 235.
46. Ibid.
47. Ibid., 'Tar Dalpaala Aamar Choitonyo' ('In Its Branches My Consciousness'), Vol. 2, p. 42.
48. Ibid., 'Prokritir Kachhey Phera' ('Returning to Nature'), Vol. 2, p. 74.
49. Ibid., 'Shikawrer Mawto Aeka' ('As Lonely as a Root'), Vol. 2, p. 200.
50. Ibid., 'Monay Monay, Gachher Shikorer Shawngey' ('In My Mind, With the Roots of a Tree'), Vol. 3, p. 120.
51. Ibid., 'Ei Shei Shingbhum, Jar Jawngoley Paharey' ('This is Shingbhum, In Whose Jungles and Mountains'), p. 120.
52. Ibid., 'Chhinnobinno', p. 120.
53. Ibid.
54. Ibid., 'Je Kishore Hridoy Boshechhey' ('The Youth Who Sits in the Heart'), Vol. 3, p. 49.
55. Ibid., 'Jwalanto Rumaal' ('The Burning Handkerchief'), p. 134.
56. Ibid., 'Gachh Kyano' ('Why Do Trees'), Vol. 2, p. 206.
57. Ibid.
58. Ibid., 'Ekhaney Kobita Peley Gachhey Gachhey Tangabo' ('If I Find Poems Here, I'll Hang it from the Trees'), Vol. 3, p. 28.
59. Ibid., 'Duti Kawthaye' ('In Two Words'), Vol. 3, p. 43.
60. Ibid., 'Upodruto Ghasher Bhetorey', Vol. 3, p. 24.
61. Ibid., 'Haratey Haratey Taakey'.
62. Ibid.,
63. Ibid., 'Manusher Moddhey Thhekey' ('Living Amidst Men').
64. Ibid., 'O Gachh, Aamakay Nao' ('O Tree, Take Me').
65. Atwood (1972).
66. Chattopadhyay (2014), 'Hey Debdarur Bistar'.
67. Ibid.

6

Satyajit Ray

Satyajit, writing about his grandfather in the introduction to Sukanta Chaudhuri's translation of his father Sukumar Ray's nonsense rhymes into English, says, 'Sukumar's father was Upendrakishore Ray, whose many-sided genius found expression in his writings, songs and illustrations as well as his work as a printer. We find in Upendrakishore a rare combination of science and the arts, the east and the west. He played the pakhwaj as well as the violin; wrote devotional songs while carrying out research in printing methods; viewed the stars through a telescope from his own rooftop; wrote old legends and folktales anew for children and pen-and-ink, using truly European techniques. His skill and versatility as an illustrator remain unmatched by any Indian.'[1] These are, of course, words of praise by the grandson, but they are also factual details that allow us an insight into the temperament of that time, when Bengalis, artists, and intellectuals, but also everyone else living in the language and its culture, were negotiating, in their own peculiar manner, the claims of European modernism and its concomitant colonialism, as well as their own tradition, that Satyajit paraphrases as 'the east and the west'.

We see this in his father Sukumar's life and career as well. After graduating in physics and chemistry (many of the illustrations in *Abol Tabol* seem like appropriations of instruments seen in science labs in college[2]), Sukumar Ray went to England to educate himself in printing technology. Soon after his return, *Sandesh*, a children's monthly, was launched by the family—Upendrakishore became its first editor. Apart from similarities in their proclivities in art, what the father and son—and, later, the grandson Satyajit—shared was the ambition to create a literature for Bengali children that was of its culture, not imported. It was a common ambition at that time—we see it in Dakkhinaranjan Majumdar, who, in his introduction to *Thakurmar Jhuli* (the grandmother's tales where we also find magical plants and potions made from them, those that cure

Plant Thinkers of Twentieth-Century Bengal. Sumana Roy, Oxford University Press. © Sumana Roy 2024.
DOI: 10.1093/9780198929314.003.0007

human infertility, a recurring theme in these stories), reveals the same ambition.[3] Rabindranath, writing a preface to this collection of folktales collected from the provinces and villages of Bengal, declares a similar ambition: 'Can there be anything more quintessentially indigenous than *Thakurmar Jhuli*? Sadly, this bag of mouth-watering tales is being supplanted by imports from England ... The worst sufferers are the children ... Can a newborn baby who is fed barley water instead of nourishing mother's milk ever grow into a healthy child?'[4]

Satyajit carries on with the same tradition when writing about his father's nonsense verse. He acknowledges the similarities between Sukumar and Lewis Carroll and Edward Lear and then quickly marks out their difference: 'The creatures in "Jabberwocky" belong to such a remote world of the imagination that they need utterly new words to describe them ... Lear, too, created many nonsense animals: the Dong, the Jumblies, the Pobble ... Their realm is virtually that of the fairy tale. The Lug-Headed Loon, on the contrary, lives in Bengal.'[5] Satyajit recognizes this easily perhaps because this is exactly his aim—his stories, even when fantastical, are placed in Bengal, a 'real' world. He also mentions his father's other important impulse: 'One of the chief purposes of Sukumar's life was to form an association of youths to revive Brahmo ideals and practices through weekly lectures and discussions. The proud history of the early Samaj inspired him; he seems to have been depressed in equal measure by certain contemporary lapses from the ideal. One detects a note of disillusionment in his late work, *Atiter Chhabi* (Pictures from the Past), a versified history of the Brahmo Samaj for children. Nowhere else in his writings do we find such a note.'[6]

Satyajit's words are important in this context—Rabindranath, Jagadish Chandra, Bibhutibhushan, Jibanananda, all of them, as I've tried to show through my reading of their work, were formed by the ideals of the Brahmo Samaj, particularly Upanishadic philosophy, but simultaneously by other currents of thought and practice. Satyajit records some of these forces through the subjects of discussion of the Manda Club that Sukumar ran with writer and scientist friends. 'The transactions of the club covered diverse matters from Plato and Nietzsche to Bankimchandra and Vivekananda, the poetry of Tagore and of the Vaishnav poets. There were also musical sessions, dinners, picnics and general merrymaking.'[7] The Vaishnav way of life, in particular, because of its rituals and a living philosophy, influenced a manner of thinking about plant life that also allowed, to use Satyajit's words, 'humour and merrymaking'.

The epigraph in *Abol Tabol* is quite unique: not only for its complete disregard for the kind of reader uninterested in entering this make-believe world, but for introducing an unfamiliar rasa, one mentioned neither by Bharata in his list of eight rasas in the *Natya Shastra*[8] nor by Abhinavagupta, who added a ninth. Sukumar Ray calls this new experience 'kheyal rasa'—a rasa bordering on the whimsical.[9] The first poem, 'Abol Tabol', makes his intent clear: 'naiko maaney naiko sur', it has neither meaning nor tune. Its rhythm is of the 'asambhab', the impossible; 'byakaron mani na', I don't care for grammar ('Khichuri').[10] Whimsy, the impossible, outside grammar, both of words and music—this is where he would play.

'Kath Buro', a poem about an old wood-man, shifts our attention to something that is usually not noticed at all: wood; yes, wood, not plant *life*, but the consequence of plant death as it were. While we—inhabitants of a world we recognize as normal and familiar, a world outside 'Abol Tabol'—eat greens, Kath Buro eats wood. He sits in the sun and licks boiled pieces of wood. His world runs to a strange causality: 'Because there are cobwebs in the sky, there are holes in wood'.[11] Kath Buro's obsession is with the holes inside dead tree trunks and branches, those that are now used as wood. Which hole tastes good, which one bad, which crack in the wood has what kind of smell—such questions occupy Kath Buro. There are others:

> He puzzled and pored over intricate sums
> Of wood that has crannies and wood that has crumbs,
> Of cracks that are bitter and cracks that are sweet,
> And cracks whose bouquet is an epicure's treat.
> One log with another he stroked and he tapped,
> Exclaiming, 'Now here's the whole picture I've mapped!
> I've given my lifetime to stumps and to sticks,
> The rascally timbers I fitly can fix,
> I know which are peaceful and which rather wild,
> The logs that are lusty and logs that are mild,
> And logs with philosophy lodged in their souls—
> The thousand-odd reasons why wood runs to holes.[12]

Sukumar makes us question the limits and limitations of botany, which is only, after all, about the personality of plants—asking questions of trees that have never been asked, about their character and personality. He is not humanizing the tree though—he is making us less anthropomorphic, and he is also subverting the scientific imagination, one perched obsessively on utilitarianism, on how scientific research can benefit human life. The holes in wood are, of course, of no benefit to man, and hence our indifference to them. The personality of logs—lusty, mild, with souls and with philosophy—would have been a continuation of Jagadish Chandra's experiments on living plants. There is both playfulness and critical thought in these queries—they make us think about the difference between plant and human life as much as the difference between life and death.

The genre of non-botanical plants that we shall meet in his son Satyajit's writing for children is introduced to the Bengali reader by Sukumar. Their distinctiveness, so different from the familiar plant world, occurs in poem after poem. In one, Bhishmolochon Sharma starts singing at the height of summer. Many things happen: the world is about to go topsy turvy because of the manner and pitch of his singing; the trees fall 'jhoop jhaap', not just dying, but making their entire species go extinct ('bongsho', dynasty rhymes with 'dhongsho', destruction, after all). In 'Chhayabaji', a poem about shadows and shadow-fighting as it were, we are given an imagined life of the relationship between trees and their shadows.

> The shadows of trees seem to utter no sound,
> We think they lie peacefully sprawled on the ground—
> But you'd be surprised if I told you the facts
> Of what my research has revealed of their acts.
> When everything's still, they will start from their sleep,
> And nuzzle around as they wander and peep.[13]

All of this might seem whimsical, as Sukumar tells us in his prefatory note to the collection of poems, but it also seems something else—a document of possibility, of alternate and unknown histories (we know too little about both shadows and plant life—our knowledge is merely scientific, nothing more). One cannot forget that his contemporaries on other continents were writing manifestos for surrealism, futurism, and dadaism. Sukumar is, without a doubt, doing the same for plant life here—if clocks can melt, why can't tree shadows 'start from their sleep'?

From time to time, hilarious and unexpected cures appear. Kumropotash (Sukanta Chaudhuri translates this as 'Pumpkin Puff'), a hybrid creature whose name indicates that it derives part of its port-manteau name from 'kumro', meaning pumpkin, while the illustration shows it to be animal-like, makes a paste of chhenchki shaag to apply on its head. It is not just these greens that are treated thus—proverbs, where received wisdom lives, are turned on their head. In 'Nyara Beltawlaye Jaaye Kawbar?', an adage based on moral instruction, that one doesn't re-peat one's mistakes, just as one with a bald or shaved head does not stand under a wood apple tree frequently, for fear of their head breaking from the hardy wood apple falling on their head, Sukumar subverts the ques-tion in a mock-statistical manner. Does the nyara stand under a wood apple tree? If yes, how many times. In our Beltala, a nyara comes to play with us approximately twenty-five days a month.[14] I paraphrase badly, of course. What Sukumar is trying to salvage, in his own humorous manner, is the reputation of the poor wood apple—why have a few species of plant life been given a bad name? He also mocks the mindless use of a few words: to 'visva', meaning 'world', a word that was coming to be over-used at that time ('Visva Bharati', 'Visva Sahitya', 'visva-bhora pran' by his friend Rabindranath, for instance), Sukumar added a most unexpected suffix—'toru'; 'visva-toru', world-tree, what did that even mean?

What is given to us through this improbable non-botanical plant world is both an alternative world for humans, only if they were able to imagine such a habitat and its rules, and a critique of social mores and conditioning, including ours in language. In 'Hulor Gaan', we are asked to imagine trees shrouded by a velvet covering in the dark night. What would this bring to the human world? It will remind us that only humans build homes that cover the sky, as if the sky were an enemy (for the tree the sky is a protector, its ceiling), of how far we have moved away from our animal life in this industrialized world, and it will show us, much be-fore Deleuze and Guattari, the artificial texture of velvet when compared to the bark, branches, and leaves of trees, none of which are 'smooth', whose beauty and function derive from friction. As someone who had been exposed to how machines were entering our daily lives, during his training as a printmaker in England, and also from the knowledge of scientific experiments at that time, his poems, couched as nonsense rhyme, are almost a warning, like Chaplin's *Modern Times*, of the intimation of technological invasion. That prescience is to be found in his creation of an imagined instrument called 'footscope', one that could scan the head for what was wrong with it; it is also to be found in the imagined new world where 'shim', broad beans, grow on neem trees. There is the cleverness of the internal rhyme of 'neem' and 'shim' there, but there is also a challenge to how the human imagination is conditioned to not accept deviant behaviour in the plant world it might otherwise accommodate among animals, including humans.

It is this unexpectedness about plant behaviour, deprived as we still are of information and understanding about plant life, dependent as we have been on scientific information alone, that Sukumar's son Satyajit imports to his writing about fantastic or non-botanical plants. Plants who think, feel, conspire, contrive, kill. Some of this does not seem so fantastical in the light of new research on plant life.[15] When I read some of this, my mind goes to something completely non-serious: a cartoon of Jagadish Chandra Bose by the painter and cartoonist Gaganendranath Tagore, nephew of Rabindranath.

The words in it, if you notice carefully, for they are hidden, are— SHAME SHAME, AGITATE, Bande Mataram.[16] The drawing and the words manifest the public response to Jagadish Chandra's experiments and conclusions about plant behaviour. 'Shame Shame' is the literal translation of 'lajja' in 'lajjabati', the tree on which Jagadish Chandra carried out many of his experiments. The instruments he designed, mocked as they were by his contemporaries, are perhaps the source for an imaginary instrument in *Abol Tabol* and some of the drawings. These ideas, many of them then just hypotheses and 'mystical' fables, particularly of colonial scientists, would have allowed both Sukumar and his son Satyajit to imagine a new planetary order for plants.

In the memoir of his childhood, writing about his holidays to Darbhanga, where his uncle and aunt lived, Satyajit mentions 'several big trees, including mango, on one side of the compound. To the left of the house, in an open space, stood another huge mango tree from which hung a swing'.[17] Below this tree, when water accumulated during the monsoons, Satyajit would float paper boats and imagine 'these boats to be the ships of the Vikings'.[18] At one level, little Satyajit is like little Opu in *Pather Panchali*, imagining an elsewhere, in time and space, but there is a primal difference—Satyajit has been raised in the city, he is largely unfamiliar with plant life and their secrets; Opu has been nourished by plant life, and is, as Bibhutibhushan takes care to remind us, almost constituted by it.[19] I make this comparison to suggest the obvious—the non-botanical plant, with powers that have to be imagined, that are not real, is a sign of the growing distance of the human from the natural world. In Shakti Chattopadhyay, it would manifest itself in the unstoppable urge to travel to forests, and in imagining and living the life of a plant; in Satyajit, and, before him, his father and grandfather, it would take a turn towards the fantastic. Upendrakishore, for instance, imagines the forest in a generic manner, without spending any energy on specificity—his forest is a sanctuary for those rejected by the human social, the reason Goopy and Bagha escape to it. 'All the people in my village are idiots. They can't appreciate good music. That is why I came to stay in the forest'.[20] It is a gentle and even benevolent forest, and, for all purposes, unreal. 'The forest had no tigers, but it did seem to have one Terrible Beast! Bagha hadn't seen it, but he had heard it roar in the distance!'[21] The Terrible Beast turns out to be Goopy's singing. It is not animals that we see but ghosts, kind as they are, granting boons. It is a fantastic forest, a place 'for rest' for humans, both living and dead.

δ

Rabindranath, a friend of Upendrakishore's, is said to have written this note in little Satyajit's diary:

> It took me many days, it took me many miles;
> I spent a great fortune, I travelled far and wide,
> To look at all the mountains,
> And all the oceans, too.
> Yet, I did not see, two steps away from home,
> Lying on a single stalk of rice:
> A single drop of dew.[22]

One notices the metaphor from plant life—the single stalk of rice—and what the little boy would make of it in his career. Also, these words, with their quality of the parable, are useful to understand the artistic ambition and ambit of Satyajit—he would make a life from Bengal, and he would turn even the most fantastical, plants or places or people, Bengali.

'Sukumar named this special vein of nonsense the rasa or spirit of whimsy. Needless to say, it is not one of the nine rasas of Indian dramatic theory. There are traces of such whimsy in the folk poetry of any nation. But authentic literary nonsense masks its caprice beneath an apparent gravity in an urbane and sophisticated manner unknown in popular rhyme.'[23] What Satyajit writes about Sukumar is true of his own work when it comes to his writing on plant life—the kheyal rasa. It's almost as if he has access to what has become a well-circulated title: the *secret* life of plants. He communicates an intuitive awareness of the mysteries that surround plant life, something unknown or not yet known to humans. In them is pharmakon, both cure and poison.

But first the stories of cure, as in 'The Magic Moonlight Flower', for instance.[24] Our interest in both 'magic' and 'moonlight', inhabitants of the non-materialist world, is founded on our half-knowledge about them—we know and do not know enough. And hence their appropriation in our poetry—Satyajit imports that sense of mystery and magic in one of the last zones where this has been preserved, in the plant world. When old Balaram falls ill in the 'The Magic Moonlight Flower' story, the doctor prescribes only one possible cure: 'He has to be given the juice of moonlight leaves . . . Nothing else will cure him. The classic name of this plant is Lunani. And the disease is called miseria.'[25] Miseria, as the name indicates, is a form of depression, being miserable; and 'Lunani', quite obviously, derives from 'lunacy'. Balaram's 17-year-old son Kanai is the only person who can save him, but it isn't easy, for the moonlight plant is not to be found 'anywhere and everywhere'.

'You'll have to go to the forest of Badra. There's an ancient abandoned temple there. Twenty-five feet to its north is a moonlight plant. But it's almost ten miles away, can you go all that way?' the doctor tells Kanai. His father is the only person Kanai has in this world, and therefore no task seems difficult when it's about his father's health. There is only one hitch however—how is he to identify this strange moonlight plant? The doctor helps him with identifying characteristics: 'It has small, pointed, purple leaves, yellow flowers and a bewitching fragrance. You can smell it twenty feet away. Its scent can beat the amaranth of paradise hands down'.[26] In other words, everything that the common rose or marigold or hibiscus is not. There is of course nothing extraordinary about cures for all kinds of human ailments coming from plant life, a source that inspires many of the stories in *Thakurmar Jhuli*, of which this story by Satyajit seems to be a descendant. There is also Ayurveda, an entire knowledge system about the curative properties of leaves and flowers, stems and roots. But Satyajit exoticizes this domestic relationship between plants and home-grown doctors when he gives the moonlight plant a combination of over-whelming characteristics—purple leaves (how many plants have purple leaves?; is he thinking of the inchplant, that is also called the wandering jew?; is there a reason he is choosing purple leaves?), yellow flowers, be-witching fragrance.

The young Kanai manages to get to the forest of Badra—twenty-five yards inside it, a whiff of that bewitching fragrance gets to him. He is re-lieved that the cure is at last at hand, but suddenly a voice calls out to him, 'You won't get what you want here'.[27] It is an old man, who lives in a peculiar cycle of remembering and forgetting. He knows, for instance, without Kanai's telling, why the boy is here, but he forgets other things. From him comes the piece of information that leaves Kanai devas-tated: 'The minister and soldiers of Rupsha have taken the plant away. Rupsha's citizens are all ill with miseria. People die in twenty days of starvation after their limbs waste away. The juice of the moonlight leaf is the only possible cure'.[28] But Rupsha is sixty miles away. And so, the kind old man gives Kanai 'three round objects—one red, one blue, one yellow'. Ray is again using colour in the most tautological way—where else but in plant life would one find such a surfeit of colours? The red one is a fruit: 'By eating this you will be able to run thrice as fast as a deer'.[29] 'All three of these are fruits', though the old man cannot remember what makes the other two precious.[30] The old man also gives him a seashell—it is a version of the cell phone; Kanai can speak to the wise man whenever he is in need of help. It is as if it's coded in the category: fruit, both noun and verb, in Bangla, must bring rewards, and what greater reward than a cure? (Satyajit is using this utilitarian idea of fruit just as his contem-porary Shakti Chattopadhyay wanted to subvert it in his poems.) Not just fruit, but red fruit.

The red fruit works its magic and Kanai is soon in Rupsha where he is struck by the beauty and splendour of the clothes in the market, their joyous weave a contrast to the sullen and morbid faces of the traders. He asks a shopkeeper, 'Why are all of you so serious? You're doing very good business so why don't you look happy?'[31]

The people in Rupsha have been afflicted by an epidemic, 'an epidemic of miseria. It's only affected the weaver's colony so far, but how long before it spreads? The weavers are all wasting away and dying because they cannot eat.'[32] Kanai is surprised because the moonlight plant, stolen from the forest of Badra, is already in Rupsha. Why are its people wasting away then? He soon finds out that the king of Rupsha is a despot and that he wants the weavers to die because they wanted to replace him with his kind son.

A series of adventures follow. Kanai manages to sneak into the royal garden full of flowers of all kinds, but he can't find the moonlight plant. His quest is short-lived because the guards capture him and put him in jail. After three miserable days in prison, Kanai hears a feeble voice coming from the seashell—the old man has suddenly remembered the function of the blue fruit. It will make him invisible. Along with this comes another important piece of information: 'a trader had sold the king an emerald for one hundred thousand gold coins seven years ago. This emerald is set into the necklace around the king's neck. It's a magic emerald and the root cause of all the evil in the state.'[33]

Blue fruit. How many blue fruits do we know? But, because we don't know any, or too many, we cannot become invisible. A personal anecdote about the colours of these fruits might help our understanding of where this might have come to Satyajit: 'The ink he (Chhoto Kaka) used to write in his diary was of four different colours—red, blue, green and black. Sometimes he used all four colours to write just one sentence. There was a reason why he switched from one colour to another, but I could never grasp it fully. All I could fathom was that descriptions of nature were to be written in green, and all nouns had to be in red.'[34]

Soon Kanai uses the invisibility fruit and gets to the prison chamber of Kishore, the young prince who has been imprisoned by his father for suggesting that the leaves of the moonlight plant be used to save the lives of the sad weavers of Rupsha. Another three days, and Kanai manages to escape from the prison with Kishore. But the moonlight plant has still not been found, and his father and the weavers of Rupsha are wasting away. It is then that Jagai-baba, the old man from the forest of Bhadra, calls on Kanai's seashell: 'Listen carefully, Kanai, this is important. You must go to the north-west corner of the garden of the inner chambers of the royal palace in the first hour of daylight tomorrow. The moonlight plant has been planted in a little island in this part of the garden.'[35]

The next morning, Kanai does find his way to the north-west corner of the garden, but a king cobra has wound itself around the precious plant and the moat encircling the little island is full of alligators. But there is the invisibility fruit—and so Kanai manages to uproot the moonlight plant. He takes a leaf and leaves the plant in the care of the poor boy Gopal. His father has to be saved—the purple leaf yields a purple juice and, after drinking it, Kanai's father is instantly revived. The young boy is back in Rupsha, where, to his happy surprise, there is smile and laughter in the weaver's colony, except on the face of one boy, the prince Kishore.

For the king has the disease too, miseria. Kanai agrees to cure the king on one condition, that he would go on a pilgrimage immediately after he is cured. After that, Kishore becomes the king and Kanai is made minister. But he is ignorant and young and inexperienced. Jagai-baba comes to the rescue again: the yellow fruit is still with Kanai, 'it will multiply your knowledge and understanding a thousand times.'[36] And good times begin for everyone.

That miseria, quite clearly a form of depression, almost mass depression, might be an early manifestation of what we know as 'climate change fatigue' does not seem like a far-fetched interpretation when one realizes that its cure is in plant life—the intimacy and proximity of plant life. Plant altruism, the ethic and behaviour that is the axis of this story, is not Satyajit's invention. It is there in folk traditions of most cultures, as we see in many stories in *Thakurmar Jhuli*. It is there in Satyajit's grandfather's stories as well: in the story 'Dukhiram', Sulakshan 'possesses a wondrous mango seed . . . As soon as the seed was planted, a sapling would appear and then grow rapidly into a tree. It would bear mangoes, which would ripen instantly and would be ready to eat! Best of all, one could take the seed out from beneath the tree and use it again';[37] in the 'Monkey Prince', eating the mangoes left by a sage for the childless king's seven queens leads to their bearing a child each;[38] in 'The Ghandosaur's Tale', which might have been an influence on Satyajit's story about the magic moonlight tree, the daughter of a king 'needs the juice of a lemon to get better',[39] but 'there was only one lemon tree in one farmer's garden in the whole kingdom! The tree had just started bearing fruit that year. And the lemons of that tree were no ordinary lemons. Each of them was as big as a pumpkin! None of you have ever seen or tasted lemons like those.'[40] In the same story, a boat is made from 'magical wood'.[41] Satyajit took care to make the taste of the cure—'medicine'—attractive to children, his target reader. This might have been from his own memory: 'As a child, I could not swallow pills whole. Once, before a visit to Dhaka, I was obligated to chew some quinine pills. Even after all these years, I can feel its horrible bitter taste lingering in my mouth'.[42] Reading this, as I was reminded of Bibhutibhushan's thoughts about the sweetness one finds in plant life, and how children, in particular, derive delight from it, I also thought about the colours of the fruits Satyajit had chosen for his story, red and yellow and purple, and how Bharata had identified them with certain rasas in *Natya Shastra*—yellow, a colour that keeps recurring in these stories, Bharata associates with adbhuta, the rasa of wonder.

δ

Like his father, Satyajit's plant thinking challenges human logic and colonial science.

Pharmakon is not just cure; it is also poison. And hence 'Beeshphool'.[43]

Jaganmoy-babu, a man taking a holiday in a non-touristy town, is greeted by a young boy's warning, 'Don't go that way, babu'. A little investigation soon reveals that on the other side of the road is a 'beesh gachh', a plant with poisonous flowers.

The little boy, whose name it turns out is 'Bhagwan', god, has a strange conversation with Jaganmoy-babu:

What's the name of the tree?
I don't know.
How do you know that it's poisonous?
They die . . .
What?
Snakes, frogs, rats . . . birds . . .

But how do they die? When they sit on the plant? Or if they eat
  the fruit?

If you go near it.

Near? How near?

Four arms away. Or five. Char haat.

You are a great yarn spinner, I see. Or do you smoke ganja at this age?
  Ask your schoolmaster. No flowering plant produces this kind of
  poison . . . I am new to this place. I'm not well, do you understand?
  Stop bluffing. No one's heard of such flowers in this land.

It's not desi. Saheb had brought it here.

. . . Which sahib?

The house that you are staying in here, he stayed in the same place.

When was he here?

The year before the famine.

What's his name?

I don't know his name. Red-faced, blonde hair.

He planted it here on this heap?

I don't know.

Then?

This plant grew only after he left. You see the forest there, he used to
  roam around there with a glass in his hand.[44]

Jaganmoy-babu takes the Englishman to be a botanist and would perhaps have spent more time idling on the thought had the boy not drawn
his attention to the skin of a snake, one 'killed' by the poison plant. He
inspects the plant and its flowers with his binoculars: yellow flowers
speckled with purple, and on that purple, tiny blotches of orange and
white and black. What was it about the purple and yellow colours in
plants that made Satyajit view them as possessing uncommon attributes?
The purple and yellow moonlight plant had cured people of miseria, and
now this plant, which was killing animals in its proximity.

Suddenly I found that I had become the Jaganmoy-babu of the story.
Like him, I was curious to know whether there were more plants like
these. It turns out that there indeed are. Where? In the forest. Was it really
possible, I began to wonder like Jaganmoy-babu, that a plant could 'ex-
hale' poisonous air? That these stories could only have been written in
the post-Jagadish Bose era is self-evident: if a plant was indeed a living

thing, if it responded to external stimuli, surely it could do other things as well? Plants need not be thought to be unconditionally benign creatures.

Jaganmoy-babu wasn't, in fact, even supposed to take a holiday in Kathjhumri ('Kath' in the name stands for wood). A bachelor with a reasonably handsome income, he had recently been diagnosed with a mild breathing disorder, and his well-wishers had, after scolding him for being a miser, suggested taking a holiday in a 'dry place'. A nephew had suggested an old bungalow owned by a Britisher as a possible resting house, and the late owner's wife, Mrs Moore, had accepted the proposal. Three days after settling into his holiday, Jaganmoy-babu is pleased with himself: the climate has helped him feel better; it is a blessing to be away from the train-tram-telephone life; Calcuttans are too homebound. He is happy with everything except the niggling question about the 'poison flower'. And hence his questions to various people: to the chowkidar who confirms that there indeed are poisonous flowers in this part of the world, and to Pabitra-babu, a tourist like himself, who even describes the flowers to him. 'This is my fourth visit to the town. I've noticed it for the last two years—the first time was when I saw a pig lying next to one such plant.' Why hasn't he written about it in the papers? asks Jaganmoy-babu. 'What is there to say? Nature has its own vagaries—can one write about them in the papers? There are thousands of poisonous fruits and insects and birds. You live in Calcutta, where the air is so poisonous that you are losing five seconds of your life with every breath. In that context, should one worry about such poisonous flowers at all?' replies Pabitra-babu.[45]

The story 'ends' with the discovery that it was only a plot by the writer to get rid of Jaganmoy-babu, so that he could stay in the bungalow where he has been spending a few months every year for the last decade. When Jaganmoy-babu gets off the train, he sees the same plant. There are three goats near it, all alive.

δ

The botanist is a recurring figure in Satyajit's stories, as it is in many stories of his contemporaries. The curiosity and wonder about plants and those who studied them was a mark of the times. In his memoir, he recounts: 'Sometimes, we used to visit the house of Sir Jagadish Bose. He also lived in Upper Circular Road, only a short distance away. Jagadish

Bose was a very famous scientist, having proved that plants have life, and had received a knighthood for this. However, we went to his house not to look at him, but to see the little zoo by the side of his garden.[46] Jagadish Bose comes up in 'The Hungry Septopus'. A botanist comes to visit an old acquaintance after many years. They had gone shooting together in the forests of Assam a long time ago. Now the hunter is a writer—Satyajit is, of course, taking a dig at the literary life that awaits former hunters, an old tradition since Jim Corbett. The botanist has, since then, spent many years in America, writing and researching about plant life. He's added specimens from his travels in the Americas to his greenhouse. Now he's come to the hunter-turned-writer Parimal for help. Talking about food, the hunter's rejection of hunting but not eating animals, the botanist Kanti-babu says, 'Do you think vegetables and greens, don't have life?' To this Parimal says,

'Yes, of course they do. Thanks to you and Jagadish Bose, I have to always remember this. But are plants and animals the same?'

'Do you think they are very dissimilar?'

'Aren't they different? Say, for instance, plants can't walk, they can't make any sound, they can't express their mind—in fact, one doesn't even know whether they have something like a mind.'[47]

Satyajit uses this seemingly inconsequential chatter to set up two things: the cultural environment of speaking and thinking about plant life; to expose, as it were, that plants do indeed have life, and that they can do all the things that Parimal believes they can't.

When Parimal visits Kanti-babu's house with his friend Abhi and dog Badshah, they are shown various species of plants. Satyajit spends a lot of energy naming and describing carnivorous plants. We see insects being eaten by the pitcher plant, the Venus flytrap, plants with teeth—all of this is only a preface to what Parimal, his friend, and the reader shall soon see. Locked in a separate workshop-like space is a tree that scares them: Kanti-babu calls it Septopus ('seven passes', he explains), its bark is smooth and brown, with marks on it. It is sleeping, says Kanti-babu, and explains why he believes it is a tree: it grows from the earth after all. He found it in Nicaragua, where locals call it the Devil Tree, he's seen it eat monkeys there, now he feeds it dead rats and other dead animals found on neighbouring streets. Kanti-babu then discloses the reason for inviting Parimal to his house—Septopus tasted human flesh a couple of days ago, the arm of the botanist's assistant, and it is possible he might turn into a man-eating tree. A terrifying situation follows: Septopus eats up the dog Badshah and attacks Abhi. Parimal shoots at the tree Septopus's 'head'.

Satyajit uses the miniature model of the pitcher plant to imagine Septopus—the pitcher plant is amplified in the body of Septopus, so that the 'pitcher' where the tree puts its food becomes Septopus's mouth, and so on. Jagadish Bose, new research on plant intelligence, all of these annotate our reading of the man-eating tree today. More than anything else, though, it sometimes seems that were trees capable of feeling revenge, we might have all been Badshahs today. As elsewhere in his plant stories, this one, too, is a tale of foreboding—of a world outside the control of science and the infrastructure of the human mind, and one where trees will outlast us as a species.

In 'Shobuj Manush', we find a reversal of this trope—I'm not completely sure whether it can be called reversal though.[48] Abanish and Narayan Bhandarkar, professors of botany and philosophy respectively, are friends. Abanish, who is also the narrator of the story, says this about himself: 'My world is the world of plants. In other words, I'm a botanist. Most of my day is spent here, in this greenhouse. The collection of the rarest orchids and cactuses that I have in my greenhouse is, in all likelihood, not available anywhere in India.'[49] Professor Bhandarkar, who'd been a student at Santiniketan when Rabindranath was alive, had spent his life and career, both emotional and intellectual, in living and preaching what was an idea and spirit common to that time: 'visva-maitri', literally 'world friendship', or a friendship among everyone, without any kind of discrimination on the basis of their social identities. Now, just back from attending a philosophy conference in Upsala, he tells Abanish that he's met someone there who's changed his worldview—he now realizes that the idea of world friendship is implausible because of basic differences between humans: how can there be similarities between the Aryan and the Mongoloid, the Nordic and the Polynesian, those from an equatorial climate and those who are desert people? Their physiognomy and environments are different—how can they think and feel in a similar way?

An argument follows, after which Bhandarkar leaves, but not before his left hand is brushed by a cactus. 'I will never forget the blood on his hand, because it was green in colour. I cannot say how long I sat in my greenhouse after Bhandarkar's departure. I couldn't sleep last night. After going to my favourite greenhouse this morning, I find no reason to live. I saw that none of my plants are alive, not a single one. Not only that, along with their lives, they have also lost their colour – green. What remains is that bland colour of ash'. [50] This reversal, not of the plant killing the human, but human malice, manifesting itself in the changed colour of blood, from red to green, killing plant life, an entire universe, a microcosm, as symbolized by the greenhouse, seems like prescience—Satyajit is telling us of the times we are now living in, of hatred between humans, identity wars, and also of a plant-less world, destroyed by the human touch. What I've taken from the story is also why green, the colour of the plant world, has come to be a semiotic for jealousy.

δ

Unlike the many humanists whose writing often supplied the germ for his films, Bibhutibhushan's for instance, Satyajit's relationship with 'nature' was one that came from a place of suspicion. Anything associated with plant life, even a scarecrow in an agricultural field, planted to keep birds away, is invested with a percentage of fear. Mystery, magic, medicine, murder: these would be his appraisal of the plant world. Plants and trees and flowers and fruits are foreign in his universe: in that sense, his gaze upon this half-understood botanical life is like a child's, viewed with wonder and unannotated curiosity. In his stories, meant as much for adults as they were for children, he often invested plant life with the paranormal. In the story 'Kagtaruya' ('Scarecrow'), Mriganka-babu, a famous writer, is invited to Durgapur for a felicitation ceremony. Train reservations are difficult to get, and so the writer decides to drive to the countryside. He stops at a place to take a smoke—from the roadside, standing beside his car, he watches out onto the beauty of the countryside. That beauty is of course only the beauty of plant life: fields of yellow mustard, a lonely tamarind tree, no guest except the breeze, no human habitation, nothing resembling humans except a scarecrow standing in the middle of the field.

Mriganka-babu is annoyed with his friend for having put him through this trouble. He wishes for the presence of a fellow human to help him with some fuel so that he can carry on with the journey, but he can't see anyone except what looks like a 'fake human' to him. But that is only the scarecrow—Mriganka-babu pities birds for their low intelligence that makes them feel scared of this still creature. That's the difference between dogs and birds, he thinks to himself. And though Satyajit doesn't say it, I can't help the thought from coming to me: do the plants who the scarecrows guard know the difference between real humans and them?

Though he cannot really be certain, Mriganko-babu notices a slight change in the 'appearance' of the scarecrow—it looks a little more 'alive'; are those legs really made of bamboo? And then suddenly the bamboo legs begin to move, the scarecrow begins to walk, and then talk. Instead of the clay pot for a face, the scarecrow now has a human head.

'Babu', the scarecrow suddenly calls out.

A shiver runs through the writer's body. It is the voice of Abhiram, his old servant. Yes, he remembers, the man was a native of these parts.

'Do you recognise me?' the scarecrow-servant asks the writer.

'Yes, I do. From your shirt', replies the writer. 'I'd given it to you, didn't I?'

'Yes, you did', replies Abhiram. 'You've done a lot for me, babu, but why did it turn out like that in the end? It wasn't my fault. Why didn't you believe me then?'[51]

It all comes back to Mriganka-babu—how this trusted servant of twenty years was accused of stealing a wristwatch, and, in spite of his pleas and protestations, was fired from his job. Abhiram says that he didn't take up a job after returning to his village. He died soon after, and his son began wearing this shirt. When it began to tear, the shirt was given to the scarecrow. Abhiram decided to become a scarecrow after his death for he was certain that Mriganka-babu would come this way once and he'd be able to clear his name of the accusation of theft. The dead can see things that the living are incapable of, he says, and so he instructs the writer to go back home and look for his watch behind the almirah where it has been lying for the last three years.

The driver returns with enough petrol to start the car, Mriganka-babu realizes that he'd fallen asleep with the notebook in his hands. When he returns home, he finds the watch—yes, it was lying exactly where the scarecrow said it was, behind the almirah.

The shadow between the real and fanciful is so thin that one cannot be sure where the scarecrow actually is—on the agricultural field or inside the writer's head alone. The scarecrow is a divisive figure: it is fearsome to birds but a protector of plants. Satyajit, even when he is only writing tangentially about plants, exhibits this compulsive urge to embed that universe with an element of mystery: was the scarecrow really a ghost of the servant Abhiram or had the writer imagined all of it in his dream? Like the plants that the scarecrow guarded, we shall never know.

In 'Kutum Katam', a banker finds a branch of wood that resembles a dog and brings it home. And then the branch of wood comes to life in this horror story.[52] Satyajit was, quite obviously, borrowing the title of his story and the idea of turning tree branches into works of art from Abanindranath Tagore. In the spirit of 'found art' of those times, Abanindranath had started collecting discarded branches of trees, seeds, and roots into sculptures, particularly into animals.[53] The name 'kutum katam'—'kutum' means relative and 'katam' would imply an association with 'cutting'—was his name for found art, and Satyajit would have noticed it during his time in Santiniketan, and, later, as decoration pieces in middle-class houses in Calcutta. It is fascinating to see how an art form, on which Satyajit bases his story, can also be seen as a premonition of the time to come, almost a century later, when perhaps only wood would remain, and, from it, the only animals that can be created, for all else would be gone, a reiteration of the relationship between our literary history and ecological history.

δ

The plant kingdom offered both medicine and cure, and especially in his stories for children, Satyajit liked to play around that binary. In his famous series of stories about the scientist Professor Shonku, for instance, he took his young readers to islands and other imaginary places where unfamiliar plant life grew. *Munroe Dweep* (*Munroe Island*) begins with a note written on 13 December 1622. 'We have discovered a strange kind of plant life on this island, one that can bring about revolutionary changes to human life because of its elixir-like qualities. Blackhole Brandon is the monarch of this island now ... If any team or group comes to collect this plant from this island, it must be ready to fight Brandon.'[54] The letter is signed by Hector Munro.

Time present is set in Skeleton Coast, Namibia. A few men are discussing this letter and researching the shipwrecks on 1622. A young man by the name of David Munro introduces himself to this research group—he's been reading about shipwrecks in Shakespeare's time and wants to write about it. When they reach Munroe Island at last, one of them notices the absence of birds on the island. Another gets fever. While Professor Shonku and the team are setting up their equipment, David Munro decides to take a walk through the island with his dog. The equipment senses the presence of something 'large' in their vicinity—that curiosity, abetted by an unfamiliar fragrance, leads them to the trees on which grow miraculous fruits. When the man who is down with fever is given one, he recovers immediately: the fruit has a miraculous combination of vitamins and other minerals that can cure the human body of ailments.

It is, however, not only the miraculous plants that Professor Shonku's team finds on the island. Littered all over the island are skeletal remains of animals, including birds. This leads them to conclude that there must be a cannibalistic animal on the island. One of them is attacked, and eventually they manage to find a way to the cave where they are surprised by the presence of human skulls and Hector Munro's diary. In the cave are also boxes full of gold coins, remains of a loot. Professor Shonku concludes that after Munro, pirates had arrived on the island, and being ill, they stopped to took shelter. They must have discovered the miracles of the unique fruit and discovered a way to disease-free and almost never-ending life.

But who was the monster that was feeding on birds and humans and other animals? An encounter in the cave brings out the truth and the 'monster', and only Professor Shonku recognizes him: it is Blackhole Branden from the seventeenth century. The miraculous elixir-like fruits of the island had kept him alive until this day, when a gunshot kills him.

Stories like these, that illustrate the magical quality of plant life, are almost typical of the Satyajit of the children's stories. In *Sapno Dweep* (*Dream Island*)—and it's a trope, how the magic is, almost in a Shakespearean manner, placed on an island, with the nature-culture binary snuck in—Professor Shonku is troubled by dreams of an island filled with the most extraordinary plant life. (In the comic book based on this story, the images of the island would remind one of Gauguin's representations of plant life in Tahiti.) Soon after, news arrives about the disappearance of seven famous scientists from Manila, Philippines. Professor Shonku was one of the invitees to the science symposium there, but, being busy with his experiments, he had had to cancel his trip. But he decides to go there now—along with the intent of helping to locate the missing scientists, there is also the urge to find out more about the 'dream island' that has been appearing in his dreams.

Eventually Professor Shonku sets sight on the island, one that his co-traveller calls a 'rainbow island', where the colour of the sand is purple. (Purple—Satyajit's rasa of magic and mystery.) 'When we leave, we must remember to carry a few of these outrageously colourful plants for our garden in Calcutta', says the co-traveller. The professor notices that he feels lighter in his head and all his scientific problems look geared towards a solution. It is then that he notices that the plants are dying in one part of the island.

The professor and his mate are surprised by the lack of smell on the island—there is neither any foul smell nor any fragrance, in spite of the presence of such colourful plant life. They find a pair of glasses that Shonku identifies as belonging to Sidney, and a little later they find the scientist Hamida with his hands inside his walking shoes, walking on all fours. Before he is able to find out the reason for such childlike behaviour, Shonku has fallen into the trap himself: all around him are the seven scientists singing and dancing to lullabies and child rhymes, one reciting 'Jack and Jill went up the hill', another jumping into the sea to the beat of 'Baa baa black sheep, have you any wool?'. A funnel shaped flower lands on Shonku's head and the results are near hallucinogenic: one flower over another comes to rest on the professor's head, and it's like a happy drug that soon puts him to sleep.

Florona, the island, is almost immediately swallowed by the sea. When they get back home to Bengal, Professor Shonku finds out that besides the eight scientists, there were several scholars and intellectuals who had the same dream about the colourful island of Florona. Why these grownup men were behaving like children on the island will forever remain a mystery. These scientists have been able to regain most of their memory and intellect over the last three months, but no trace of that island has been found in spite of several underwater searches. The name 'Florona', deriving as it does from 'flora', is a sign of Satyajit's belief in the plant world being a secret world, not accessible through reason alone.

How Abinash ('Abinash' means something that cannot be destroyed), the professor's friend, managed to remain unaffected also remains a mystery. This man, whose lifelong ambition had been to accompany Professor Shonku on an expedition, managed to do something really significant though: he has carried a petal from the flower that had sat on Shonku's head and turned him into a happy child. The scientist reveals that the 'anatomy' of the petal is terribly complex, and is similar to the structure of a human brain. Shonku speculates that Florona might have been debris from a planet, and then observes how in spite of the passage of so many months, the colour of the 'petal' remains unchanged. Abinash-babu, his friend, coaxes Shonku into 'killing' the petal with 'Annihilin', a variety of gun invented by the Professor himself. The story ends with a piece of friendly advice from Abinash-babu: don't stress your brain so much that it becomes an easy nest for wayward thoughts; look at me, the flowers couldn't make a home on my head. In a story such as this one, Satyajit posits two kinds of Other against the human—the extraterrestrial and the plant world. In them there is the same impulse: a tragic unknowability. Perhaps it is this that makes him subvert the conventional iconography of the tree root as the equivalent of the human head: in the rainbow-coloured flowers is the human brain's perfect equivalent.

Reading some of the Professor Shonku stories, and the unnatural colours described in them, I wondered whether they had come to Satyajit from his great uncle Kuladaranjan, whom he called 'Dhon Dadu'. His 'main occupation was enlarging photographs', and little Satyajit noticed how he was able to not only enlarge faces from group photographs, particularly after the person's death, but to make black and white photographs reveal the unexpected colours of life in them: 'on one occasion, I remember he was able to bring out the green in the surrounding plants.'[55]

δ

Satyajit would go to the forest to make his films, released in successive years—*Goopy Gyne Bagha Byne*, in 1969, and *Aranyer Din Ratri*, in 1970. Both the films were based on stories by other writers—the first by his grandfather, the second by Sunil Gangopadhyay. The forests in the films, though, couldn't be more dissimilar. Ray's first film for children was shot mostly in Rajasthan—the forest is an interlude, even an excuse, and, quite honestly, Goopy and Bagha could have met the ghosts and their king anywhere. The forest gives it background and history—the background of colonialism, the different kinds of ghosts, the 'foreign' ghosts, and the confrontation of afterlives: there are many tree ghosts in the forest, for the forest allows the dead to live with the living in a way human social spaces don't—only the living are allowed residency, it's called 'living quarters', after all. In the end, though, it is the ghosts of humans we remember from these scenes, not the trees, which, in its faithfulness to Upendrakishore's story, remain generic.

Aranyer Din Ratri, a film released a year after *Goopy Bagha*, is based on an autobiographical novel.[56] Sunil Gangopadhyay writes about a trip he took with his friends to the forests of Palamau. One cannot read Sunil Gangopadhyay's novel without the awareness—and sometimes even the baggage—of a hundred years of Bengalis writing about their encounters with and in the forest. There's Sanjib Chandra Chattopadhyay's *Palamau*, one of the first books in the genre, and there's also a novel like *Kapalkundala* by his brother, Bankim Chandra Chattopadhyay.[57]

The forest becomes a bohemian's retreat in *Aranyer Din Ratri*—the four friends, separated by economic class and the ambit of their desires, almost force their way into a government forest bungalow. During their stay they discover two kinds of women, set up almost as binaries: the sophisticated Bengali women, those who read books, listen to cricket commentary on the radio, sing, and debate, and Doli, a forest dweller. The woman of the forest has always been a luxuriant patriarchal metaphor, whether in *Kapalkundala* or in *Aranyer Din Ratri*. The forest becomes a dope for the men, their sexual freedom, and their becoming 'jungli', a Bangla word that means 'wild' and even 'unrestrained', one that derives, evidently, from 'jungle'—it is telling that the city dwellers become 'jungli', one of the men trying to trick and rape Doli. As I've said elsewhere, 'Untamed and unfamiliar flowers often have their characteristics described as "*buno*", forest like. This falls in line the common idiom of forests living on the margins of civilisation. The presence of trees, for some inexplicable reason, seems to skin away the human's accrued and conditioned reserves of civility and sophistication to turn them beast-like. What is it about forests that make men reverse the evolutionary path temporarily, to become more animal as it were? Is it the forest's ambivalence about hiding and revealing that abet men on to become ancient versions of themselves?'[58] The jarring inequality is presented to us by Satyajit—the forest dweller willingly takes on the role of the servant, cleaning the room, buying groceries, all for a pitiful sum of money. Satyajit, who took liberty with Sunil Gangopadhyay's story in his script, would have been acting as much from the spirit of the novel as he would have been from his memory of *Aranyak*, where the narrator Satya says:

> Whatever history that India had, became subsequently the history of this Aryan civilisation—the history of the vanquished non-Aryan races was not written down anywhere, or perhaps, it was written only in such secret mountain caves, in the darkness of forests, in the lines of calcified skeletal remains. The victorious Aryan had never been anxious to decipher that script. To this day, the vanquished wretched tribes continue to be ignored, shunned and disdained. Aryans, proud of their civilisation, had never spared them a glance, never sought to understand their way of life and they do not try to do so even now.[59]

When I think of the film, I remember the tree near the well, close to the forest bungalow where the men from Calcutta are staying. It is, for want of a better word, majestic, and gives the sense of being watchman and time-keeper. Satyajit's camera rests on it as a side glance often. Then there are the trees of the forest, tall and spear-like, poking the sky—we never see their ends—which seem to move with his camera, as they look for the man who's been struck by a male forest dweller. The trees close in, shrinking space—suddenly the freedom one associates with the forest has disappeared.

Satyajit's contemporary Ritwik Ghatak used trees in his cinematic frames in a way that has perhaps never been done in Indian cinema. It is possible to identify almost each of his films with a particular tree or, at least, a particular frame of a tree. What were these filmmakers trying to do? Was it pathetic fallacy alone, particularly as it played out in the melo-dramatic and epical tradition of Ritwik's cinema, that they were using trees—or even grass and tea plantations, as Ritwik did in the picturization of 'Akash bhawra shurjyo tara'—to show the unease of humans?[60]

δ

What about the botanical imagination among Satyajit Ray's contemporaries in Bangla literature? Mahasweta Devi, in her short story 'Arjun', turns the tree into a political space—a local political leader, who uses both violence and financial power to control a 'tribal' population in Purulia, largely dependent on forest resources, needs the arjun tree to be cut.[61] Lies by one group, gossip by another, the invocation of its significance to the forest dwellers, all of these circulate. The ancient tree is cut, and, with it, a thought system and pre-colonized archive of plant life is gone. Syed Mustafa Siraj's story 'Gachh-ta Bolechhilo' ('The Tree Said') is about a tree that speaks in its own dialect—while it reminds one about Jagadish Bose's desire to record the plant script, this one is not necessarily audible to everyone, as if to remind the reader that there should be a shared language between plants and humans.[62] Whether the arjun tree as political site or the prescience of plant life that can predict death, or the aswattha in Bimal Kar's story with that title, where a sacred fig seems to control a woman's relationship with her family, we see the rise of a non-botanical imagination, one that is close to Satyajit's, where plants are imagined beyond the scientific and spiritual.[63] Simultaneous with this is the emergence of the figure of the botany professor, such as we see in Bimal Kar's story 'Udbhid' ('Tree'), and a questioning of the space of the garden,[64] both in this story and in Subodh Ghosh's 'Cactus', where we observe, with dismay, disappointment, and disbelief, a retired judge's obsession with growing a Latin American cactus, bought for quite a significant sum of money, how his desire to have a beautiful garden makes him indifferent to the plight of humans.[65] The garden is critiqued in these stories and also obliquely, such as in Satyajit's 'Piku', a place where human control is so visible that it indulges greed and lust more than calm.[66] Then there are stories such as Banaphool's 'The Tree' and Narayan Sanyal's 'Gachh Ma' ('The Mother Tree'), based on Shel Silverstein's parable about the apple tree, that were already in circulation, stories that, while based on the morality that could be quite easily derived from the plant world, also encouraged new ways of looking, beyond both the Romantic and the functional.[67] Satyajit was, therefore, only part of a new cultural climate of moving beyond the botanical, beyond beauty that was to be had from the natural world, beyond an understanding of a gentle plant world, as we find in Bibhutibhushan, to one that could turn hostile. Bangla literature was moving towards the apocalyptic tone, a movement that can be seen in many literary and cinematic cultures across the world at that time.

δ

For a moment I think of the tree in Satyajit's sketch book. No, it is not his drawing. It is by his 'Leela Pishi'.[68] I also think of his teachers at Kala Bhavan, Nandalal Bose and Benode Bihari Mukhopadhyay, whom Satyajit often credited for his visual imagination, and their relationships with trees. It was Satyajit, who, while making a distinction between Eastern and Western art, shared with the world that Nandalal had said that the difference between two cultures could be seen in the way they drew trees. The Europeans drew a tree top to bottom, Indians—possibly most Oriental cultures—drew a tree as it grew, from bottom to top. 'A tree grows upward; it is driven by a singular urge to spread towards the sky— trunk, branch and leaf', Nandalal explains in the opening line of 'The Structure and Characteristics of Plants and Trees'.[69] In drawing a tree, one should *become* a tree: 'All its branches and all the leaves and flowers on its twigs and stems grow in such a way as to get as much sunlight as possible; this is why its branches, its twigs, flowers and fruits emerge in a spiral motion from the (parent) trunk, branch or twig, respectively. To absorb, as much as possible, the rays of the sun, its life-giver, with all its body, then grow big and bear fruit is its natural urge.'[70]

Satyajit would have heard all this from his teacher, how a painter had to understand a tree's body to be able to understand how to draw it. I know of no comparable art pedagogy that was unconsciously aimed at such a multispecies understanding of life: 'the trunk is like the tree's backbone'; the banyan tree's 'numerous mouths'; 'the edges of scars resulting from stripping of barks from tree trunks seem to have sewn up and repaired'; tree-branch joints compared to human elbows and shoulder points; how a paisley has the shape of a woman sitting inside it, the Buddha 'the bell of the lotus', a drawing of a woman has 'many angular breaks like petals or flowers', mountains like lotus beds.[71] K. G. Subramanyan, who collected and translated Nandalal's lectures from Bangla into English, shares this episode. Talking to a student who is studying a tree he says,

Watch the tree for some time. Go and sit near it, morning, noon and evening, even in the darkness of the night. That will not be easy. After sitting for a while you will feel bored. You will feel that the tree is telling you in annoyance, 'What are you doing here? Go away! Get lost!' Then you will have to coax the tree. And say, 'My teacher has asked me to. I cannot but heed him. Please bear with me. Be nice to me, show yourself to me.' If after a few days of such effort you feel you are seeing the tree, then go home, close yourself up and paint that tree.[72]

This understanding of the botanical anatomy, as comparative species, a metaphorical manner of thinking where one was trained to see one species through another, a lotus as mountain or a tree with mouths like the human's, the holes in a tree trunk as the human ear, would naturally condition a way of seeing as we find in Satyajit, where the botanical and the fantastic, the scientific and the imaginative, would come together instinctively, as they did to his teacher Nandalal and his other students.

Sunit Sengupta, in *Satyajit-er Chhobi O Kheror Khata*, writes about Nandalal and Benode Bihari's influence on Satyajit.[73] One important lesson that he learnt from them was 'Before setting a story in a certain place, it was necessary to know the nature and natural characteristics of the place'.[74] In the same book, we discover Benode Bihari telling Satyajit 'To study nature is to analyse life', to find many 'signs of truth',[75] the same Benode Bihari who continued to paint even after he went blind, who told his student Satyajit about a tree when the latter was making a film on him.

'You will show khoaai in your film, won't you?'
'I certainly wanted to—but all the khoaai seems to have vanished.'
'There is one place where it still exists. Taltorh. Neat Prantik station. And you'll find some more if you go towards Cheep Sahib's bungalow. Don't leave the khoaai out. A stretch of khoaai, and in the middle of it, a solitary palm tree. That's all. If you wish to look for my spirit, the basic essence of all that my life stands for, you will find it here. You could say, I am *it*!'[76]

Perhaps because one's default mode is now to punch operative words into search engines, I Googled for 'Satyajit Ray' and 'tree'. Among all the results, one stood out. Satyajit Ray's last drawing, from his hospital bed in 1992, had apparently been one of a tree: in that sketch of a benevolent tree with drooping branches were hidden the faces of twelve 'important' personalities in India, presidents and prime ministers, and so on. I felt it was too uncanny to be true—a man in hospital drawing a sketch of a tree, turning it into a parliament. I wrote to the historian Chandak Sengoopta who confirmed it was a 'classic fake', an expression that made me smile for its having no equivalent in the plant world. I was neither disappointed nor alarmed: I just realized that there were others like me who had observed Satyajit Ray's relationship with plants and had reached nearly the same conclusion that I had, even if in different ways. That in imbuing an unexplained mystery to the world of plants, by making them behave like humans, Ray was perhaps silently rebelling against the self-serving humanism of the last few centuries, that which had also marked his films. In Satyajit Ray's theory of evolution, man was to evolve into a tree. The 'classic fake' had intuitively got that correct.

Notes

1. Ray in Ray (1997), introduction.
2. Ray (1923).
3. Majumdar and Tagore (2012 [1907]).
4. Ibid., p. xii.
5. Ray in Ray (1997), introduction.
6. Ibid.
7. Ibid.
8. Muni (1951).
9. Ray (1997).
10. Ibid.
11. Ibid., p. 2.
12. Ibid.
13. Ibid., p. 8.
14. Ibid.
15. See, for example, Simard (2021).
16. https://bengaluru.sciencegallery.com/phytopia/exhibits/can-you-hear-her-speak.
17. Satyajit Ray (2021), p. 52.
18. Ibid., p. 53.
19. Bandyopadhyay (2019).
20. Roychoudhury (2014), p. 6.
21. Ibid.
22. Ray (2021), p. 36.
23. Ibid.
24. Ray (2014).
25. Ibid.
26. Ibid.
27. Ibid.
28. Ibid.
29. Ibid.
30. Ibid.
31. Ibid.
32. Ibid.
33. Ibid.
34. Ray (2021), pp. 41–42.
35. Ray (2014).
36. Ibid.
37. Roychoudhury (2014), p. 41.

38. Ibid., p. 55.
39. Ibid., p. 67.
40. Ibid.
41. Ibid., p. 70.
42. Ray (2021), p. 7.
43. Ray (1981). Translation mine.
44. Ibid.
45. Ibid.
46. Ray (2021), p. 13.
47. Ray (2012), 'The Hungry Septopus', n.p.
48. Ray (2012), 'Green Man'.
49. Ray (2012), p. 71. Translation mine.
50. Ibid., pp. 73–74. Translation mine.
51. Ray (2012), 'Kagtaruya' (Scarecrow), n.p.
52. Ray (2012), 'Kutum Kutam.
53. Ray (2015), 'Munroe Dweep' ('Munroe Island').
54. Ibid.
55. Ray (2021), p. 11.
56. Gangopadhyay (1968).
57. Chattopadhyay (1881); Chattopadhyay (1989).
58. Roy (2017).
59. Bandyopadhyay (2017).
60. Ghatak, *Akash Bhawra Shurjyo Tara* (movie).
61. Debi (2018).
62. Siraj (date), 'Gachh-ta Bolechhilo' ('The Tree Said').
63. Kar (date), 'Aswattha'.
64. Kar (date), 'Udbhid' ('Tree').
65. Ghosh (2022).
66. Ray (2012).
67. Banaphool, 'The Tree'; Narayan Sanyal, 'Gachh Ma' ('The Mother Tree').
68. Ray, 'Leela Pishi'.
69. Bose (1999).
70. Ibid.
71. Ibid.
72. Ibid.
73. Sengupta.
74. Ibid., p. 15.
75. Ibid., p. 116.
76. Ray (2005), p. 197.

7

Anonymous

Being around Maya-*mashi* was like living in a forest.

She was short enough to be taunted as a dwarf by children, thin enough to have her shadow be mistaken for a reed's. Poverty had marked her face and skin and hair in such a manner that she seemed like the oldest person to all the children in the neighbourhood. And we were cruel, like only children can be.

My playmates and I called her names and annoyed her with the most ridiculous rhymes. I still remember one:

Maya mashi aagachha
Maya mashi-r nei pachha

Maya mashi is a weed
She doesn't have a butt.

The '*aagachha-pachha*' rhyme must have been an invention of the playground, but I now wonder where that weed metaphor came from. How did a middle-aged Bangladeshi refugee, abandoned by her husband and, later, her own family, come to have this effect on teenage children in a small town in sub-Himalayan Bengal? It is possible that this happened because Maya-mashi spoke in plants. Compulsively, every day, she expressed herself in botanical idioms and proverbs. Her Bangla was a thing of leaves and fruit and stems and roots – her forest.

I loved and hated Maya-mashi in equal measure – but I kept the love private, because I thought it would make me look weak in front of my playmates.

Like most female domestic workers of the time, Maya-mashi did not have a surname. This was the common destiny of women who worked as household help in Bengal, subject as they were to the callous gulf of

Plant Thinkers of Twentieth-Century Bengal. Sumana Roy, Oxford University Press. © Sumana Roy 2024.
DOI: 10.1093/9780198929314.003.0008

privilege that such work entailed. Their surnames were unimportant to their employers, and so they severed them easily, like nails, and instead quickly acquired suffixes that denoted virtual relations: often 'didi', or sister, but most commonly 'mashi', or maternal aunt.

Maya became 'mashi' to both my parents and me—a strange relationship, the kind that is possible only in mythology. She had two boys that she had brought with her from Bangladesh, with rhyming names that made us laugh – Mongol, or Mars, and Jongol, or jungle. Chhaya, her eldest child and daughter, whose name meant shadow, she had left behind with her mother in back home, hoping to bring her to this new country after she had settled here. It must have been more than a decade since she left, but Maya-mashi still hadn't found the opportunity to fetch her daughter. It is this bit of history that first made me curious about Maya mashi—how could a mother abandon a daughter like that? It made me scared for myself—could my mother abandon me like that as well?

The daughter's nickname was Lata, which meant a creeper. Every afternoon, as Maya-mashi cleaned the dishes or scrubbed the red oxide floors in our old house, that name appeared and disappeared on her lips like a chant. We grew used to it like the way one does to a grandparent's chronic coughing—a metaphor that came to us from my father's friend, who, fond of annoying Maya-mashi, proposed to marry her daughter, the never-seen-but-always-spoken-about Lata.

I remember Maya-mashi's reply because I did not understand what it meant. 'Anarash bawley kathhal, bhai tumi bawro khoshkhoshey'— The pineapple tells the jackfruit that its skin is rather harsh to the touch. It made my father's friend go silent.

As I grew older and the more secretive implications of idioms and proverbs began to make sense to me, Maya-mashi began to change in my eyes from an awkward and annoying person to someone mysterious, a person worth tenancy in my curious teenage mind. I'd begun to find her means of self-defence oddly attractive—when scolded or taunted, she lashed back with a Bangla proverb. And that proverb was inevitably about plant life.

It was my mother who brought this to the family's attention over dinner one day. And she, a teacher, because she treats the world as her schoolchildren, explained and bolstered her observation immediately: Maya-mashi's daughter's name was Lata, her son's Jongol. That was a psychological giveaway; it was 'abnormal', my mother concluded, her attachment to plant life.

I was at an age when the psychological life seems unattractive, even a burden, when compared to the riches of the material, of smell and skin. I didn't bother with these deductions. I didn't think Maya-mashi's lexicon unusual. There were already many proverbs from plant life that surrounded us. My mother was herself fond of using one for us: 'Aek laphey gachhey otha'— Climbing the tree in one leap. tIt was her schoolteacher's way of instructing my brother and me to shun shortcuts.

When I was 12, I came down with a series of ailments that left me confined to bed for months. Every morning, my working parents and my school-going brother left me alone at home to befriend the day. Pity is a great lodestone, and so Maya-mashi—usually harsh and pungent, especially with children—began to spend significant portions of time by my bedside.

I was too weak to be interested in anyone besides myself and my ambitions to return to the life I had left on the playground. Her stories whirred like the ceiling fan above my head, never making a home inside me. To grow up to be a detective was my life's aim, and I liked to think of people around me as detectives of their own kind. The doctor was a disease detective; my father, a banker, was a money detective; a botanist a plant detective, and so on. In this world, I did not know where to place Maya-mashi. She couldn't be a detective of pots and pans, neither of dirt and dust. Then what?

It must have been to answer this conundrum that I began spying on Maya-mashi's words. A severe moralist frustrated with an unfair world, she was seeking justice in the natural law of plant life. For what else is there in our proverbs about plants? 'Trinobomonnotey jawgot'. These polysyllabic words leaked out of her from time to time: The world is in a blade of grass.

There were others she used to pass judgement. One of these, delivered with great scorn in her voice, was 'Aapon cheye pawr bhalo, pawr cheye jungle bhalo'—The stranger is better than dear ones, and the jungle even better than the stranger. My school education had only equipped me with the awkward, exclusionary expression 'law of the jungle', one that invoked fear and privileged animal life over plants. Maya-mashi's jungle, with its ecosystem of justice, was a universe of plants rather than animals.

Hence her fondness for forest proverbs, the saddest of which I now use in my complaints to my loved ones: '*Bone porey shawbai dyakhey, mone porey keu dyakhey na*.' Everyone sees the forest burning, they don't notice the heart burning.

Maya-mashi's biography, which she gave away for free, was composed of such self-pitying morals. '*Nyara bel-tawlaye aekbari jaaye*'—The bald man stands under a wood apple tree only once—was deployed when my mother asked her to consider marrying again. Maya-mashi was firm— she was not going to be a fool to stand under a wood apple tree and injure her bald head again. When the process of acquiring ration cards for her looked difficult, or when she pined for the taste of sweet-water fish of the rivers of her old Bangladesh, another plant proverb would escape out of her: '*Aek gachher chhal onnyo gachhey jora laagey na*'—The bark of one tree cannot become the bark of another.

When my mother scolded her—uselessly of course—for her lack of family planning and bringing three children into the world, Maya-mashi used a self-mocking tone. '*Agachhaye phawl beshi*', she said— Weeds produce more fruits than fruit-bearing trees—simultaneously calling herself a weed and praising her own reproductive strength. When my mother asked her to take care of her skin and passed on a vial of cosmetic cream or body oil, Maya-mashi refused, making her argument with another plant proverb: '*Upokari gachher chhal thhakey na*'— Medicinal plants rarely have their barks left on. Maya-mashi refused to take any criticism, even if it was for her own good. She likened herself to plants who had no use for suggestions from gardeners and admirers.

When her husband came to visit her from Bangladesh and she refused to go back with him, the man beat her up, leaving open gashes on her back and neck that she showed to my mother the next morning.

'*Aada shukaleu jhaal jaaye na*', she explained to my mother—Dried ginger does not lose its heat. And then came up with a consolation herself: '*Taap baarey jhopey aar khejur baarey kopey*'. The heat abets the growth of the bush just as the date palm tree needs to be hurt and wounded to bear fruit.

There was little to separate her sons from the daughter, she said, explaining her children's lack of affection for her: '*Shawb roshuner aek-i koya*'—All the pods in a garlic are the same.

A great devotee of Time, she always asked us to be mindful of its grace and rhythm. For this too her instructions came from the behaviour of plants. Her words were annoying, particularly on the eve of examinations, when she scolded us for staying up late to study instead of pacing our study schedule evenly through the year. If my brother or I or our playmates said something inappropriate to our age, two words would come rushing out of her: 'Awkal pokko', prematurely ripe, which is ripeness without taste or consequence. Or this saying, which I did not understand for years, and whose meaning I was scared to my mother about: 'Awkaley kheyechho kochu, monay rekho kichhu kichhu'—You've eaten an unripe yam, you'll remember a few things. There is another one which I find myself using now, especially when I see people coming out of the gym or going through crash diets—'Kiliye kathal pakano'. Beating a jackfruit to make it ripe.

Maya-mashi and my mother created an ecosystem of such sayings, one borrowing from the other—though, of course, my mother's stock was meagre. Both shared a dislike of flamboyance and fantasy and were sadly intolerant of daydreamers. 'Gachhey kathal gNophey tel' was thus a favourite indictment of theirs—The jackfruit's still hanging from the tree, but he has oiled his moustache in anticipation of the sap sticking to it. They used it particular for a young neighbour I called Robi-kaku, someone who had failed his school-leaving exams a few times but harboured dreams of becoming a successful doctor.

Robi-kaku passed his tenth-grade exams eventually—he had, perhaps to avoid looking older than the boys in his class, shaved off his moustache by then. But Maya-mashi's adage did not stop stalking him. In fact, another one joined it soon, when Maya-mashi discovered Robi-kaku smoking weed with a group of older men in an abandoned school building. 'Kaacha bashey ghoon dhorley, rokkha nei tar kono kaaley'—if the young bamboo attracts weevils, there is no escape for it.

Gradually things began to change about the way I saw people. Their names, their hobbies, their habits, even their jobs, receded into a blur. Instead, the plant proverb that Maya-mashi had used for a person came to direct my consciousness and became their visiting card, as it were.

When someone scolded her sons for being naughty in school, I heard her saying this under her breath: 'Chandey kawlonko aachhey, golap-ey kawntok'—the moon has its flaws, the rose its thorns.

But her worldly wisdom also made her see the inequality in plant life. 'Not all fruits or vegetables are worth a life in proverbs', she explained, before reciting a list where some fruits and vegetables were privileged over the rest. *Aam* over *aamra*—mangoes over hog plum. The jackfruit, taro, toddy palm, and paddy kept recurring in these sayings, as they did in the work of the poet Jibanananda Das. Tasty or nutritious—these were praised only for their usefulness to humans. This made her angry, this expectation to be useful to humans, and the 'human' for her was inevitably an educated, salaried person. Sometimes she asked our family physician—she believed doctors knew everything—if there was a plant that humans hadn't found any use for.

I must have been too young to understand Maya-mashi's permanent state of anger. It couldn't only have been the obvious differences of socio-economic class that made her feel like an outsider. She endured jibes about her hygiene and the quantity of rice she ate, and, often, also threats about her precarious legal status in this new country. That none of us knew her surname is also telling—'mashi', as used for domestic helpers, had been turned by the Bengali middle class into a caste and class category. I can now remember a neighbourhood uncle trying to guess Maya-mashi's caste from her high cheekbones and short build, and, in the end, calling her a 'tribal'. This hierarchy – and its irrational and ruthless codes – was like a sport that everyone liked to play, both adults and children. It conditioned us to see her behaviour as outrageous and even an assault on the confidence of her employers.

It would have been this conditioning that made me find Maya-mashi's superior air annoying. She often contrasted what she saw as the muscular and robust intelligence of the poor with the supposedly effeminate ways of the wealthy, comparing the latter to decorative house plants. '*Tumi phero daaley daaley aami phiri paataye paataye*'— You move through stems while I move between the leaves, she would tell someone who she thought was trying to cheat her. She suffered from a persecution complex, forever racked with the anxiety of being cheated for being illiterate. Among all things she envied in the rich, foremost was the intelligence that came to be a custodian of their lives after school and university.

Yet she tried to show herself as superior. '*Dhaaney aekgoon, ghashey shawtogoon*'—Paddy has one virtue, grass a hundred, she would say, taunting her middle-class employers whenever they made her feel low and lowly. Or, when reprimanded for her obtuse behaviour, she'd confront them with '*Lebu kawchlabey jawto, hawbey teto tawto*'—The more you squeeze a lemon, the more bitter it becomes.

In fact, most of her conversation with her employers was tit-for-tat and bristly. But, perhaps because it was melded with the workings of the natural world, her sharpness did not cause long-term damage. She would happily call herself a '*dumurer phool*', the flower of a fig tree that did not reveal itself, when she reappeared after a long period of absence. As I grew older, I began to enjoy this, her unbending nature, her refusal to bow to the employer's commands, the kind of rebellious streak that teenagers find attractive. '*Shukno daal bhangleu noye na*'—The dry branch of a tree breaks but does not bow, she told an employer once before quitting.

Her smallness was a gift to her at times, but allied with it was the fear of big things—big people, big families, big trees. When my parents asked her to quit all her other jobs so that she could stay with us and save herself the exhaustion of working in several houses, she refused. She didn't want to put all her eggs in one basket, she meant, but her choice of adage was '*Bawro gachhei jhawr laagey*'—A storm strikes the big tree. Another recurring fear, given her fragile legal status, was of living a parasitic life, and she held her independence, however tattered it might have looked to her employers, with great pride. '*Bawro gachher tawlaye baash, daal bhanglei shawrbonash*'—If you live under a big tree, even the breaking of a branch might be the end of you.

When the municipal authorities came to raze 'illegal' settlements on the riverbank where she lived, she led the protesters, shouting '*Gachh tultey shawbai aachhey*'—Everyone will join you in uprooting a tree. For a neighbour she did not know very well, but about whom she had heard rumours of corruption and miserliness, she could casually say, '*Gachhero khaaye tawlar-o kuroye*'—he eats from the tree and gathers fruit from the ground beneath it as well. This same neighbour, who would have been in his early sixties, suddenly began wearing a wig. Maya-mashi shouted out to my mother as he passed by our house: '*Mawra malonchey phutlo phool, taakey aabar uthlo chool*'—Flowers have arrived on a dead branch, hair has sprouted on a bald head.

There were a few people for whom she reserved her most astringent self. The milkman was one of them. And perhaps because I hated milk and my own dislike for the milkman seemed the most natural corollary,

I did not mind Maya-mashi's jokes at his expense. I can only remember a few of those now. When the milkman appeared with a swollen face one morning and explained to my mother that he had been kicked by a cow while trying to milk it, my mother came up with a common adage: The cow that kicks is also the cow that gives you milk. Maya-mashi came running from the garden to say that the swollen face suited the skinny man; '*Shaadher kawmol tultey giye haatey phutlo kaata*'—Trying to pluck the desired lotus has resulted in the thorns on his hand. Before the milkman could respond, out came another proverb: '*Phool-er shobha bhomra, gai-er shobha chamra*', the beauty of flowers is to be seen from the bees around it and the beauty of a cow is to be found in the quality of its leather.

Who could convince Maya-mashi that this had been an inappropriate use of the proverb? She was adding her own life to these sayings, using them to make sense of her destiny, which she likened from time to time to that of Bangladesh: a small place, its birth snatched out of violence.

I remember asking her about where she had learnt these proverbs.

The question made her angry at once. 'Whoever taught the trees?' she lashed back. This she shared proudly with the trees—a happy illiteracy. In this, she also seemed to be driven by the compulsive need to pare down the egotism she associated with formal education.

Once, when teaching my brother, my mother said, 'All the sounds that we need are to be found in the alphabet'. To this, Maya-mashi added, as if it was a complementary statement, 'All the learning that is to be had is to be found in the plant world.'

Also, she never apologized, no matter what the circumstances. Plants did no wrong, they did not understand the apology.

Maya-mashi worshipped many gods, but was frustrated with the Hindu temples for not hosting a god whose portfolio was rebirth. In her imagined instalments of rebirths, she saw herself as a tree. This current life, lived amidst proverbs using the behaviour of plant life, was, for her, a training for the next one, where she would be a plant. Once, when I asked her if she missed her surname, having been reduced to everyone's 'mashi' in a new country, she said she didn't. Plants did not need surnames, she said, and this was their safeguard against violence caused by surnames—the violence inherent in the differences of caste and community, manifest in surnames.

My parents did not fight her idiosyncrasies. When she began working for us, for instance, she demanded a huge salary. I remember my mother telling me later how they tried to reason with her, but Maya-mashi demanded a surprisingly large salary. I remember my mother telling me later how they tried to reason with her, but Maya-mashi just would not give up. Her explanation came much later—instead of an annual increment, she would take an annual decrement. 'Like trees,' she said. 'Young people need more money than the aged. Haven't you seen how saplings need more care and water than old trees?'

I was a high-school student in Calcutta when my mother last saw Maya-mashi. Everyone knew she was dying, but Maya mashi refused to believe doctors and well-wishers who told her so.

When my mother asked her about her ailment, the older self returned: '*Baash mawrey phooley, manush mawrey bhooley*'—the bamboo dies for flowering, man for his mistakes.

Maya-mashi had been my mother's closest confidante when our family moved to this small town. 'You know that I don't have a birth certificate', she sat up on her bed to tell my mother. This was not news, my mother had heard this multiple times before. The concept of a birth certificate was then quite new in the Subcontinent, where written records were still uncommon in rural areas.

'Sometimes I wonder how people will remember me, if at all', Maya-mashi whispered.

My mother later told me that she thought she'd given a very intelligent and poetic answer when she said, 'People will remember you like they remember a tree.'

Maya-mashi held my mother's hand and said, '*Bherendao brikkho*', Bherenda—a weed—is also a plant.

Bibliography

Atwood, Margaret. 1972. *Surfacing*. McClelland and Stewart.

Axelby, Richard. 2011. 'Calcutta Botanic Garden and the Colonial Re-ordering of the Indian Environment', *Archives of Natural History*, 35 (1): 150–163.

Bandyopadhyay, Bibhutibhushan. 2017. *Aranyak of the Forest*. Translated by Rimli Bhattacharya. Seagull Books.

Bandyopadhyay, Bibhutibhushan. 2018. *Restless Waters of the Ichhamati*. Translated by Rimli Bhattacharya. Rupa Publications India.

Bandyopadhyay, Bibhutibhushan. 2019 [1929]. *Pather Panchali: Song of the Road*. Translated by Rimi N. Penguin.

Basu, Satyendra Kumar, and Rammohan Dutta. 1957. *Trees of Santiniketan*. Santiniketan, West Bengal: Visva-Bharati.

Bhattacharya, Arupratan, and Sailen Chakrabarty, ed. 2013. *Jagadish Chandra Basu Rachana Sangraha*. Calcutta: Dey's Publishing.

Boehme, Jacob. 2013. The *Signature of All Things: Signatura Rerum*. Createspace.

Bose, Jagadish Chandra. 2007 [1896]. 'Niruddeser Kahini' ('The Story of the Missing One'), in *Sera Kalpabigyan* (*Best Science Fiction*). Anish Deb. (ed.). Kolkata: Ananda Publishers Limited.

Bose, Jagadish Chandra. 1895. "On a new Electro-Polariscope." *The Electrician* 36.

Bose, Jagadish Chandra. 1899. *Rachanasangraha*. Kolkata: Dey Publishing.

Bose, Jagadish Chandra. 1901. 'To Jagadis Chandra Bose from Rabindranath Tagore'. Translated by Manmohan Ghosh. http://www.jcbose.ac.in/assets/uploads/8d6ce2cef 73e06e0fff070e483d179e5.pdf. Last accessed 23 March 2023.

Bose, Jagadish Chandra. 1907. *Comparative Electro-physiology: A Physico-physiological Study*. London: Longmans, Green, and Co.

Bose, Jagadish Chandra. 1922. *Abyakta*. Createspace.

Bose, Jagadish Chandra. 1927. *Plant-Autographs and Their Revelations*. New York: The Macmillan.

Bose, Jagadish Chandra. 1929. *Growth and Tropic Movements of Plants*. London: Longmans, Green, and Co.

Bose, Jagadish Chandra. 2011. *Acharya Jagadis Chandra Bose in Modern Review*. A.K. Mukhopadhyay (ed.). Kolkata: Progressive Publishers.

Bose, Jagadish Chandra. 1922. 'Udbhider Jonmo O Mrityu' ('The Birth and Death of Plants'), *Abyakta*. Kolkata: Bahu-Vijyan-Mandir.

Bose, Nandalal. 1999. *Vision and Creation*. Translated by K. G. Subramanyan. Kalkota: Visva-Bharati.

'Buddhadeva Bose: Forty Years On', *The Daily Star* website, 22 March 2014. https://www.thedailystar.net/buddhadeva-bose-forty-years-on-16646. Last accessed 8 October 2022.

Chattopadhyay, Debiprasanna. 1979. *Uttarayan-er Bagan O Gachhpala*. Rabindra Bhavan, Visva-Bharati.

Chattopadhyay, Sanjib Chandra. 1989. *Palamau*. Biswasahitya.

Chattopadhyay, Bankim Chandra. 1881. *Kapalkundala*. Calcutta: New Sanskrit.

Chattopadhyay, Shakti. 2014. *Padya Samagra* (**Collected Poems**), Vols. 1–7. Calcutta: Ananda Publishers.

Chattopadhyay, Shakti. 2018. *Very Close to Pleasure There's a Sick Cat.* Translated by Arunava Sinha. Seagull Books.

Chaudhuri, Bishnu Pal. 1992. *Cremate Me, O Fire* (movie) https://youtu.be/q4uC_OV4Jw0.

Das, Jibanananda. 2018 [1957]. *Rupashi Bangla.* Createspace.

Das, Jibanananda. 2018 [1942]. *Banalata Sen.* Createspace.

Das, Jibanananda. 2019. *The Scent of Sunlight: Poems by Jibanananda Das.* Translated by Clinton B. Seely. *Parabaas* website. https://www.parabaas.com/jd/articles/seely_scent.shtml. Last accessed 8 October 2022.

Das, Jibanananda. 2022. *Malloban.* Penguin.

Das, Jibanananda. n.d. 'Bengal the Beautiful'. Translated by Clinton B. Seely. *Parabaas* website. https://www.parabaas.com/jd/articles/seely_scent.shtml. Last accessed 8 October 2022.

Dasgupta, Alokranjan. 1995. *Jibanananda.* Calcutta: Dey's Publishing.

Dasgupta, Sugata. 1962. *A Poet and a Plan: Tagore's Experiments in Rural Reconstruction.* Thacker Spink.

Das Gupta, Uma. 2022. *History of Sriniketan: Rabindranath Tagore's Pioneering Work in Rural Reconstruction.* Niyogi Books.

De, Anil Kumar, ed. n.d. *Prakriti Path* (**Nature Study: Teachers' Manual**). Np: np.

Devi, Mahasweta. 2018. *Arjun.* Shristi.

Devi, Mahasweta. 2021. *Our Santiniketan.* Translated by Radha Chakravarty. Seagull Books.

Dutta, Krishna, and Andrew Robinson. 2009. *Rabindranath Tagore: The Myriad-Minded Man.* I. B. Tauris.

Elmhirst, Leonard K. 1975. *Poet and Plowman.* Visva Bharati.

Frost, Robert. 1936. 'Desert Places' (1933), *A Further Range.* Henry Holt & Co.

Frost, Robert. 1969. *The Poetry of Robert Frost.* Henry Holt & Co.

Gangopadhyay, Sunil. 1995. *Proshongo Shakti Chattopadhyay.* Calcutta: Dey's Publishing.

Gangopadhyay, Sunil. 1995. *Aranyer Din Ratri.* Calcutta: Ananda.

Ghatak, Ritwik. 1961. "Akash Bhawra Shurjyo Tara," in *Komol Gandhar* (movie). https://www.youtube.com/watch?v=8kpW2tOoRjw.

Ghosh, Subodh. 2022. *Cactus.* Re Publishers.

Gruntman, M., and Novoplansky, A. 2004. 'Physiologically Mediated Self/Non-self Discrimination in Roots', *Proceedings of the National Academy of Sciences*, 101: 3863.

Guha, Bhumendra, ed. 2017. *Kusumkumari Daser Dinalipi.* Calcutta: Dey's Publishing.

Guha, Ranajit. 1999. *Elementary Aspects of Peasant Insurgency in Colonial India.* Durham: Duke University Press.

Haque, Masdul. 2011. *Jibanananda Das O Onnyanyo.* Dhaka: Ityadi Grantha Prakash.

'Jagdish Chandra Bose', **New Word Encyclopedia**, 2021. https://www.newworldencyclopedia.org/entry/Jagdish_Chandra_Bose. Last accessed 4 April 2023.

Kamrisch, Stella. 1952. *Rathindranath Tagore: An Exhibition of Printings and Woodwork.* Calcutta: Government College of Art and Craft.

Kar, Bimal. [1995] 2013. *Panchasti Galpa (Stories).* Calcutta: Ananda Publishers.

Milton, John. 1896. *Paradise Lost.* Cambridge: At the University Press.

Mitra, Pradyumna. 1983. *Jibananander Chetona Jagat.* Calcutta: Dey's Publishing.

Mitra, Pradyumna. 2000. *Kobitar Garo Enamel: Jibananandar Kabya Bhabana.* Kalkota: Dey's Publishing.

Moon, Beth. 2014. *Ancient Trees: Portraits of Time.* Abbevile.

Mukhopadhyay, Pratul. 'Ami Banglay Gaan Gai' ('I Sing in Bangla'). https://www.yout
ube.com/watch?v = jTDZVq5kxvU. Last accessed 8 October 2022.

Muni, Bharat. 1951. *Natya Shastra*. Translated by Manomohan Ghosh. Calcutta: Asiatic
Society of Bengal.

Ray, Sukumar. 1923. *Abol Tabol*. Calcutta: U. Ray and Sons.

Ray, Sukumar. 1997. *Select Nonsense of Sukumar Ray*. Translated by Sukanta Chaudhuri.
Oxford University Press.

Ray, Satyajit. 1970. *Aranyer Din Ratri* (movie).

Ray, Satyajit. 1981. *Poison Plant*. Calcutta: Ananda Publishers.

Ray, Satyajit. 1998. *Childhood Days: A Memoir*. Translated by Bijoya Ray. Penguin.

Ray, Satyajit. 2005. *Speaking of Films*. Penguin.

Ray, Satyajit. 2012. *Pikur Diary O Annanyo*. Calcutta: Ananda Publishers.

Ray, Satyajit. 2012. *The Collected Short Stories*. Penguin.

Ray, Satyajit. 2014. *The Magic Moonlight Flower and other Enchanting Stories*. Translated
by Arunava Sinha. Rupa Publications.

Ray, Satyajit. 2015. *The Mystery of Munroe Island and Other Stories*. Introduction by
Victor Banerjee. Penguin.

Roy, Sumana. 2012. 'On Eating: Rabindranath Tagore's Dis(h)courses', *South Asia: Journal
of South Asian Studies*, 35 (1): 33–47.

Roy, Sumana. 'Dalit Plants', *Warscapes* website, 6 August 2014. http://www.warscapes.
com/column/sumana-roy/dalit-plants.Last accessed 8 October 2022.

Roy, Sumana. 2017. *How I Became a Tree*. Yale University.

Roy, Sumana. 'Tree Time', *The Paris Review*. website, 30 August 2021. https://www.thepari
sreview.org/blog/2021/08/30/tree-time/. Last accessed 8 October 2022.

Roychoudhury, Upendrakishore. 2014. *Goopy Gyne Bagha Byne*. Translated by Rushir
Joshi. Penguin.

Sayeed, Abdul Mannan, ed. 2010. *Banalata Sen: Jibanananda Das*. Dhaka: Abosar.

Seely, Clinton B. 1976. 'Doe in Heat: A Critical Biography of the Bengali Poet
Jibanananda Das with Relevant Literary History from the mid-1920s to the mid-
1950s', unpublished PhD dissertation for the University of Chicago.

Sengupta, Samir. n.d. *Kobi Shakti*. Patralekha.

Sengupta, Sunit. n.d. *Satyajit-er Chhobi O Kheror Khata*. Calcutta: Gangchil.

Shepherd, V. A. 2005. 'From Semi-conductors to the Rhythms of Sensitive Plants: The
Research of J. C. Bose', *Cellular and Molecular Biology (Noisy-le-Grand)*, 51: 607–619.

Shivani. 2021. *Amader Shantiniketan*. Translated by Ira Pande. Vintage Books.

Simard, Suzanne. 2021. *Finding the Mother Tree: Discovering the Wisdom of the Forest*.
Knopf.

Singh, Rajinder. 2009. 'J. C. Bose and the German Scientific Community: Scientific and
Political Context', *Current Science*, 6 (3): 419–422.

Siraj, Mustafa Syed. 2014. *Sera Panchasti Galpa* (A Collection of Bengali Stories).
Kolkata: Dey Publishing.

Sukanta, Chaudhuri, ed. 1997. *The Select Nonsense of Sukumar Ray*. With an introduction by Satyajit Ray. Oxford HED.

Tagore, Abanindranath. 1905. *Bharat Mata*. Water colour painting, 10 ½" × 6".
Victoria Memorial Hall, Kolkata, India. https://artsandculture.google.com/asset/
%E2%80%98bharatmata%E2%80%99-abanindranath-tagore/oAEeunKSH5SPag?hl=
en. Last accessed 8 October 2022.

Tagore, Rabindranath. 1943. "The History and Ideals of Sriniketan," *The Modern Review*.
Calcutta.

Tagore, Rabindranath. [1905] 1962. **Swadeshi Samaj.** Calcutta: Visva- Bharati.

Tagore, Rabindranath. [1913]. *The Gardener*.

Tagore, Rabindranath. 1963. *The Religion of an Artist.* Visva- Bharati.

Tagore, Rabindranath. 2010. *Three Women.* Translated by Arunava Sinha. Random House India.

Tagore, Rabindranath. and Mitra Majumdar, Dakshinaranjan, ed. 2012 [1907]. *Thakurmar Jhuli.* Manuscript Publication.

Tagore, Rabindranath. 1919. *Sadhana: The Realisation of Life.* New York: Macmillan.

Tagore, Rabindranath. 2020 [1922]. 'The Religion of the Forest' in *A Confluence of Minds: The Rabindranath Tagore and Patrick Geddes Reader on Education and Environment.* Bashabi Faser. (ed.). Luath Press.

Tagore, Rabindranath. n.d. *Banbani.* Kolkata: Visva-Bharati.

Tagore, Rabindranath. 1878. 'Golap phul phutiye achhe', *Tagore web*, https://www.tagore web.in/Songs/prem-o-prakriti-258/golap-phul-phutiye-achhe-6378. Last accessed 3 April 2023.

Tagore, Rabindranath. 1881. 'Basanto probhate ek malatir phul' *Tagore web*, https://www. tagoreweb.in/Songs/natyogiti-516/basanto-probhate-ek-malatir-phul-10120. Last accessed 3 April 2023.

Tagore, Rabindranath. 1883. 'Bane eman phul', *Tagore web*, https://www.tagoreweb.in/ Songs/prem-235/bane-eman-phul-5749. Last accessed 3 April 2023.

Tagore, Rabindranath. 1913. 'Nutya tomar je phul phote', *Tagore web*, https://www.tagore web.in/Songs/pooja-233/nutya-tomar-je-phul-phote-4745. Last accessed 3 April 2023.

Tagore, Rabindranath. 1927. 'Shiuli phul shiuli', *Tagore web*, https://www.tagoreweb.in/ Songs/prakriti-236/shiuli-phul-shiuli-5239. Last accessed 3 April 2023.

Tagore, Rabindranath. 1933. 'Phul bale dhanya ami', *Tagore web*, https://www.tagore web.in/Songs/chadalika-gitabitan-514/phul-bale-dhanya-ami-9616. Last accessed 3 April 2023.

Tagore, Rabindranath. n.d. 'The Champa Flower (Supposing I Became a Champa)', *Tagore web*, https://www.tagoreweb.in/Verses/the-crescent-moon-192/supposing-i-became-a-champa-2574. Last accessed 3 April 2023.

Tagore, Rabindranath. n.d. 'Chhoto phul', *Tagore web*, https://www.tagoreweb.in/Verses/ kori-o-komol-5/chhoto-phul-2200. Last accessed 3 April 2023.

Tagore, Rabindranath. n.d. 'Phul photano', *Tagore web*, https://www.tagoreweb.in/Ver ses/kheya-54/phul-photano-1839. Last accessed 3 April 2023.

Tagore, Rathindranath. 1958. **On the Edges of Time.** Calcutta: Visva-Bharati.

Tandon, Prakash Narain. 2019. 'Jagdish Chandra Bose & Plant Neurobiology', *Indian Journal of Medical Research*, 149 (5): 593–599.

The Englishman, January 1896. London: Open Court Publishing Co.

Trewavas, A. 2003. 'Aspects of Plant Intelligence', *Annals of Botany*, 92 (1): 1–20.

Index